STONEHENGE

and the Origins
of Western Culture

to
the memory
of
Olaus Wormius
1588–1654

Anno ÆTAT: 38. OLAUS WORM D. MEDICINÆ IN ACADEMIA REGIA HAFNIÆ PROFESSOR PUBLICUS. 1626

Externam, WORMI, tibi sculpsit jmaginis umbram,
Sed mentem Glyptes sculpere non potuit.
Nec decuit, Cur non qværis? Dicam. Qvia doctâ
Tu melius Glypte hanc exprimis ipse manu.
Hæc docet et Medicum te Philosophumq̀ vocari:
Hac primus Danos TEMPORA prisca doces.

Sereniß: Daniæ, Norveg: etc. Regis sculptor Simon de Pas sculpsit. | M· Iohannes Erasmi
Phyſ. prof. P.

STONEHENGE

and the Origins of Western Culture

Leon E. Stover & Bruce Kraig

HEINEMANN: LONDON

William Heinemann Ltd
15 Queen Street, Mayfair, London W1X 8BE
LONDON MELBOURNE TORONTO
JOHANNESBURG AUCKLAND

First published in Great Britain 1979

SBN 434 39745 8

Printed and bound in Great Britain by
Cox & Wyman Ltd,
London, Fakenham and Reading

It is remarkable that whoever has treated of this monument has bestowed
on it whatever class of antiquity he was particularly fond of.
—Horace Walpole, *Anecdotes of Painting*, 1786

contents

Plate 1. The brutal stones of Stonehenge at a distance, seen from the northwest.
(Hans Schaal)

Introduction

Stonehenge has been standing on Salisbury Plain in the Wessex district of southern England for thirty-five centuries. Books have been written about it for nine centuries.[1]

Ever fascinated by the authority of its strong grey stones, men of each age have seen in that monument whatever strength of purpose has animated their own society.

In the twelfth century Geoffrey of Monmouth, England's first national historian, treated Stonehenge as a group of memorial stones raised by Merlin the Magician for a British cemetery of war dead fallen in the name of post-Roman patriotism.

In the seventeenth century Inigo Jones, the king's surveyor general, who returned Italian architecture to Britain for the glory of its monarch, saw in Stonehenge a Roman temple dedicated to imperial grandeur.

When English monarchy again flowered under Charles II, Walter Charleton, his physician, saw in Stonehenge a place where early kings were crowned.

When liberal philosophy went against the idea of monarchy, exploding finally in the violence of the French Revolution, the antiquarians John Aubrey and William Stukeley saw in Stonehenge a temple of resurgent nativism directed by British Druids against the Roman conquest.

In our own day when 1 out of 120 working Americans is employed in the research and development industry, an astronomer at the Smithsonian Astrophysical Observatory in Cambridge, Massachusetts, Gerald S. Hawkins, finds in Stonehenge a scientific observatory for the prediction of solar and lunar events. We build electronic computers, so the ancients must have built rude prototypes anticipating our own concern with science and technology.

But what did Stonehenge mean in its own time? The question rarely has been asked. Yet all that is required for an answer is a consultation with the builders of Stonehenge who lie buried all about it. We cannot

Plate 2. Stonehenge from the southeast. (Hans Schaal)

consult them directly, of course, but we can attend their bones, their grave goods, and the cultural tradition these artifacts share with archaeological remains found elsewhere in prehistoric Europe. These in turn fit into a time sequence of things dated earlier and things dated later, with continuities well established by archaeology. Later artifacts move out of the realm of prehistory and up into the realm of ethnohistory when they are associated with behavior recorded in written documents. These include the observations of ancient Greeks and Romans who visited barbarian Europe when it was still inhabited by peoples descended from the builders of Stonehenge and their cultural relatives, all of whom we identify as Indo-European peoples. Relevant documents also include recorded versions of Indo-European oral literature. Working our way back through this tangled skein of epic literature, classical observations, and archaeology, we find something suggestive of our own conclusions in each of the major theories sketched above.

We admit the astronomical significance of Stonehenge, but would qualify this by saying that its status as an observatory is conceived too professionally by Hawkins, who dwells upon scientific interests special to him and his time. We find instead *cosmological* significance in Stonehenge, something rather more imprecise, in keeping with the mythic interests of the ancients. It is these interests that John Aubrey and William Stukeley captured in their restoration of Stonehenge as a Druidic temple, whose keepers reflected upon celestial events for the religious purpose of relating them to earthly affairs. Because religion and its priesthood must always work in the service of some *political* order, we can also accommodate Walter Charleton's theory that Stonehenge answered to a place where ancient kings were crowned; or, as we would say, where Indo-European chieftains were installed by Druids in the name of tribal solidarity and tribal alliances. Monumental architecture, raised by religious leaders as a political theater in which chieftains may enact their power, returns us finally to the magical skills of Merlin, who raised Stonehenge in the midst of a royal cemetery where the king's loyal followers lay buried; or, as we would say, where chiefs and warriors belonging to the Indo-European tradition of heroic society lay buried—adding that the monument itself was no dead pile of memorial stones but a living stage set on which big men acted out issues of tribal power such as war making and alliance making. This stage set included not only the monument itself but the whole plain on which it rests, filled to the horizon with groups of enormous grave mounds. Here did Indo-European chieftains meet to do their tribal business in parliamentary session—political business made serious by the presence of dead heroes buried all about the place in tombs containing the bodies and war finery of the chief's predecessors, the allies of his predecessors, and their warrior followers. What parliament of strong men ever met on more hallowed ground! It was sanctified by centuries of tomb building under the supervision of priests wise in cosmic knowledge, the same who supervised the construction of the monument itself with its own sepulchral forms derived from the architecture of great megalithic tombs belonging to the long ago, when men lived a simpler, peaceful, communal life and were buried in collective graves; when warring interests had not yet taken form with the ambition of aristocratic chieftains, who found their rest in single heroes' graves.

Our conclusions, hinted at here, are advanced along the following line of argument, chapter by chapter:

Chapter 1. History of Ideas about Stonehenge. At the outset we mean to show that the astronomical theory set forth by Hawkins and now widely accepted is prejudiced by the temper of its time, as were all other preceding theories. This chapter establishes the point of departure from which our own theory, anthropological in viewpoint, takes leave. The science of anthropology, to be sure, is also symptomatic of our day, scarcely one hundred years old; but it is a skeptical science that appreciates the relativity of cultures in time and space, and even questions some of the values of Euro-American society out of which it springs. Whereas the other theories are hopelessly culture bound, tied to the values and predispositions of their propounders or their patrons.

Heroic burial (round barrow) near Stonehenge. From Edgar Barclay, *Stonehenge and Its Earthworks*, 1895.

Other round barrows in the Stonehenge cemetery. From Barclay, 1895.

Round barrows, like the long barrows that preceded them, are more than tombs for the dead. They also mark out social territories of the living, enforcing claims to the land by supernatural means. If Irish folklore allows that spirits and fairy folk live in these mounds, it is a memory of ancient rituals and ghostly warnings to intruders upon family or tribal lands. The big cemetery at Stonehenge, however, tells more. Evidently it was the focus of intertribal alliances over a wider region, because other than local dignitaries are buried there.

Stonehenge in 1895 as drawn by Barclay.

Chapter 2. Europe before Stonehenge. Here we introduce the roster of prehistoric cultures that must enter any anthropological discourse on Stonehenge. This chapter is therefore a kind of Who's Who of ancient Europe, in which we identify the cultural dramatis personae that appear on and off throughout the later chapters. Above all in importance is the culture we identify as that of the first Indo-Europeans.

Chapter 3. Political History of Stonehenge. Stonehenge was constructed in three main phases over a period of many centuries by a series of peoples who entered Britain at different times. These people differ not only in culture content but also in their level of political organization, which ranges from communal to aristocratic.

The first phase, Stonehenge I, was built by a pre-Indo-European people whose economy was based on mixed farming, and which was spurred to widen its intercommunity relations by way of trade in stone axes. Politically, the Stonehengers of phase I lived in a communal society based on tribal egalitarianism, or so we deduce from their practice of burying their dead in the stone chambers of megalithic tombs, which are collective tombs.

The second phase, or Stonehenge II, was built by a proto-Indo-European people known as the Beaker folk, whose farming economy took on a pastoral bias. Politically their tribal equality was modified by the presence of a warrior caste, in addition to a priestly caste that used to sanctify a communal way of life in the previous phase.

The third phase, or Stonehenge III, was built by a fully pastoral Indo-European people known generally in Europe as the Battle Axe folk and in southern Britain as the Wessex warriors. Politically their society may be characterized as a chiefdom, led by a warrior caste topped by an aristocratic chief whose leadership was associated with control of a trade in metal axes begun in the previous phase. The Indo-European chiefdom is a heroic society of the sort celebrated in the later works of Indo-European epic literature, such as the *Rig Veda* from Aryan India, the *Iliad* of Homer, which recalls Mycenean Greece, and the so-called "Iliad of Europe" from Celtic Ireland, the *Táin Bó Cúalnge.* These epics will be treated in chapter 5 for their relevance to the heroic society lived at Stonehenge III.

Chapter 4. The Stones of Stonehenge. The construction of the various Stonehenges is described here, stage by stage. The architectural forms of Stonehenge III are compared with structural elements derived from megalithic tombs by way of showing that the final phase of Stonehenge harks back for its cosmological meaning to conservative religious concepts carried forward by priests from the days of Stonehenge I. At the same time, we examine the astronomical theory in detail and find it not so plausible in the light of a cosmological interpretation.

Chapter 5. Indo-European Warriors and the Heroic Tradition. Only two hundred years separate the composition of the first Indo-European epic (the *Rig Veda,* 1800 B.C.) and the building of Stonehenge III (2000 B.C.) The other epics come considerably later, but all have bearing on the culture of the Wessex Warriors who built it. The Indo-European tradition of heroic society is a long and conserving one, going back to Beaker times (associated with Stonehenge II) and coming forward as late as Celtic times, when barbarian Europe was finally absorbed by the Roman Empire, itself built on Indo-European foundations. Stonehenge is not as remote from us as we might suppose. The culture of its architects is to some extent still with us, insofar as the Battle Axe people may be said to be the very originators of Western culture.

Chapter 6. Stonehenge: Parliament of Heroes. Here is presented our conclusion that Stonehenge, in its later phases, was an Indo-European assembly place where pastoral chieftains and their warrior followers were brought together annually to do their tribal business, at the time of the autumn cattle roundup, itself a tradition going back to the first phase and even earlier. Each intrusive people found the host culture agreeable with its own, making for continuous use of the Stonehenge site throughout every phase, whatever the difference in emphasis. At last it became the political center of a powerful chiefdom, drawing in others like it by way of tribal alliances. Evidence of this process may be found in the groups of burial mounds that represent areal interests outside the Stonehenge region.[2] That the monument to this process never was completed tells us that the stones of Stonehenge were erected in a premature effort to achieve peace among warring interests. They stand as relics of a prehistoric parliament, the father of the mother of parliaments, that great legislature of Great Britain and model for the few surviving democratic nations of our time. Sad to say, the model is on the defensive against a multitude of rivals, great and small, who reject it in favor of something its originators tried to overcome. Stonehenge seems to signal the decline of the West long before it was noticed. May it not be so.

Western rulers, all ye feeble:
Finish Stonehenge, save your people.

Reconstruction by Barclay (1895).

1. History of Ideas about Stonehenge

Every age gets the Stonehenge it longs for. When British history first began to be written, Stonehenge filled the need to dignify the national past with a memorial to patriots felled by a national enemy, the Saxon pirates. This explanation carried authority for over five centuries. After that, just before the French Revolution, Stonehenge was all classical architecture and courtly, flushed with the joys of monarchy. After the Revolution, Stonehenge fell into the wild, jagged ruins of the romantic vision, relics of a liberal Druidism that helped throw off the Roman yoke. With the Druids fading away in this age of science, now is the time for Stonehenge to be taken over by research scientists as a celestial observatory and eclipse computer.

Merlin's Magic[1]

Britain had been a Roman colony since A.D. 43, in which year the emperor Claudius landed on the island and easily subdued the war bands of the native Celts. The occupation brought Roman civilization with its city building and province-wide political institutions. Although Rome in time abandoned her colony, during the years of catastrophe which saw the

1

barbarian sack of Rome, Britain never returned completely to the pre-conquest condition of heroic society and competing rustic princelings. As the imperial legions were withdrawn, marauding Germanic pirates attempted to fill the vacuum. The resultant struggle, between the end of Roman rule and the emergent Saxon kingdoms of the late sixth century, lasted for more than 150 years, a struggle between the intermittent pressure of the invading barbarians and a mixed population of Romanized and insular Celts.

During one of the lulls in this contest for the island, a British monk named Gildas in 539 wrote *De exidio et conquestu Britanniae (The Destruction and Conquest of Britain)*. Addressed to the errant rulers of Britain, it rebukes them for their evil ways; it is their drinking, wenching, and murderous squabbling that foretell the ultimate fall of Britain. For Gildas, the fall is the triumph of divine providence by which wicked men are judged, sinful nations are punished, and the forces moving history are revealed. In Britain's fall they sinnéd all.

With the twelfth century Renaissance, historians returned to classical models of explanation and description. Despite its tissue of fancy and folklore, this is the pattern behind Geoffrey of Monmouth's *Historia regum Britanniae,* written about 1135. History for Geoffrey is not, as it was for his Dark Age predecessor, Gildas, a lesson in theology. Personal sin does not have national consequences. Supposedly a chronicle of the kings of Britain, the *Historia* begins with a heroic founder, Britto, a descendant of Aeneas, and ends with the death of Arthur. Britain falls, but not before Arthur establishes himself as a great warrior and national hero who conquers Western Europe. Arthur returns home, only to meet the treachery of his fellow countrymen; but the message is not that evil men cause the fall of a nation. Rather, a nation's history is something apart from evil men who on occasion rule it.

It is fashionable today to criticize Geoffrey as an unscrupulous writer of bogus history whose entertaining lies gained him the promotion from Augustinian canon in Oxford to bishop of St. Asaph. But how could Geoffrey possibly have known anything about the pre-Roman past? And what did he have to draw upon for post-Roman Britain other than Bede, Gildas, Nennius, the Welsh chronicles, and folklore? Fiction purporting to be history, yes; but no longer history as a hortatory tract, calling for national repentance. The nation is greater than any individual, and will survive. It is in this light we ought to see Merlin's role in building Stonehenge. Merlin stands for human greatness creating human history and its own destiny.

No other work before Geoffrey offers to explain Stonehenge. To be sure, the first recorded words about it do occur in 1129 in the first edition of *Historia Anglorum* by Henry, archdeacon of Huntingdon. But Henry of Huntingdon merely denominates Stonehenge as second of the four wonders of Britain, and confesses that no one can imagine by what art, and for what purpose, such large stones could have been erected.

The story Geoffrey tells provides both method and purpose. Aurelius Ambrosius, king of the Britons, wishes to erect a memorial to those of his subjects slain by Hengist the Saxon and who had been buried in the convent at Amesbury. He sends for Merlin, a magus famous for prophecy and engineering skills. Merlin recommends the following:

> If you wish to honor the grave of these men with an everlasting monument, send for the *chorea gigantum que est in killaro monte hybernie*, the Giant's Dance which is in Kildare, a mountain in Ireland. For there is a stone structure, which no one today could raise without a profound knowledge of the mechanical arts. They are stones of a vast size and wonderful quality, and if they can be brought here they will stand forever.[2]

Ambrosius accordingly sends an expedition to Kildare, defeats the Irish in battle, and acquires the stones, which Merlin transports over sea and land by his magic arts to Salisbury Plain and there reerects them as Stonehenge.

Modern students of Stonehenge, looking into Geoffrey's *Historia* for some glimpse of real history, like to point out that the composition of the so-called bluestones at Stonehenge, when examined in microscopic section, is identical to that found among a unique formation of spotted dolerite atop Mount Presely in Pembrokeshire. Therefore, Geoffrey's account of the movement by sea of stones from Ireland in the time of Ambrosius could have been drawn from a garbled memory of an actual waterborne shipment from Wales in prehistoric times. But new geological evidence shows that the bluestones were, after all, native to Salisbury Plain, brought there by the same glacial movement that deposited their brethren on top of Mount Presely.[3] But the *Historia* is less a text from which actual happenings in British history can be taken than it is a guide to the intellectual climate of Geoffrey's day, when the moral approach to history was changing in favor of a secular approach. Merlin's special powers to perform magic deeds are given in the service of national progress. Man makes himself. This new insight into history was sufficient to carry the contents of Geoffrey's book for several centuries. The Stonehenge story held good until 1620.

"A Roman Thought Hath Struck Him"[4]

In 1620, Stonehenge attracted the attention of King James I during his stay at Wilton House, near Salisbury, the seat of the earls of Pembroke. It was here that Shakespeare and company played before King James in 1603. Wilton House is rich also in the memories of Sir Philip Sidney, Ben Jonson, Holbein, Vandyck, and Inigo Jones, England's most famous architect who designed a new front for Wilton House in 1633. To answer the king's curiosity about the local ruins, his host sent for Inigo Jones whom the king ordered "to produce out of his own practice in architecture, and experience in antiquities abroad, what he could discover concerning this of Stonehenge."

The antiquities Jones had studied abroad were Roman ones in Italy, where he traveled under the patronage of William, earl of Pembroke, the same who summoned Jones into the presence of the king. Jones began his

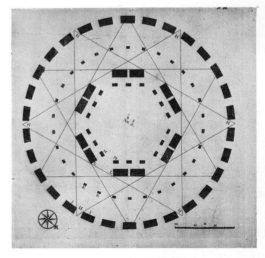

Ground plan of Stonehenge III (Inigo Jones).

career as a stage designer for masques written by Ben Jonson, lavish productions performed within palace walls to enliven the long, dull evenings of royalty during winter. He may very well have designed costumes for Shakespeare. In any event, he rose to become His Majesty's Surveyor General and in that capacity gave English architecture a new direction with his buildings in the Italian style. With justice he was in his own time regarded as "the Vitruvius of the Age."

Jones returned from Italy with the revolutionary conviction that a building, to be beautiful, must conform to the ideals of ancient Rome. Shakespeare might have said of him (*Antony and Cleopatra* act 1, scene 2):

> *on the sudden*
> *A Roman thought hath struck him.*

The same thought struck him with regard to Stonehenge, which he placed at the time of Agricola in A.D. 79. He concluded that "this ancient and stupendous Pile must have been originally a Roman temple, inscribed to Coelus [Uranus], the Senior of the Heathen Gods, and built after the Tuscan Order." A fantastic inference. But perhaps Stonehenge for Jones was no more than a source of artistic inspiration, something to be improved upon with the imagination rather than surveyed with precision. For Stonehenge appears in one of his masques, *Coelum Britannicum*, as "The ruins of some great city of the ancient Romans, or civilized Britains."[5]

At the center of the actual site are Stonehenge's most spectacular features, the five trilithons, each a massive construction of two upright stones supporting a horizontal stone. A few of the stones have fallen among the standing ones, but none are missing and the ground plan of the original design is impossible to overlook. The five trilithons once stood in a horseshoe shaped array. Inigo Jones has *six* trilithons arranged to form a hexagon, which not only involves the addition of an extra structure, but the replacement in a new position of all but one of the others. The outer ditch and embankment Jones has trisected with three entranceways where there is only one, all three flanked both inside and outside the ditch with a pair of pyramidal monoliths where the remains of none have been found. All of this, and more, is spelled out with punctilious but wholly fictitious measurements.

In his drawings of Stonehenge restored, Jones provides a smooth and regular finish to the whole that, despite weathering, could not have been other than rough and craggy in its original condition. Jones claims that Stonehenge was built in accordance with the rules of the Tuscan order, as set forth by Marcus Vitruvius Pollio, the first century B.C. Roman architect and author of *De architectura*, a ten volume encyclopaedic work consulted by Italian Renaissance architects during the classical revival. Jones did the same in England after two trips to Italy. Successful in redirecting English architecture, he simply projected the elements of his success onto Stonehenge.

The Tuscan order, as specified by Vitruvius, shares three properties in common with the Doric, Ionic, and Corinthian. The columns are round, tapered toward the top, and set on pedestals. The columns that form the

Classical Stonehenge (Inigo Jones).

outer ring at Stonehenge do not in the least conform. They are broad and flat, the tapering is highly irregular or nonexistent, and there are no pedestals. Specific to the Tuscan order are the dimensions of height and intercolumniation. The height is supposed to be six diameters of the column's thickness in its biggest part a little above the bottom, and the distance between columns four diameters. These proportions are not to be derived from any measurements Jones himself provides: uprights 15½ feet high by 3 feet deep and 7 feet wide, with a distance between them of 9 feet.

In fairness to Inigo Jones, it must be said that he himself did not publish these results. This was done from notes after his death by John Webb, his disciple, nephew, and son-in-law, groomed to succeed him as surveyor general. Jones died in his eightieth year in 1652; Webb published the book in 1655 as *The Most Notable Antiquity of Great Britain, Vulgarly Called Stone-Heng, on Salisbury Plain, Restored, by Inigo Jones, Esquire, Architect General to the Late King.*[6] The reference to the "late king" is Charles I, executed in 1649 by Oliver Cromwell during the Puritan Revolution. This was a long time after Jones visited Stonehenge in 1620, during the reign of James I.

It is therefore likely that Jones was unhappy with his conclusions, which may even have been thrust upon him as a pet theory of royalty by King James, and that he somehow managed to avoid publication of them during his lifetime. The book is wholly of Webb's composition, based, as he himself admits, on "some few indigested notes" of his master. Indeed, Webb published a second book in 1665, *A Vindication of Stone-Heng Restored,*[7] after the first was repudiated by a physician to Charles II, Dr. Walter Charleton.

"'Tis Now Become a Throne"[8]

Dr. Charleton published his confutation in 1663 with *Chorea Gigantum, or, The most Famous Antiquity of Great-Britain, Vulgarly called Stone-Heng, Standing on Salisbury Plain, Restored to the Danes.*[9] Although restoring Stonehenge to the Danes may seem one degree less silly than restoring it to the Romans, Charleton introduced an authority who still holds our respect for the careful description he gave many archaeological sites which have since perished, the Danish antiquary Ole Worm.

That Charleton knew of Worm's writings is a tribute to his wide reading, not to mention his own voluminous output, some twenty-nine books in both Latin and English. In fact, it has been said of Dr. Charleton that his academic success was injurious to him as a physician by encouraging him to spend more time at the writing desk than at the bedside of his patients. This did not prevent him, however, from taking up the presidency of the College of Physicians. He was no Harvey, although he added to his contemporary's work on the circulation of the blood some good remarks on the connection between arteries and veins. It was his exactness of description and method of observation, rather than new discoveries, which gave him a scientific reputation, as in his *Physiologia* (1654) and his

Portrait of Walter Charleton.

Natural History of Nutrition, Life, and Voluntary Motion (1659). He contributed to atomic theory by pointing out that the microscope shows the divisibility of matter; and since the letters of the alphabet permit 295,232,-799,039,604,140,847,618,609,643,520,000,000 permutations, it is obvious that an infinitely more numerous combination of atoms may produce all known forms of matter.

In addition he published a novel, several works on theology, some philosophical dialogues, a translation of Epicurus, a book on wine making, and *A Character of His Most Sacred Majesty Charles the Second* (1661), a eulogy describing that profligate king as one in whom no more perfect union of religious piety, clemency, justice, intelligence, fortitude, and magnanimity was ever matched. But then again, only an uncompromising royalist would be admitted to serve the king as physician-in-ordinary, which Charleton did from the outset of the Restoration.

Charleton's approach to the Stonehenge problem is appropriately wide-ranging for one of the first elected Fellows of the Royal Society, a polymath among polymaths. He first reviews the classics for evidence of monument building in antiquity and reduces the motivations for building them to psychological and political ones. Next he systematically eliminates every feature of Roman design claimed by Inigo Jones. Then he draws on an obscure (if unauthenticated) account of the discovery, in the time of Henry VIII, of a metal plate at Stonehenge inscribed in letters unreadable to the learned men of the day. The writing, therefore, cannot have been Latin, so no Romans built the monument. The writing had to be in a barbarian script, which he airily evidences from stone inscriptions elsewhere in England. Runic or Gothic characters being the most common form of barbarian writing known to him, he turns to an expert in runes and stone monuments, a fellow physician, his counterpart in attendance upon the king of Denmark, the great Dr. Olaus Wormius.

In an exchange of letters, Worm provides Charleton with a classification of stone monuments. There are two types, inscribed and uninscribed. Among the latter are:

> *Sepulchra* (tombs)
> *Fora* (places of judicature)
> *Duelorum strata* (places of camp-fights)
> *Trophea* (battle monuments)
> *Comitialia loca* (election places)

Taking this last as his clue, Charleton point by point compares Stonehenge with "Ancient Courts of Parliament in Denmark." He then concludes that Stonehenge was built by the Danes, after overthrowing King Alfred, as a "Court Royal, or Place for the Election and Inauguration of their kings."

Charleton dedicated *Chorea Gigantum* to King Charles and presented him with the first printed copy, bound in red morocco, with the double crowned "C" on both sides, which is preserved in the British Museum. Like the work of Inigo Jones, this book seems to be a response to the royal person's curiosity. The dedication says as much.

> Your Majestie's Curiosity to survey the Subject of this Discourse, the
> so much admired Antiquity of Stone-Heng, hath sometime been so

great and urgent, as to find a room in Your Royal Breast, amid Your weightiest Cares; and to carry you many miles out of Your way toward Safety.

The king's "weightiest cares" were escaping to France following the defeat of his army by Cromwell at the battle of Worcester in 1651. On his way south, he stopped overnight in the home of a royalist in the vicinity of Stonehenge, but not before making a ruse, for the benefit of the servants, of pressing onward. In the interval, His Majesty spent the afternoon hiding among the ruins of Stonehenge where, according to Samuel Pepys, his company "found that the king's arithmetic gave the lie to the fabulous tale, that those stones cannot be told alike twice together."[10]

Chorea Gigantum celebrates the Restoration of 1660, as does John Dryden's "Epistle to Dr. Charleton," which closes with these lines:

> These Ruins sheltered once *His* Sacred Head,
> Then when from *Wor'sters* fatal Field He fled;
> Watch'd by the Genius of this Kingly place,
> And mighty Visions of the Danish Race.
> His *refuge* then was for a *Temple* shown:
> But, *He* Restored, 'tis now become a *Throne*.

Dryden's epistle, originally prefixed to the book, has been called the noblest poem in which English science has been celebrated by an English poet.[11] But Charleton's science was not sufficiently royalist for John Webb, who so advised the king in his dedication to *A Vindication of Stone-Heng Restored*. Webb complained that "Your physician dreameth it is a place for ELECTION OF KINGS: when all your just and Rightful PREDECESSORS . . . have held DOMINION over their Island by unquestionable and indubitate RIGHT OF SUCCESSION: in no Age by popular and tumultuary clamour." What is more, "this Doctor" has traduced the architectural taste of royalty by allowing barbarians to build so noble a thing as Inigo Jones has shown Stonehenge to be. "Your Architect conceived Stone-Heng to be a TEMPLE Dedicated to the Gods: when SOVEREIGNTY, though to Idol-Deities, spared no TIME, no LABOR, no COST, to make sacred STRUCTURES famous." No, the Danes and their "riff-ruff Rubble" will not do. Webb, as he develops his argument, will yield to "no roving and uncivilized people, for permanent works of Divine Art."

Chorea Gigantum (Walter Charleton).

Liberalism and the Druids[12]

In the same year Webb published his *Vindication*, John Aubrey completed a manuscript that marks the beginning of the next line of thought, "Monumenta Britannica; or Miscellany of British Antiquities. Vol. 1, Section 1, Templa Druidum; Stoneheng."[13] Aubrey's antiquarian researches are commemorated today in the Aubrey holes, the ring of chalk-filled pits just inside the circular embankment at Stonehenge. His efforts to link Stonehenge with the Druids, however, were premature so long as kings were eulogized. But the Druids were at hand, ready to appeal to those liberal feelings of disrespect for monarchy that exploded in 1789 with the French Revolution.

William Stukeley.

Druids by name derive from the plural forms *druidas* in Greek and *druidae* or *druides* in Latin. These are the words used by the classical authors such as Athenaeus the writer of miscellanies, Strabo the geographer, Diodorus Siculus the historian, and Julius Caesar in his commentaries on the Gallic War. The picture of life in Gaul drawn by these authors is for the most part borrowed from a lost work of the Greek historian and ethnographer Posidonius, who died in 51 B.C., the year of Caesar's commentaries. The Druids themselves in these sources are described as a class of priests associated with the war chiefs of barbarian Europe; they are a class of learned men, repositories and oral transmitters of tribal wisdom concerning gods and men, the composition of poetry, the skills of calendar keeping, the rites of sacrifice, and the interpretation of omens. That Druidical sacrifices and omen readings called for human victims, killed by stabbing and holocaust, is well attested by Posidonius, a fact romantic apologists for the Druids have squeamishly avoided.

Druids were rediscovered together with the Greek and Roman classics during the Renaissance. The first books about them appeared in the sixteenth century by continental writers who looked to the pre-Roman past for a national mythology. Respectable ancestors could be made out for the Gauls if only their priests could be laundered of barbaric crudities, which was accomplished by holding that Druids really loathed human sacrifice and stood by it merely as a duty to tradition, their minds on higher things. In England, the ancient Britons came to be appreciated, after the Elizabethan encounter with the Red Indians of America, as a part of barbarian Europe elevated to civilization by the Roman conquest. Primitive ancestors then could be ennobled by comparing them with noble savages found abroad. Distance lent romance to the American Indians that exactly filled the need to establish a primitive Golden Age at the beginning of national history. Druids were added permanently to the national folklore of England in 1740 with the publication by William Stukeley of *Stonehenge, A Temple Restor'd to the British Druids.*[14] Stukeley's association of Druids with circular stone structures, by no means justified from the classical texts, was preceded by John Aubrey. In a published sketch of the ancient Britons of Wiltshire, Aubrey wrote of the Druids:

> Their religion is at large described by Caesar. Their priests were Druids. Some of their temples I pretend to have restored, as Avebury, Stonehenge, &c., as also British sepulchres. Their waie of fighting is lively sett down by Caesar. . . . They knew the use of iron. They were two or three degrees I suppose less savage than the Americans.[15]

Aubrey's "Monumenta Britannica," however, remained in manuscript, its influence limited to Stukeley who in 1718 transcribed a copy, twenty-one years after the author's death. By 1740, Stukeley's *Stonehenge* and his republican Druids found a ready market, only forty-nine years before the French Revolution.

Like Inigo Jones, Stukeley places Stonehenge in Roman times, in 460 B.C., but assigns its construction not to Roman architects but to British. His drawings of Stonehenge in ruins comported with the eighteenth century attitude toward moldering abbeys and crumbling castles: the triumph of time over the tyranny of monks and barons. That Stonehenge, before it lay in ruins, was itself a power center, from which Druids led a resistance movement against Roman oppression, is an inconsistency only the romantic mood can resolve. Another romantic, Adolf Hitler, required his architect, Albert Speer, to construct a model of Nuremburg Stadium in ruins a thousand years hence, so that the Fuehrer could enjoy both monument to power and wistful retrospection of its eventual decay.

Romantic Stonehenge (engraving by David Loggan, 18th Century).

The Druidic fantasy was expanded into a three-volume novel in 1842 with *Stonehenge, or, The Romans in Britain,* by a pseudonymous Malachi Mouldy.[16] A Roman soldier in the days of Nero travels alone across the high downs. He looks for a place to lay him down for the night, sees firelight in the distance, advances toward it. There he discovers bearded men in white robes, sacrificing an assortment of white heifers and bloody soldiers behind the rude, rocky portals of Stonehenge: Druids at their equinoctial meeting. The Arch Druid seizes the intruder, bares his chest, poises the sacrificial knife for cutting out the hero's heart—but wait. What is that birthmark? No. Yes. It's the Arch Druid's lost son, orphaned by the hazards of the Roman occupation. Father and son rejoined, they set off together to subvert imperialism, combining priestly mysteries with the practical crafts of Roman soldiery.

By now, the old British priests have had their day. The Ancient Order of Druids, fabricated in the nineteenth century out of the rites of Freemasonry and the ideas of the romantic antiquaries like Aubrey and Stukeley, is moribund. But the pathetic sunrise ceremonies of today's self-invented white-robed Druids live on in the white laboratory coats of ancient computer programmers Gerald Hawkins has discovered tuning Stonehenge to the stars.

Space Age Mythology

In *Stonehenge Decoded,*[17] Gerald Hawkins claims, among other things, that Stonehenge was built to monitor not only the turning of the midsummer sun, but also the rising and setting points of the moon in summer and winter. Critics point out that the points of observation are conflated from different phases of construction, hundreds of years apart.

In addition, Hawkins claims that by moving counters in the 56 Aubrey holes, lunar eclipses were predicted for cycles of 56 years. This number, however, can mean anything. Two other scientists, from the laboratory of Applied Physics at Johns Hopkins University, think that the Aubrey holes were not meant for counting years, but months, and that twice around for a 112-month cycle would predict the setting of the summer new moon.[18] But as the Aubrey holes were excavated during the first phase of Stonehenge when it was nothing more than a circular enclosure, it might just as reasonably be inferred that 56 indicates the number of social units involved in throwing up the embankment, and whose families were entitled to dig one of the holes and use it to inter the cremated remains that in fact have been found in some of them.

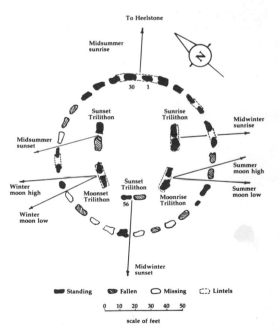

Astronomical Stonehenge: the alignments.

This notion would at least depart from an abstract numbers game, played on a flat sheet of paper inscribed with ground plan and azimuthal arrows, and better fit the concrete facts of archaeology, which show that the people who built the enclosure and its Aubrey holes were pastoralists who lived in a fairly wooded environment (their cattle in browsing the floor of the forest had not yet reduced Salisbury Plain to the treeless expanse we know it to be today); and without grassland to provide fodder they had no means of tiding the bulk of their animals over the winter. Very likely they rounded up the surplus at autumn, slaughtered it, and enjoyed a season of feasting that brought isolated families together in ceremonious reunion from all parts of the region. This is exactly what many prehistorians believe to be the case, and that the center of activity was the enclosure, a cattle pen and ceremonial place, associated with the first phase of Stonehenge. Future phases would naturally grow out of this cultural base line as later peoples specialized more in pastoralism, given the progressive denudation of forestland and the opening up of grassland.

Yet Stonehenge has been accepted as a celestial observatory and eclipse computer by the National Aeronautics and Space Administration (NASA). The opening scenes of *Moonwalk One,* NASA's official documentary film justifying the American space program, dramatize Hawkins's theory with no reference to the natives of Stonehenge nor to its phased construction. Surely this is special pleading, to take the building of a monolithic Stonehenge as prelude to the immense funding, by government and industry alike, of large-scale scientific research and engineering development.[19]

The Stonehenge of *Stonehenge Decoded* is taken to be a primitive computer, one mark on the long road of progress toward microminiaturization and the on-board computers that took Apollo spaceships to the moon, the very object of prehistoric calculation. If the idea of progress is a modern one, to read back into Stonehenge the scientific mystique of research and development is to project contemporary interests and longings as did the classicists and romantics.[20]

The mathematicians necessary to compute lunar eclipses do not exist in a cultural vacuum; they can exist only in a literate society whose population is large and dense enough, and whose division of labor is complex enough, to include occupational specialties of some refinement. Astronomers literate in numbers first appeared with the emergence of civilization in Mesopotamia. But even among the Babylonians, eclipse prediction was not perfected until the sixth century B.C. It is no rebuttal to conjure up, as did another astronomer in defense of Hawkins—Fred Hoyle of Cambridge University—an exceptional group of prehistoric Newtons and Einsteins endowed with the genius to solve the problem, all by themselves, fifteen centuries in advance of the Babylonians and their supportive civilization.[21] But even so, this answer does not resolve the numbers game. Hoyle attributes to the Stonehengers a different set of calculations, even a different method of calculating, than does Hawkins. Hoyle speculates that light and dark counters, representing dawn and evening, were moved around the ring of Aubrey holes in a leap-frogging manner that not only served as a digital computer but inspired the game of checkers![22]

Society in ancient Britain, even when the large stones of Stonehenge were erected, centuries after the Aubrey holes were dug, was not civilized. It lacked cities, and even a sufficient agricultural base for the support of cities. The Britons who built the final phase of Stonehenge were a pastoral people known to archaeology as the Wessex warriors, a branch of the Battle Axe people identified with a zone of Indo-European occupation stretching at one time or another from India to Ireland and from northern Europe to the Mediterranean. The battle axes of the Wessex warriors are interred with them in the burial grounds of Stonehenge; their deeds of combat and cattle reiving echo in the oral literature of a great variety of other Indo-European warrior heroes, as recorded in the *Iliad*, the *Rig Veda*, and the *Táin Bó Cúalnge* (toin vo kú-ling-ee). Homer's *Iliad* was set down in the eighth century B.C. on the basis of an oral tradition recalling the Mycenaean heroes of ancient Greece in 1500 B.C. The *Rig Veda* recalls the invasion of India by city-sackers at about the same time, in an epic poem faithfully transmitted orally by Brahmins until recorded by colonials during the British conquest. And the *Táin Bó Cúalnge* ("Cooley's Cattle Raid") recalls the heroic character of an Indo-European society that survived in Ireland, isolated even from the Roman conquest, until penetrated by Christian missionaries in the fifth century A.D. We are indebted to the monks who recorded the *Táin*, for they have provided us with an oral tradition that—incredible as this may seem—opens a window on the distant past and blows life into the bones of the Wessex warriors of southern Britain, buried in 2000 B.C. If Homer's Mycenae—the most advanced of the heroic societies—is an unlikely place for an astronomical observatory, how much less likely is barbarian Britain five-hundred years earlier.

Above all, space age mythology is patronizing, in so far as it is taken to show the intellectual capacities of a "primitive" people to be the equal of ours. To deny the barbarian builders of Stonehenge their share of science matching our own interest in research astronomy is somehow felt to impute inferiority. But we rather find them no less our human equals for their politics and cosmology.

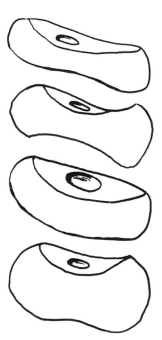

Types of stone battle axes buried with the Wessex warriors in the heroic graves of Stonehenge cemetery.

2. Europe before Stonehenge

As we have seen, previous authors have looked at Stonehenge as an object built in one constructive act for one purpose. Only recently have prehistorians come to appreciate that it is a composite monument of three main phases (Table 1 and figures) added to over the centuries by a succession of differing populations, and that it served a train of purposes. Its builders are not fixed in time like insects trapped in amber. Pushed by the universal movers of history, internal development, external influence, or both, their culture evolved. They move in time, no less than does the monument. For Stonehenge is nothing if not the expression of changing thought patterns, evolving with the generations of men who built its consecutive phases.

Stonehenge, in short, is a monument to the very process of culture change itself. But that is our view of it, looking back on the past, not the builders'. The readiness of modern intellectuals to explain the crashing reality of change all about us, and to see process in all things, is quite unlike the outlook of idea men newly risen with the dawn of philosophy. To find plausible our attempt to recover ideas from the ruins of Stonehenge, that difference must be accepted.

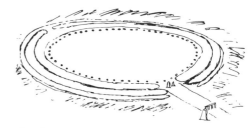

Stonehenge I.

Phases	Architecture
IIIa 2000 B.C.	trilithons sarsen ring Station Stones Slaughter Stone bluestones removed
II 2100 B.C.	double bluestone circle Avenue
I 2900 B.C.	ditch and bank Aubrey holes Heel Stone

Table 1. Stonehenge building sequence

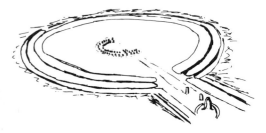

Stonehenge II.

Ancient wise men in the guise of priests, shamans, Druids, or whatever, directed the building of monuments to the heavens, the earth, and even the underworld; and they did so without reference to change. In their perception, they were building monuments to a timeless order of things, a stable order associated with the idea of the sacred. To them the material and the immaterial, the realities at hand and the distant cosmos, were one and indistinguishable. In this world view nothing is mutable, the universe is static or at best cyclic, repeating itself in endless patterns of return and renewal. Stonehenge, then, is the substantiation of a mythic world view; and like holisms known from other archaic or preliterate sources, it is the product of "a symbolic articulation of institutional structures and communal thought."[1]

In this work we have set out to reconstruct the social life of the Stonehengers as they intellectualized it and made it solid in their monument. We have done so out of many disparate elements, pulling together knowledge of cultures much later and much earlier in time. We have placed the various stages of Stonehenge society on a continuum of cultural evolution, for we recognize that each flourished at but one shifting point in time, as one passing scene in the ever-unfolding drama of human history.

This has permitted us to explicate the final Stonehenge monument and the Wessex warriors who built it in at least two ways. The first is the standard historical approach to past cultures, a perspective that combines the descriptive data of archaeology with reconstructions based on analogies derived from ethnographic and ethnohistoric data. The second is rather more imaginative, the cognitive approach, that strives for empathy; whereby we hope to reconstruct the ambient mentality of the Wessex people, and even of their predecessors, and feel the vitality of ideas that moved them to build the various Stonehenges. We are far less interested in the artifacts they left behind than in their ways of life and especially their outlook on the world, seen and unseen. Knowing we can never begin to fully explicate the cultural climate of those vanished societies, yet do we hope to have illuminated and made vivid a few aspects of it sufficient for us to say: here are peoples whose life-ways and monuments make sense, not in our terms, but in theirs.

This work will suggest that at least Stonehenge III, the final phase, was built by warrior herdsmen belonging to an ancient form of European society, a heroic society. If this is not exactly the Iron Age Celtic version witnessed by Roman and Greek writers and remembered in epic poetry, then it is formative to these well-known later ones. Historians both ancient and modern have seen Europe as divided into two zones, northern and southern, barbarian and civilized. Thus, the barbarism and insecurity of heroic society are the obverse of corporate civil life in the ancient Near East and Mediterranean. Yet the two are related; both spring from the same roots and through history constantly impinge on one another. We now know that the formation of heroic societies is very old, dating at least to the fifth millennium B.C., and probably growing out of a mixture of agriculturalists and older hunting-gathering folk somewhere in the western zone of the Eurasian steppe. These societies are mixed herding and farming complexes who always reckoned their wealth in cattle. It is essential to understand that heroic warrior societies do not simply appear like Athena, sprouting fully armed from her father's forehead. In common with all cultures they go an evolutionary progress, though in truth pastoral ones may change almost as swiftly in time as the people themselves move in space.

The essential structure of the heroic age is a stratified tribal society—a chiefdom—of warriors, priests, and husbandmen/farmers in which the warriors fight for their chief, the priests sanction and praise the chief and his band of followers, and the husbandmen herd the cattle and provide grain and ordinary crafts for all. These graded obligations lie behind the more elaborate formulas of medieval feudalism. Just as one needs to understand the structure and history of heroic society in order to understand the Middle Ages, in fact to understand Western civilization as we know it, so the precursors of the barbarians must be known. The basis for the heroic age is the Neolithic Age, a state of culture first established in the Near East by the tenth millennium and in Europe since the eighth. Neolithic means self-sufficient village life based on garden agriculture (i.e., horticulture) mixed with some degree of animal husbandry. But the Neolithic, too, has an even longer history as it emerges from and blends with mobile hunting and gathering folk. We must, therefore, begin at the beginning, and assign Stonehenge its proper place in the continuous history of mankind.

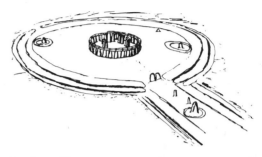

Stonehenge III.

Paleolithic Hunters

The most powerful centers of mankind today are the highly urbanized, industrial nation-states. Factory industrialism began with the Industrial Revolution in England about three-hundred years ago. Urbanism began with the cities of Mesopotamia in 3000 B.C. But this urban revolution presupposed support from a Neolithic countryside. Agriculture, in its turn, began with the so-called Neolithic revolution in villages that first arose among hilly regions flanking the Mesopotamian valley in about 9000 B.C. Before that, man everywhere was a hunter of wild game animals and a collector of wild vegetable foods, from about two to three million years ago.

This is the story of man run backwards, with all its decisive revolutions, although in truth they were not sudden revolutions but gradual changes, each new state of culture slowly emerging out of an older one. The end result, however, has not been uniform for all men. Today all men are not citizens of a great nation-state, dwelling in its cities, laboring in its industrial workshops, or on its mechanized farms. Most humans by far still live in a Neolithic state of culture, in the horticultural folk villages of Asia, Africa, and Latin America. Some of these villages exist to feed only themselves (such as those isolated in the tribal wilderness of the Amazon Basin or the interior of New Guinea), while others exist to feed also the urbanites in nations still undergoing the process of industrialization (such as the peasant folk of India). And some men, a tiny fraction, are still living in a hunting and gathering state of culture, notably the Bushmen of the Kalahari desert in Southwest Africa and the Aborigines of Australia.

We observe that the cultures of contemporary man coexist in various stages of development. We see not only coexistence, but interaction on a global scale, as between the nations of the industrial West and their former colonial possessions who now seek nationhood and industry for themselves, often with unlike results.

Thus it ever was, as soon as cultures in one region evolved beyond those elsewhere, they began to mutually influence each other. Interaction of this sort took place within the confines of the Stonehenge region for a good many centuries and contributed to the outcome of the final monument, as we shall see. By the time Stonehenge III was completed, the region had seen interaction between at least three different "ages." There were finally the warrior herdsmen who dominated the place and who are identified with the Bronze Age. They arrived in two major waves: the Beaker folk who built Stonehenge II and after that the builders of Stonehenge III. The people they more or less dominated were farmers of the Neolithic Age who supplied grain and stone axes. There were, therefore, two stages of the Neolithic. The first was the Wessex farmers, offspring of the Danubian pioneers; the second was the Windmill Hill folk, a product of the interaction between Wessex farmers and native Mesolithic peoples. The point of contact among all these groups was trade, at first in greenstone axes, later in metal axes and daggers. The hunters, in their turn, are identified with the Mesolithic Age, the era of skilled hunters who replaced the original hunters of the Paleolithic Age, who in turn pioneered the human way of life.

In Britain, the last of the Paleolithic hunters disappeared by the end of the Ice Age around 10,000 B.C., as they did almost everywhere else. Yet they, too, contribute to the Stonehenge story insofar as they passed on to their Mesolithic pupils a fundamental religious idea about the dead that we find memorialized in the stones of Stonehenge as well as in the surrounding burial ground.

Beginning with the emergence of man and the manufacture of the first stone tools some three million years ago, the Paleolithic Age lasted throughout the Eurasian continent south of the January frost line and in Africa up until the end of the geological Ice Age. It is usually subdivided, at least in Europe (to which we shall confine our attention), into three periods: Lower Paleolithic, with the earliest species of true men (*Homo erectus*) having differentiated from the animal world, and the usage of cutting tools made from stone cores; Middle Paleolithic, the time of Neanderthal Man, directly ancestral to modern man, and the usage of flake tools; Upper Paleolithic, from about 30,000 B.C., with modern *Homo sapiens*, and a proliferation of tool types (including the first tools with which to make tools), and the cave art of western Europe. During this last period man first occupied cold regions north of the frost line and colonized the New World and Australia.

The term Paleolithic, which means "Old Stone Age," was coined in the early days of anthropology to designate the first stage in the technology of stone working, but today has social and economic significance as well. Paleolithic in the narrow, technological sense refers to the so-called hand-axes (actually butchering tools) made from flint or quartzite. In this process a lump of such material is shattered with a hammerstone until the core is shaped to a cutting edge. It would be wrong to assume that this simple technology was crude or static. The former, at least, is an aesthetic judgment made from a modern point of view. It is apparent from the great length of time these core tools were in use that they were perfectly adequate to the needs of our ancestors who made them. Furthermore, they developed new forms over the course of many millennia, such as flake tools out of the waste matter of core tools, possibly in response to a growing scarcity of raw materials as well as to new hunting conditions.

In the wider usage, Paleolithic means the most ancient state of human culture belonging to the nomadic life of the earliest hunters. This involves the pursuit of large game over, at first, wide geographical areas, later over narrower ones. Hunting contrasts with the prehuman condition of man's primate ancestors which, like the living monkeys and apes, foraged for food, each individual and each sex for itself. The primates have an ecology, but only man has an economy. The human revolution is associated with the emergence of a hunting economy, which includes a feature universal to all mankind, a sexual division of labor. The males pioneered a new activity, the killing of large game animals, while the females continued to gather plant foods in the manner of both sexes in prehuman times, bringing their pickings home to a campsite, marked by fire, for sharing with their family or band—home, family, and band organization being other cultural features of the human revolution. The hunting way of life as such is still viable among the Bushmen and the Australian Aboriginals. Bushman males hunt antelope, females gather mongongo nuts; Australian males hunt kangaroo, females go on daily foraging expeditions.

These two hunting cultures, however, are not Paleolithic. They represent a culmination of its Upper period in the skilled hunters of the Mesolithic Age. Mesolithic hunters go back to the end of the Ice Age, when the large game animals of the extensive tundra zones that once

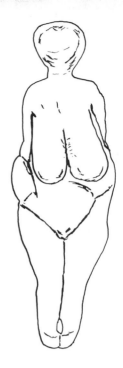

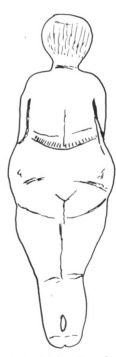

Female figurine from Kostenki, Russia. A standard item in the inventory of Upper Palaeolithic art, such a figurine has been found at Dolní Věstonice.

Head of a female, carved from ivory, Dolní Věstonice, Czechoslovakia. This object was found in a hut separate from the rest of the hunter's settlement which also contained a female buried under red ochre together with objects which seem to have had religious import. This would seem the first example of religious specialization, some 25,000 years ago.

characterized most of Europe disappeared, and waters from the melting glaciers broke up the landscape in many places with new streams and ponds. Hunters thus had to adjust to the pursuit of a more varied quarry of smaller postglacial fauna, including fish and other aquatic species, limited to pockets of regional distribution. Associated with these new pursuits are the domestication of the dog as a hunting companion, the invention of the bow and arrow, and a more flexible tool kit.

The Mesolithic way of life took place in ever more localized areas of the world and within Europe itself. As a result, a great number of variations on the Mesolithic way of making tools grew up among different regions, each with its own method suited to local resources. Some Mesolithic hunters, given the opportunity to fish streams that passed through game-rich forests, or to combine hunting with the seasonal harvesting of wild grain, were able to achieve the beginnings of residential stability. Sedentary life is crucial to the possibilities of organization inherent in human society; they are foretold even among certain hunters during Upper Paleolithic times.

In Upper Paleolithic sites ranging from Czechoslovakia to southern Russia and dating back almost 30,000 years, archaeologists have found what amount to villages, although not agricultural ones. Perhaps the best known of these is Dolní Věstonice in southern Moravia which dates somewhere between 30 and 25 millennia in age. Rather than ranging over wide territories for their hunting, the inhabitants of this remarkable site preyed on mammoths and reindeer that ran nearby in abundant herds. If the people migrated they did so seasonally and within a restricted zone. The presence of well-made huts and circular earthen lodges indicates a long established community. Two of the lodges give evidence of advanced social organization. One is larger with five hearths in it, and it was assumed by the excavators to have been the community center. The other contains a burial located under the floor and covered with red ochre, together with a human figurine carved in bone. This figurine, interpreted as female, with many other human and animal figures found elsewhere in the site, carved in mammoth ivory or baked in clay, testifies to a lengthy cultural tradition native to a settled place.[2]

Dolní Věstonice has something to say about the process of cultural evolution, which process we shall apply to the rise of Stonehenge. First, it is clear that human societies over time adapt themselves ecologically to varied environments and thus develop different forms. Second, given conditions for settlement, community life of a sort more permanent than that of transitory hunting camps will emerge. Last, we may infer that settled life, however primitive, will give rise to a new element of social organization beyond that of the sexual division of labor. In the case of Dolní Věstonice, it was a religious specialist concerned with tendance of the dead and their souls, treated as extensions of living members of the community, which likely was based on kinship. While we have evidence of deliberate burials in some Neanderthal caves of the Middle Paleolithic, we have nothing to indicate religious practitioners. This we have at Dolní Věstonice, the oldest site which we can claim for the archaeology of religion. The burial under red ochre at this site not only indicates a belief in an afterlife, red being the color of blood and historically of eternal life; the female figurine associated with the burial may well indicate a shamanistic person, a specialist who communicates with supernatural forces and mediates between the living and the dead. A few pictures of shamans at work (who may be of either sex, depending on cultural tradition) may be seen in Upper Paleolithic cave art.

Mesolithic Hunters

Mesolithic means "Middle Stone Age," a type of industry sandwiched between the end of the Paleolithic and the start of the Neolithic. It is marked by tiny flakes set in wood, horn, or ivory so as to form compound tools such as harpoon heads and sickle blades for the cutting of wild grain.

In wider economic terms, the Mesolithic Age may be viewed either as a culmination of the hunting tradition or as a transitional period of "incipient food production."[3] It had its briefest term in western Asia, where farming evolved shortly after the last of the glaciers retreated to their present positions in about 9000 B.C. In Britain, the transition from Mesolithic food collecting to Neolithic food producing did not take place until the later part of the fourth millennium, with the entry of nomadic farmers (the Danubians) who set the example for native hunters.

One of the oldest Neolithic sites in the world is Jericho, near the Dead Sea, where Mesolithic campers learned to exploit local resources with such intensity and skill that they found themselves living in a substantial town even before they learned how to grow crops and domesticate animals. For some two thousand years, beginning in the tenth millennium, they had combined hunting and fishing with the gathering of seed plants, the wild ancestors of einkorn and emmer wheat. By the ninth millennium, a Mesolithic campsite had become a Mesolithic townsite of mudbrick houses enclosed by a stone wall. A florescence of religious ideas made possible by settled life, anticipated at Dolní Věstonice, followed. Buried under the floors of individual houses are human skulls, their flesh modeled in plaster. The work on these skulls is spectacular from an artistic point of view; but more importantly they are a social measure of the extent to which belief in the afterlife has been elaborated in some kind of ancestor cult, linking the dead with a community of the living. Other buildings seem to be shrines, evidently under the supervision of full-time religious specialists, in which the attention of this cult was focused.[4]

At Jericho, agriculture evolved out of a settled version of Mesolithic life. The same potential for this development must therefore have existed in other Mesolithic localities, to be realized by way of example from the outside if not by growth from the inside. Indeed, the same change took place over and over again all over Europe, but whether by internal growth or by external contact it is not always easy to say. Wherever the Neolithic example was easy to follow, there also independent change was latent. Both ways of change, however, are two aspects of the same general process of cultural evolution, as we shall illustrate with two Mesolithic cultures in Denmark. Side by side, one somehow went Neolithic while its neighbor stayed Mesolithic. They are the Maglemosian and the Ertebølle cultures; the latter settled in with its resources while the other kept on the move, living from camp to camp. Together, these two cultures comprehend the whole Mesolithic spectrum in Europe, from culminating hunters to incipient farmers.

The Maglemosian culture, located inland, was adapted to the heavy woodlands that covered most of Europe during early postglacial times. Its artifacts include core axes made useful for woodwork by setting them in antler hafts, dugout canoes, bone fishhooks, and animal figurines carved in amber, raw material received in trade from the shores of the Baltic Sea. The remains of Maglemosian dwelling sites in Denmark and everywhere else in northern Europe often consist of house platforms laid down with felled trees at the edge of what used to be swamps and lakes. The houses indicate villages, but only occasional villages, reoccupied campsites. Perhaps the most famous, certainly the best explored site of this type is Star Carr in Yorkshire, northern England, dating back to 8000 B.C. Star Carr was the intermittent home for a band of some twenty-five people who followed the seasonal game trails of deer herds.

Ertebølle culture was coastal, marked by permanent villages built on great shell middens, the garbage of these people's favorite seafood and basic diet.[5] They achieved a settled life out of the Mesolithic potential for it, whereas the Maglemosians retained their essential hunters' mobility, wooden houses and villages notwithstanding. In achieving this, the Ertebølle food collectors were able to pass on directly their tool types, houses, and settlement pattern to the food producers of a successive "age," the Neolithic, which makes its appearance in late Ertebølle sites. These contain the bones of what are taken to be domesticated cattle and sheep, as well as grains of domesticated cereals and shards of pottery. What is more, this pottery is identical to the earliest Neolithic type known from northern Europe, *Trichterbecker* (TRB) or funnel-necked beakers. Its makers had made themselves the neighbors of the Ertebølle folk, but of what happened next we know only the end result.

Yet the general pattern of change is clear. Some Mesolithic peoples, like the Ertebølle, found it easy to settle into places where they could collect food at the same rate Neolithic peoples could by cultivating it. The resulting villages were not unlike those of farmers who later migrated into the same region. Food production then was taken up by the indigenes when and if it suited them. Not only was the new economy taken up by a people ready to accept it; they were similar enough to take in the new people who imported it. If not, room enough there was for both economies. Maglemosian type hunters remained in woodlands all over Europe long after the Neolithic way of life appeared there.

From this lesson we may now propose three principles of culture change that will help us explain the evolutionary phases of Stonehenge. One is internal development seen in the change a Mesolithic folk, the Ertebølle, made on their own from a nomadic to a sedentary pattern of

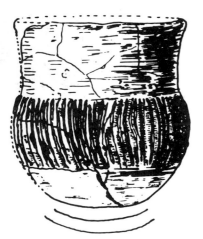

Pottery of Ertebølle type and funnel beaker (TRB) from northern Germany.

food collection. Another is external contact, witnessed in the TRB farmers who settled next to these folk and provided them, by Neolithic example at least, with an alternative basis for settlement. Last, and perhaps most important, the natives may have absorbed the newcomers, or the reverse; the result in either case would be, as we know it was at Stonehenge with the arrival of the first farmers and even later migrants, a melding both of cultures and their carriers.

Mesolithic cultures thus played an on-going role in the formation of the European Neolithic; the latter was not simply imported wholesale from a source in Western Asia as once believed. Local elements carried over were traditions in stone working and perhaps woodworking. Above all were religious ideas concerning burial of the dead and the afterlife. In France, the great collective tombs of the Neolithic period coincide geographically with the best established and longest lived Mesolithic tradition. It is possible that words in the languages of native hunter-gatherers remained as place names or as substrata in the speech of Neolithic newcomers. Assuming a local melding of peoples, that is not unlikely.

Neolithic Farmers

Neolithic or "New Stone Age" was originally coined to describe the technology of making cutting tools by grinding, pecking, polishing, or otherwise abrading pebbles of compact stone. The strategic tools in this technology are the axe for clearing the land (already a Mesolithic tool, as among the Maglemosian and Ertebølle cultures, although the head was not polished but knapped of flint), the adze for carpentry, and the hoe or mattock for tillage.

But Neolithic is also the name for village society in which a few hundred residents pass their lives together caring for their domestic plants and raising stock. Basic variations include dispersed settlement and a preference for either cultigens or animals. Cultures specific to these often leave the mark of their passing only in the remains of their craft traditions, usually pottery types, which is why we make reference to the technical vocabulary of ceramics. But what holds our attention is the new way of life from which these Neolithic variations spring: effective farming villages based on the "wheat-barley-sheep-goat-cattle-pig complex" that has supported the whole of western society to this day.[6]

Seen from today, the changeover from Mesolithic hunting to Neolithic farming seems revolutionary. One of the great men of modern archaeology, V. Gordon Childe, used precisely that term to describe the change.[7] "Neolithic Revolution" is now thought to be too strong a term for what was in fact a slow and tangled evolutionary process, yet the advent of agriculture remains the single most revolutionary change in the history of man, the one that opened up the potential in human society for political organization and which therefore laid down indispensable conditions for the rise of civilization. If the evolutionary principles already mentioned are applied—those of internal development, external contact, and amalgamation—the transition to a Neolithic state of culture will be

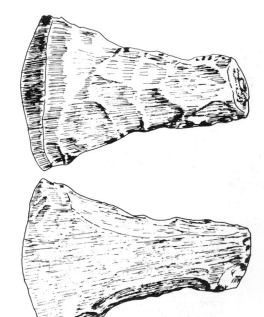

Mesolithic flake axe, Ertebølle culture, Denmark (after Klindt-Jensen). (See next page for Mesolithic core axe.)

Mesolithic core axe, Ertebølle culture, Denmark (after Klindt-Jensen).

seen to be a very complex process indeed. In fact, it is now known that there is not just one Neolithic phenomenon, but several, each adding something to our total picture of European prehistory and each touching in some way on the builders of Stonehenge. At least three traditions may be discerned in the archaeological record, those of Old European culture,[8] the nomadic Danubian farmers, and the Kurgan pastoralists. These will be discussed in the following three sections.

But first a few general words about them. They represent economic and social variations on a Neolithic theme brought about by realistic adaptations to widely different ecological factors such as climate, soil type, and population density. Human beings are the most adaptable of all animals because they are cultural animals; and one definition of culture is the total means by which a society, humans in association, copes with its chosen environment. But once having made that initial adaptation, it becomes traditional. The three versions of the Neolithic tradition mentioned above developed as highly conservative societies preserving intact many of their culture traits over hundreds, even thousands, of years.

The conservative impulse may be seen at work today in those surviving Neolithic villages in Latin America, Asia, and Africa that resist new and more productive ways of seed selection, plowing, planting, and harvesting. The old religious customs associated with their way of life also remain unchanged. So long as a culture continues to cope with its environment at even a marginal level of success, it will tend to retain basic features of the old working formula. This dictum is not confined to farmers; after all, hunter-gatherers all over the world continued to live an unchanging way of life for many millennia. The major difference between sedentary populations and nomadic ones is that the latter can move while the former must adjust their life to cope with a fixed locality. If hunters need something for their economy—such as a good game trail, a berry patch, a stand of wild grain, fruit trees, a flint mine, and so on—they have only to move themselves to the source of the desirable product. But the early farmers who made the transition to settled life had somehow to find a way to move the products. The answer to this problem was trade. In time, the new way of life with its hoeing and herding, permanent settlement, and trade would entail changes not alone in social organization but in its supportive mythology. Because man's adaptive genius is in tension with his conservative longings, elements of the old way of life will have always remained, especially nonmaterial elements—religious ideas and mythology. If economics is the most adaptive department of any culture, religion is its most conservative counterforce.

This tension is universal to all human societies. Sometimes it conflicts with the reality principle, sometimes it does not. When it does not, we have the example of unleavened bread used as a communion wafer in Christian church services, or else matzo in the Jewish celebration of Passover; where in both cases the hidden and long forgotten event that is memorialized is the original transition from a Mesolithic to a Neolithic way of life, whose immortal symbol has been bread, unleavened bread, the first prepared food basic to the new diet. To go back even further, the

idea of an afterlife, conceived by Middle Paleolithic hunters (the Ne-
anderthals), is still with us, as is the Upper Paleolithic provision (at Dolní
Věstonice) of a religious specialist to serve that idea. The afterlife, however, has lately come in conflict with the organizing principles of the
Union of Socialist Soviet Republics, following the Bolshevik revolution,
which seeks to accommodate a number of local states within the union by
abolishing their mutually hostile religious creeds, replacing them with
atheism, a government-led idea common to all.

Famed for its example of conflict between religious conservatism and
economic reality is the sacred cow of India. In the absence of an adjustment enforced by the Indian government, numerous cattle are free to
wander out from the Neolithic countryside and into the streets of Calcutta
and other cities, never chased out and certainly never butchered—nor are
they in the villages, under a taboo against the eating of beef. The explanation for this by some western anthropologists is that the taboo is,
after all, still adaptive. The taboo against butchering cattle is rationalized
from an economic standpoint—sacred cows provide vital manure, used
both as fertilizer and domestic fuel, and traction power in an energy-poor
society. If their numbers were reduced for the provision of food, the result
would be even greater impoverishment.[9] This rationale is no longer relevant. Cow manure fertilizes nothing in the streets of Calcutta, nor is there
ground to plow. The resistance to eating beef is religious, whose credo is
taken by Indian peasants to be of more importance than a ready supply
of protein, much less urban sanitation. Modern solutions to the problem of
food and energy supplies are at hand. But any one of them would wreck a
system of traditional ideas, once cohering with good practice, that no
longer is adaptive, given a new urbanism connected with the developmental economics of nationhood and factory industrialism. The point is
that once a culture finds its initial solution to an ecological problem, it
finds difficulty in adjusting to new ones. Humans are adaptive, yes; but
once they make a success in the formative period of their respective cultures, they go conservative. This explains why the "lasting character of
each people has its roots in the basic culture of the time when the people
first came into being."[10] This also explains why it is possible to trace back
the early form of Indo-European society at Stonehenge from later Indo-
European epic literature.

There is one great exception to the conservative picture drawn here.
Change may come very fast to any society if its internal contradictions allow the young to challenge the authority of the old. When the old prove
too weak to resolve the tension between adaptive and conservative forces,
the young take over, and political change is the result. This may be a
simple-minded explanation for political revolutions, but it does bear some
validity when applied to societies under stress. One might state it this
way. As long as the society remains stable, changeovers in its political
leadership also will remain stable with the new leadership reflecting the
same values as the old. In case of instability, the challenge to leadership
may be violent and changes made by the takeover generation will be radical in terms of established ways, as was the challenge to the classless Neo-

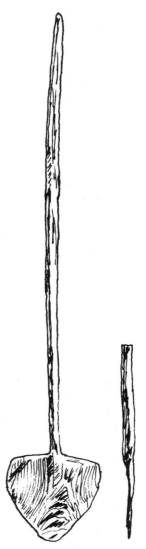

Wooden spade from Erteb⁄lle
culture, northern Germany.

lithic societies we are about to describe. When the old communal order was transformed into a stratified one, that political revolution was accomplished by young warriors. The epic poetry of the heroic age is nothing less than an exuberant celebration of young barbarians. We might even say that when the new heroic societies of barbarian Europe pitted themselves against the older civilized societies of the Mediterranean, the same pattern obtained: youth culture against the wisdom culture of age.

The preceding Neolithic Revolution, however, does not fit this pattern. A mistake in dating the European origins of Neolithic village life, by underestimating its great antiquity, led an earlier generation of archaeologists to describe in radical terms what in reality was a process of extraordinarily long duration. The break with Mesolithic hunting never was a revolution for any living generations of men as was the conquest of Neolithic communal life by the sudden rise of heroic society. Radiocarbon dating has rectified this error, a method itself lately corrected. A recent correlation of the Carbon-14 system with the growth rings of a long-lived species of pine tree in California has added hundreds of years to already quite old dates.[11] The oldest Neolithic traditions in Europe are now seen to date from about 7000 B.C. to 3500 B.C., lasting as integrated and interrelated cultures for some 3500 years! Given the increased time depth for the European Neolithic, outside its supposed origins in western Asia, its emergence out of a local Mesolithic setting by a very slow and conservative process of development is easier to visualize than rapid diffusion from an original source, the old theory. The question of ultimate origins, however, remains controversial. Nonetheless, agriculture in Europe is marked from the beginning by indigenous qualities summed up by Marija Gimbutas as "Old European Civilization,"[12] which we shall call Old European culture. The word "civilization" for us implies social stratification, a high culture, and the state.

Old Europeans

Only recently defined as a unitary world centered on the Balkans, Old European culture encompassed a region from the Adriatic and Aegean across southeastern Europe to Poland and the Ukraine, with at least five regional variants (see Map 1). Old European peoples lived in large townships the remains of which are found in huge mounds (*tulul*, plural of *tell*), the accumulated debris of thousands of years of occupation. Some *tulul* are up to fifty feet in height. Some are located on high points overlooking rivers, others are on plains. From the earliest period these settlements adjoined rich soils with plentiful water, occupying river valleys all over their part of Europe. It is also apparent, though none have yet been found, that some kind of plough must have been used. The potential for population growth is demonstrated by Tal'Noe in southern Russia. Dating to the early fourth millennium this site, a virtual urban center, covered seven-hundred acres, had some one thousand five hundred houses and a population of twenty-thousand.[13] Old Europeans obviously dwelled in towns more complex than Jericho when it was still a Meso-

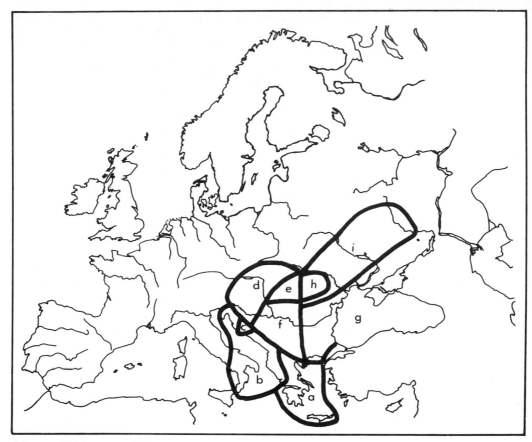

Map 1.   Old European Cultures, fifth millennium B.C. (after Gimbutas). A. Aegean; B. Adriatic; C. Butmir;
D. Danube; E. Tisza; F. Vinca; G. E. Balkan; H. Petresti; I. Tripolye.

lithic town, but the question is, precisely *how* complex? Certainly craft
and religious specialties were practiced by the Old Europeans. They exchanged objects with neighboring peoples in Anatolia and the Mediterranean, including obsidian (a black volcanic glass), alabaster, shell, and
marble. Later, in the fifth millennium, copper objects came to be exchanged in the same way. Few authorities, however, think that Old European communities were governed with any political sophistication.
While many probably had around one-thousand inhabitants, there is no
archaeological evidence for social stratification. At Nea Nikomedia in
northern Greece, for example, four rectangular houses (about twenty-five
feet wide by twenty-five to thirty-three feet long) were found grouped
around one larger house. This latter contained female figurines, axes of
greenstone and clay (which were cultic, not banausic objects in this culture), and pottery different from a domestic sort found in the other
houses. It appears to be a shrine central to the village. No warrior equipment, no lavish palaces or great halls here. Social control cannot have
been formalized but must rather have been based on personal relations of
the sort we know about in folk villages today or in the recent past.[14] Community decisions probably were made by village elders with the help, or

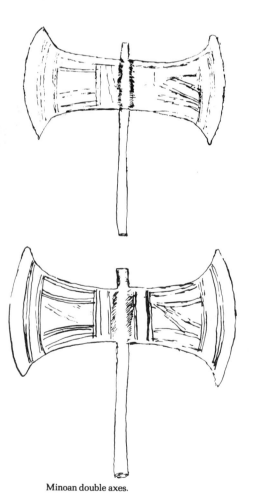

Minoan double axes.

under the guidance, of a shaman working out of a "prototemple." With small populations (most people in these places were probably related to each other) and stable environmental conditions, there would have been no need for elaborate decision-making machinery—therefore, no formal states, though Professor Gimbutas has suggested that the proximity of mounds in the Martisa River valley in Bulgaria (two to three miles apart) may indicate some sort of alliance system.

The nearest analogy to the political organization of the Old Europeans may be found among the Pueblo Indians of the southwestern United States. Each Pueblo community is separate and individual, governed by a most rudimentary political system, which is centered in a special meeting place, an underground lodge called a *kiva*, where decisions with supernatural sanction are made. Here men of high status (elders, mainly) gather to commune with the spirits of their ancestors, mediated by a shaman. While most *kivas* are small and part of each Pueblo settlement, an abandoned one in the ruins of Mesa Verde is quite large and once stood at the hub of an extensive road network. Clearly this was a supracommunal meeting place for several Pueblo villages in the area; as such it points to a nascent political structure. The same kind must have governed Old European townships. As we shall see, organization of a similar level may be inferred from one or more early phases of Stonehenge.

Although the level of social organization indicated here in no way approaches that more elaborate one of the political state, it must not be imagined that Old Europeans were unsophisticated in other departments. To the contrary, a highly developed religious culture is indicated, whose belief system is connected with certain ideas built into Stonehenge, especially those with cosmological/astronomical meaning.

It is now evident that many religious elements in Old European culture passed into post-Neolithic periods. The most obvious example of continuity is to be found in the classical Greek civilization, outwardly an Indo-European product, but submerged within it Old European iconography recurs again and again, as in the cult of Demeter, the minotaur story, and the very name of Athens itself. What is more, it would seem that Old European religious ideas were shared by a variety of Neolithic peoples all across Europe and that these, too, formed a basis for later religious thought.

Professor Marija Gimbutas has argued forcefully for a continuity of Old European symbolism based on what, in her opinion, was developed within the context of a coherent and unified theology. If her argument is followed we find that the most important religious idea of the Old Europeans was dramatized in the cult of the "Great Mother," a vegetation goddess who manifests herself systematically in many avatars, but whose main function in each must have been fertility.[15] Recognition of a pan-European "great goddess" dates from the earliest days of archaeology and studies in mythology when female figurines were first discovered in Neolithic excavations. Related to the "Mother" cult, which may have been associated with human sacrifice, are the double-axe and the bull, both of which are characteristic of Minoan civilization. Other religious symbols include pigs and bears. These two are evident associates of people who adapted Neolithic life to a forested setting, and both pass into Greek mythology, pigs representing the fertility cult of Demeter, bears the hunting goddess Artemis. The snake, spiral meanders, and concentric rings are other symbols that relate to the sun and thus have most direct astronomical associations. In fact, the whole nexus of symbology and worship reflects cosmological, hence astronomical, theory.

Both the sun and the moon appear frequently in the small art found in all Old European, Greek, and Minoan sites. The moon goes with the bull cult and seemingly with the huntress aspect of the "great goddess." This particular association is found throughout western European mythology. Artemis, the huntress of the Greeks, and Diana, the same goddess among the Romans, were both moon goddesses. It is possible that the German Freyja, the Celtic Brigit, and even the Indian Kali are also avatars of the same goddess.[16] The moon always is entrained with fertility cycles (witness the *Old Farmer's Almanac* for a modern example). It is not surprising, then, to find a major aspect of the fertility goddess of Neolithic peoples taken up with the moon. It is even likely that astrology may have had some of its roots in Old European culture. The zodiacal bull is but one example.[17] The builders of Stonehenge may have detected the same symbols in the sky, the bull in spring, the Pleiades (seen as sparks of fire burning between the bull's horns) in winter.

The sun, too, has its equally powerful symbols, such as those famous snakes grasped by the hands of priestly women figured in Minoan sculpture. With the advent of metallurgy, copper casting to begin with, the smith's fires and the color of both finished copper and beaten gold must have added luster to the sun's own. We will discuss later the pan-European extent of the solar cult in association with the spread of metallurgy. But metal use may not be the only connection. Apart from the obvious power of the sun to grow crops, it appears from earlier Neolithic burials to be related to an afterlife, perhaps even to the idea of reincarnation. The dead, especially children, were buried in a crouched or foetal position, and covered with that oldest symbol of eternal life, red ochre. In the catalogue of Old European art, figurines of the turtle and the toad abound, both symbolizing the full round of life and death among many later European peoples. The toad is still regarded as a token of birth among certain Baltic peasants.[18] A toad figurine has been found even in a Mesolithic site of Maglemosian Denmark. What has this to do with the sun cult? Simply that the return of the sun in spring, the very return of the sun daily, signifies eternal rebirth. This seems to have been so from at least Mesolithic times.

It is apparent from the rich iconography and elaborate ritual that had to go with it, that the Old Europeans employed religious specialists. They may have formed a class of hierophants, as did priests in the rising urban centers of Mesopotamia. On the other hand, they may bear closer resemblance to a familiar figure among the Plains Indians, that of the medicine man. This figure, and others like it from other tribal cultures, is general-

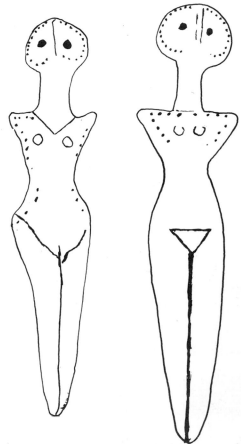

Female figurine, Tripolye Culture, Russia. This is the all pervasive female deity which figures so prominently in the art of Old Europe.

ized in the anthropological literature and called a shaman. Among Old Europeans the exact nature of their religious practitioners, whether priests or shamans, is hard to determine. Doubtless they held themselves apart as a sacred caste. Shaman/priests certainly did so among their better known neighbors to the east, Indo-European peoples to whom the Old Europeans lent some of their religious concepts.[19] Whatever the case, religious specialists are everywhere the conservators of bygone ideas, and as such they represent mankind's first professional occupation. In a precivilized state of culture, they would have been the only persons qualified beyond generalized economic activity to supervise the construction of Stonehenge in its every phase. Certainly they would have provided the rationale for that undertaking, a cosmic rationale.

The solar and lunar symbolism mentioned above imply that Neolithic shaman/priests spent considerable time observing the sky and working out a cosmological system of ideas. If analogies to early peoples in Europe about whom we have records and to preliterate peoples alive today are any guide, this cosmology would explain how the heavens and the earth were bound together in one sacred order. That rationale would have been verbalized in a mythology (which is, after all, the intellectual way primitives comprehend their natural world), which in turn would have been materialized in works of art, both secular and religious. These works leave us with but a fragmentary view of their intellectual context; yet we can be fairly certain that a corpus of celestial observations had been built up over the centuries. Some mental traces of these ancient studies probably remain in the astrological zodiac and in symbolic images assigned to the constellations. It is not that such a body of knowledge was crucial to the practical working of Old European society—that lies in economic experience—but that a cosmic superstructure was thought by them to be of vital importance in providing a higher rationale for work-a-day life. Such knowledge was the natural outgrowth of the need by an agricultural people to understand meteorological events in some way or other, in what we shall call farmers' astronomy.

Nevertheless, Mesolithic hunters and early pastoralists give strong evidence of similar concerns. The people who designed and built the later phases of Stonehenge must have built up a like body of cosmological knowledge, perhaps in some ways closely related to the work of Old European sky watchers. There is enough evidence to suggest this was so. It is also possible, but not demonstrated, that cosmic symbolism was present in Britain when the earliest henge monuments were built, of which the first phase of Stonehenge is only one example. Perhaps the symbolic representations have gone unrecognized hitherto or, because put on perishable material such as wood or painted on stones, they have been lost. Such are the problems of prehistoric archaeology in northern Europe.

The decline of Old European culture came about as the result of perhaps two basic forces. One might have been internal: transition to a stratified chiefdom as the result of the population outgrowing the political dimensions of its folk townships. This was now an age of copper use and, as we shall see, trade in that metal had much to do with helping to build layered societies. The other possibility, external, is that the towns were over-whelmed by an influx of pastoralists, possible relatives of the Old Euro-peans, from the east. We call these migrants Kurgan folk, who will be discussed shortly, for they are ancestral Indo-Europeans. Both models are valid, both may have occurred from place to place and time to time. Whatever the cause, towns were fortified, eventual centers for copper-using chiefs.

Danubian Pioneers

Old European culture was not the only Neolithic tradition in Europe, but it is the oldest. Its beginnings may very well coincide with those of western Asia, which place we are accustomed to think of as the "original" source of food production. If so, by what channel was the example trans-mitted? Nobody knows. The Mesolithic potential for it existed at more than one place, as we know from Ertebølle, not alone at Jericho and there-about. But this need not detain us.

Of interest here is the fact that Old European culture was itself an example for at least two other Neolithic traditions on its outer fringes. One lies to the east of the Balkans, the aforementioned pastoral Kurgan folk; the other to the northwest among nomadic farmers of the Middle Danube: the Danubians.

While Old Europeans lived a sedentary life for century upon century, building up mounds tremendous in both size and number (five-hundred in the East Balkans alone with internal lives of more than one-thousand years each), Danubian people evolved their culture on the move. They were once a Mesolithic people, subsisting by fishing and hunting along river banks, who took the idea of cultivation from their settled neighbors. The Danubians are known archaeologically as Banderkeramik (Linear Pottery) folk and are identified by the spiral meanders with which their ceramic ware is decorated.[20] From out of their homeland they moved through the center of Europe, a nomadic people who farmed, clearing forestland for dispersed settlements as they passed. By the early fifth mil-lennium they had reached Britain, where they are known as the Wessex farmers. In each area they pioneered they mixed with the native popula-tion, everywhere producing local variants of the Neolithic tradition.

It is interesting to see the way in which the Danubian version of Neo-lithic culture differs from its parental model. The Old Europeans culti-vated the heavy soils of river valleys with increasing intensity while the Danubians practiced slash-and-burn agriculture, or swidden, across the forested loess belts that stretched over wide areas of Europe. Loessial soil, a thick rock dust blasted off and carried from glacial moraines by wind, is quite light and porous, holding its moisture near the surface and easily worked. Swidden consists of clearing a field, if not by cutting down trees then ringing them so they die, and burning it over before planting. The burning is done just before the wet season so that rain may wash the fer-tilizing ash into the soil. This requires enough farmer's astronomy to pre-dict seasonal weather conditions.

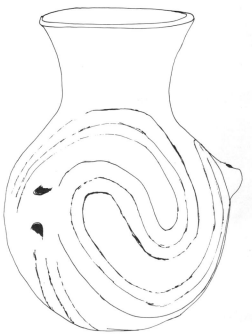

Danubian pot with swirling (linear) design. The round bottom and lugs on two sides show this pot was meant to be carried or hung. The design must indicate its use as a vessel for water or some other liquid.

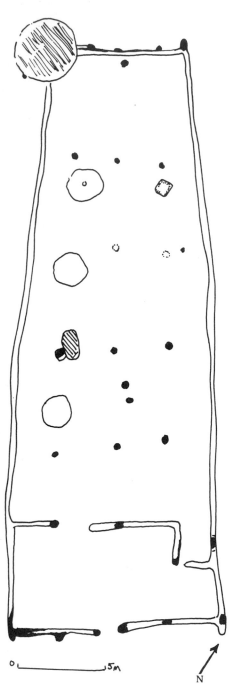

Plan of trapezoidal long-house at Postolprty, Czechoslovakia (after Ashbee, 1970).

Swidden is still practiced in tropical regions of the world, where intensive cultivation is not possible whatever the technology because the soil, once denuded of its forest cover, is leached out by the hot rains. In Neolithic Europe, however, the significance of swidden is that it carried forward the mobile residential habits of Mesolithic hunters. Homesteaders made use of local resources and when they were depleted moved on. As we have seen, the Danubian folk were formerly hunter-fishers who took up agriculture from the Old Europeans, but who did so as pioneers who didn't settle for keeps.

Danubian culture was adapted to heavily forested land and a concomitant climate. From the late sixth millennium, when the Danubian expansion began, Europe was in a climatic period called the Atlantic, a period warmer and more moist than at present. Under such conditions slashed and burnt forests will easily regenerate themselves and, as long as populations remain stable, this economic pattern can continue for a long time. We are reminded of the Mayans of the Mexican and Guatemalan lowlands who not only practiced this kind of agriculture for many hundreds of years, but who built an extraordinary civilization on that seemingly narrow base.[21]

Moving peacefully along the loess belts with their small herds of cattle, sheep, and pigs (the latter forest-browsers par excellence), and planting the most primitive form of cultivated wheat (einkorn), together with barley and a few legumes, Danubians by 4500 B.C. arrived in the Low Countries, and from thence others entered Britain. They were the first farmers in western Europe, indeed farmers only, for they seem not to have done any hunting or fishing on the side for all their Mesolithic-style mobility. They differed from Old Europeans not only in lacking residential permanence but in their family and community life as indicated by their house building tradition. Balkan townsmen most often built houses of mud-brick and of a size to accommodate single family units. The Danubians built great long-houses with gabled roofs and plastered walls, from 30 to 120 feet long by about 20 feet wide, of all timber construction. Such construction is, of course, another forest adaptation, but beyond that its size points to social organization based on extended families. Many of the Danubian farmers must have migrated in family units of this type, scattering themselves in small clearings throughout great forests. In places where a concentration of houses made for a village, it was never anything but quite small. The most famous example comes from a site in Germany, Köln-Lindenthal. This village was occupied seven times, after the farmland had lain fallow for sufficient intervals, over a period of from six hundred to nine hundred years and at its height contained twenty-one dwellings and as many extended households.[22] The population at this time cannot have numbered more than five hundred, well within the size limit for an egalitarian, communal society.[23] Again, as in the Balkan townships, we have political life confined to an informal level of organization, but one in which only a single community and its own families participate. Later, as Danubian society evolves, its social territory will grow larger until it includes clans and tribes organized across a number of communities.

Owing to their mobility, if nothing else, the Danubians stayed in contact with other peoples, trading with them. Of particular interest to the Danubians was a kind of green schist for making axes, adzes, and hoe blades, which they then traded over extensive areas of Europe. These tools obviously are those most important to a woodworking folk who also practiced horticulture. We should not be surprised to find these implements had religious as well as economic significance.

Shell from the Mediterranean also forms a part of their material culture. The means of trade by which they acquired it cannot be thought to be mercantile, carried out for profit by specialists in the business. Given a different way of doing things in the example of living primitives, we can view Danubian trade as ritual exchange, a form of business that must have gone on in Europe and western Asia since remotest times. More than likely the very idea of Neolithic food production was accompanied by certain objects, traded ceremoniously between one Mesolithic group and another, long before they achieved the economy these objects represented. At all events, Danubians traded their favorite greenstone axe heads (ground and polished in the manner of Neolithic technology), no doubt for the same combination of pious and banal reasons.

The best known analogy comes from Melanesia in the ethnographic work of Bronislaw Malinowski.[24] He describes a system of ritual exchange of ornamental necklaces and bracelets from island to island, passed around in a ring of trade called *kula*. The *kula* ring serves to bind islanders together by the mutual obligation of gift giving, backed up by supernatural qualities imbued in the items themselves. We view the *kula* ring as a model for the distribution of material resources done for a social not an economic purpose, a purpose we detect in the rise of European chiefdoms, insofar as it is geared to a like exchange of items made of copper, with all the symbolic associations that go with that metal and the forms in which it is cast.

For Danubian tribesmen engaged in trading out their greenstone axes, the ritual of exchange made for peaceful relations with others; between themselves it served to unite a society widely scattered in small islands of separate steads cut out of deep forests. It was a way of keeping in touch, and a means of covering trade in real goods, as do the Melanesians in yams and fish, beneath the religious pieties of exchanging ornaments.

The greenstone axe was the functional equivalent of the *kula* amulet. As such it remained a sacred object even for Bronze Age Europeans. From debris found in European workshops we can be certain that these axes were made by specialized craftsmen in places where greenstone is native and then were traded out over wide areas. Likewise, Neolithic pioneers who reached Britain would trade for greenstone axes manufactured at the mines of Lancashire, for use at seasonal gatherings of tribal folk elsewhere in the country. We may be sure that if the rationale for these gatherings and the exchange of cultic greenstones was religious, the practical interests of real trade, social reunion, and feasting were covered by that rationale in carnivals held under shamanistic auspices (carnival means literally a festive elevation of meat eating). The carnival grounds were first causewayed camps, then henge monuments. These lat-

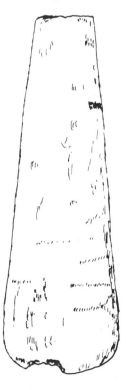

Greenstone axe, Hampshire.

ter were provincial henges before the great one at Stonehenge acquired its stones and its authority as the center of a powerful chiefdom uniting or attempting to unite all others in the region.

Kurgan Pastoralists

While the Danubians advanced their timber longhouses across western Europe, a variety of other nomadic farmers cut the same kind of rootless settlements out of forests growing in the rich black earth of the Ukraine. They are collected, in their variety, under the name Tripolye. Like the Danubians they once had been hunter-fishers before they mixed with Balkan farming folk, directly to the west of them. Unlike the Danubians, however, the Tripolye kept up their hunting and fishing even after they took on plant cultigens and pigs, sheep and cattle. Further to the east of the Old Europeans, beyond the Tripolye, along what is now the Pontic Steppe on the north coast of the Black Sea, lived yet other swidden farmers, who cleared less fertile ground but who made up for the difference with a greater reliance on stockbreeding. By the fifth millennium, these eastern peoples had evolved a steppe culture known as *Kurgan*, from the Russian word for their characteristic burial mounds. They are formative to cultures that would crystallize as Indo-European, and as such they are ancestors of the warriors who built the final two phases of Stonehenge. We already have indicated that Indo-European warriors are pastoralists; their distinctive way of life permitted the Kurgan folk and their many cultural offspring, flowing for centuries east and west over the Eurasian steppeland from their center of origin, to move in small groups very rapidly.

Pastoralism depends on two innovations: the development of herding (not merely the stabling of barnyard animals or the release of forest browsers) and domestication of the horse. Both novelties grew out of nomadic farming practiced in a steppe region, once covered by trees, the result of Neolithic life adapted to a new environment, itself the combined product of nature and man's exploitation of it.

The new environment evolved this way. On the far fringes of settled Neolithic towns, beyond the provinces of Old Europe, small groups of pioneering farmers cleared forest land in the swidden manner. But forests do not everywhere recover from the axe. Evidence from several parts of Europe indicates that once a forest growing on lighter soils is cut, the replacement cover is grass, not more trees. In western Europe, Denmark, and parts of England, this was the case during the course of the fourth millennium, as the climate shifted to a drier and warmer phase called Sub-Boreal.

Pastoralism, then, waited for its rise upon deforestation. The process began with early swidden farmers cutting out small clearings not only for their garden plots, worked by hoe, but for their domestic cattle. If the cattle population grows too dense, however, more than twenty to thirty head per square kilometer, it will denude more of the area on its own. Before long, various stands of the forest, species by species, will have been

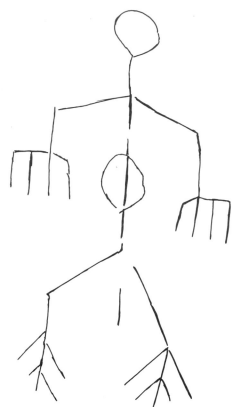

Dancing figure on Danubian pot from Czechoslovakia. This is likely a shaman engaging in a fertility rite of some kind, or so the phallic symbollism might imply. The presence of a male figure such as this in the inventory of Old European iconography speaks of religious specialists who very probably were men. We would be wrong to suppose that the cult of the female deity prevalent in the Neolithic was controlled solely by women, precisely the converse may have been the case.

destroyed: first ash, then maple, elm and oak in succession. At the same time domesticated cattle will replace wild animals used to a wider range of feeding. By comparison, roe deer in modern Denmark require as much as seventy square kilometers per head.[25] Perhaps this example provides one explanation for the lack of hunting among the Danubians.

Other reasons for massive deforestation may be supposed, the action of wind on upland soils, for example, but more likely the first destructive wedge to strike into the ancient forests of Europe was driven by man; climatic factors and animal foraging did the rest. We might add that not only was the great stone monument at Stonehenge manmade, so too were its environs: once wooded, now pastureland.

By the fourth millennium wide tracts of forest had been reduced all over Europe. In combination with that, a Sub-Boreal climate was ideal for the rise of pastoral economies, with its mild winters and long growing season for grass. Farmers on the Pontic steppe found their familiar landscape slowly disappearing. Its soil had been easily worked, but was not the richest. Fertility had been maintained by the dissolved ashes of burnt-over clearings; with shrinking forests, swidden was no longer feasible. Cattle manure could have taken the place of ashes, but instead Pontic

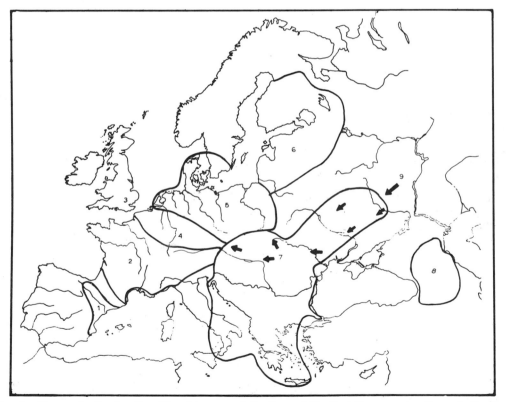

Map 2. Europe in the fourth millennium B.C., at the time of the first Kurgan migrations. 1. Iberian Neolithic; 2. Western Neolithic; 3. Windmill Hill; 4. Late Danubian; 5. Funnel Beaker; 6. Baltic; 7. Old Europe; 8. Kuro-Araxes; 9. Kurgan.

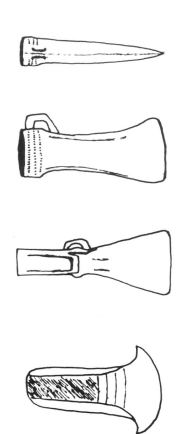

Development of metal axe types
from flat, open mold axes...

farmers drifted into becoming Kurgan herdsmen as they grazed their cattle on the stubble of the expanding grassland, depending more and more on their cattle and less on their gardens. The transition was a natural one, for moving stock from region to region is not unlike swidden farming, which itself is not far removed from the Mesolithic way of life. Indeed, Mesolithic peoples living all across Russia took up pastoralism from those who evolved it without themselves having passed through an agricultural phase. Herein is the origin of the classical nomads of later centuries, the Turkic and Mongolian peoples (see Map 2).

The pastoralism of the Kurgan folk is thus yet another version of the Neolithic way of life, subdivided out of a Danubian type economy. But the relationship to agriculture is more than historical; it is ongoing. Pastoralists complete their specialized herding economy in the craft skills and agricultural products of farming folk. Even when herders dominate farmers within a single layered society, that one-sided relationship holds true to form. So much is clear, as we shall demonstrate, from epic literature, which extols pastoralism and explains why its advantages are difficult to surrender. Once liberated to their way of life, herders do not readily return to the heavy, dull work of farming. At the same time, Neolithic villagers, settled on fertile soil with tremendous amounts of time and labor invested in their estate, prove resistant to pastoral life. It is more than simply a reckoning of work that insulates the two life-ways from each other; each generates a holistic world-view out of its culture that makes it and keeps it integral. Yet the two closely interact, especially when arranged vertically within the same space by way of social stratification. That interplay between herders and farmers is one theme of this book.

Bronze Age Metallurgists

Bronze is an alloy of copper whose optimal proportions are nine to one. A higher proportion of tin renders it brittle. The advantages of bronze over copper, which it succeeded as a material for making tools and weapons, are that it is harder, has a lower melting temperature, and is easier to cast without flaws. Its main disadvantage is that tin deposits are scarcer and more widely scattered than are copper deposits. A relative scarcity of tin means that trade had to be organized to get it. The making of bronze, and its accompanying trade in raw materials as well as in finished products, defines the Bronze Age, one of three metal "ages" sandwiched between those of copper and iron.

In space and time, the Bronze Age centers upon and nearly coincides with the world's first civilizations, which arose along the Tigris-Euphrates valley (Mesopotamia) and along the Nile (Egypt) sometime during the later fifth and fourth millennia. The technologies that made this possible included the wheel and the sail for long distance commercial trade; writing which in Mesopotamia grew out of the need to keep track of the business of trade; and, of course, smelting. These inventions made for a complex reorganization of Neolithic life, resulting in the so-called "urban revolution," which took place (significantly) in areas of sparse natural metal resources. We call the new order "corporate, civil life." Outside this primary area of civic development, the advent of metal working gave Neolithic societies in Europe proper, especially central Europe, a quite different turn—a barbarian turn—although their technology was every bit as good as that practiced in Near Eastern cities.

Before turning to that dynamic interplay between barbarian and civic societies, another and related theme of this book, it is important to note that Bronze Age civilization at its source did not spring up all at once but evolved gradually, as did all the other states of culture we have described. The beginnings of the Bronze Age lie in the first uses of copper and the slow refinement of copper technology. Only after that long process had reached the stage of tin alloying did commercial trade—no longer ritual trade—get started. The first step toward the Bronze Age, then, is the Copper Age (or Chalcolithic), which in turn is nothing other than Old European culture. All over the provinces of the Old European domain copper appears increasingly after about 5500 B.C., although these are not the first places it was used. In Anatolia, some Neolithic villages started using copper objects as far back as 6900 B.C.! But a major center for copper metallurgy would have emerged near the Carpathian Mountains where nuggets of the stuff are found. Or used to be found, since surface deposits of raw metal have long since been picked clean by the ancients. We moderns have to dig for copper ore deep in the earth; nor are we the first to have done so. Old Europeans mined copper, too, in much the same manner as their Neolithic cousins in Belgium and England mined flint.

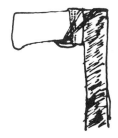

The first objects made of copper were cold hammered into shape out of small natural fragments; soon thereafter heat was applied because simple hammering without annealing makes the metal brittle. The next step was smelting. This cannot have been very difficult to achieve, given the great heat available in pottery kilns, a device basic to every Neolithic village, if not every household. Only a small amount of smelted copper could have been produced in this way, and this is obvious from the small objects made from it. Bracelets and spiral-headed pins of copper, and also of gold, which is even easier to anneal, appear almost at once. They were exchanged all over the provinces of Old European culture for shell, obsidian, and flint. The new substance began its career as material for jewelry. But some few implements also are known, such as fishhooks and sickles.[26] Perhaps only the fishhooks were banausic, the sickles cultic.

But surely the first practical tool whose raw material was smelted for mass production was the flat hammer axe, its rough form cast as a thick blank and then its blades hammered to an edge. Casting calls for rather higher temperatures than does the working of annealed metal, and thus for hotter ovens.[27] From this technical innovation, as basic for the Bronze Age as was the baking of bread for the Neolithic, we may expect some religious overtones. We have them. The copper axe attained to sanctity, with the Minoans as with the warrior groups who would later cross western Europe; and it was cast by metal smiths whose job was sacrosanct. The smelting of metals was a mysterious, hence a sacred, activity: something more akin to the specialist work of the shaman, not the generalist work of

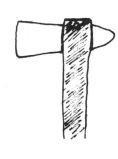

. . . to socketed close mold axes.

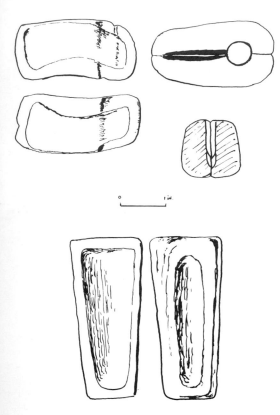

Axe molds from Kurgan Culture, Russia (after Mongait, 1956).

the hunter or farmer. Be that as it may, early metallurgists went on to invent the shaft-hole axe, made from two-piece molds (see figures) and lastly the very complicated lost wax method.

The development of casting went hand in hand with the mastery of alloys. The first alloy mixed with copper to make it harder was arsenic. Tests made on arsenical bronze prove it to have been reasonably hard and durable, but a side effect must have been the slow and sure poisoning of the smith. In fact, chemical analysis of the bones of the first metal smiths in western Europe, the Beaker folk, reveals a high level of arsenic poisoning. Learning from this failed experiment, later generations of metallurgists combined tin with copper, which then set the standard for bronze. But tin was not as easily available as arsenic, so therefore its use led to an increasing search for it.[28] In the stable, growing city-states of Mesopotamia this would lead to great trading expeditions and, with the rise of kings, to imperial wars. In Europe the same impetus would lead to the movement of small groups of metal working peoples over wide geographical areas. Together with population growth and the melding of farmers and herdsmen in layered societies, the need for metals and the desire for metal goods would further permit the rise of warrior chieftains.

To where the origins of metallurgy may be traced is not certain. Its center of innovation used to be credited to the Near East, as any of the influential books written by V. Gordon Childe will testify. But now it seems more likely that copper was smelted independently among the Old Europeans with another center in the copper bearing region of the Caucasus Mountains, sometime around 4500 B.C. Axe blades cast in open molds were at first modeled after woodcutting celts of polished stone, or at least this was the case among the Old Europeans. But it is in the Caucasus region where metal *weapons* begin to appear. Alongside the Araxes river at Kul-tepe in Azerbaijan, a famous site belonging to the Kuro-Araxes culture, a copper dagger was found dating back to the middle of the fifth millennium; in form it resembles flint daggers known among Neolithic peoples in the steppe country of upper Mesopotamia. Perhaps the metal version indicates a rising warrior society; more likely its use was cultic. In time the Kuro-Araxes culture went on to develop a high standard of smithing, which put it in contact by way of trade to the south with Mesopotamia and to the north, across the mountains, with the emerging Kurgan pastoralists. By the middle of the fourth millennium, if not somewhat earlier, Kuro-Araxes metallurgists had invented the bivalve mold, with which they turned out a great quantity and variety of ornaments and weapons. Both types of finished copper goods, but especially weapons, were traded northward over the mountains to the Kurgan folk in growing numbers. Favorite products were the shaft-hole axe and the tanged dagger, its blade cast with a prong for seating into a socketed hilt.[29]

While the Kuro-Araxes folk lived peaceful Neolithic lives in settled villages, the Kurgan folk did not. They were the warrior herdsmen who would dominate Europe, stratifying Old European cultures and raiding well down into Mediterranean lands as far as Egypt. In the next chapter we shall see how the new technology of metal worked with changing social patterns to produce such a people.

Cultural Evolution

After the industrial revolution left its mark on the world, as did the urban and Neolithic revolutions before it, modern thinkers came to see these others as prelude to a culminating event: the steam engines and belt-turned wheels and smoking chimneys of nineteenth century factories. Indeed, it was in the nineteenth century that the "ages" of prehistory were formulated, leading in a straight line upwards toward the era of modern technology and nationhood, the climax of the story of man. All else before was more or less inadequate. Factory industrialism was the outgrowth of a teleological impulse for completion, a seed planted in darkness, that flowered its way into the light of day after pushing up through the dim reaches of antiquity, from Stone Age tribalism, through Bronze Age kingdoms and Iron Age empires, and finally to the age of steam, power machinery, and the sovereign nation-state.

Although the nomenclature for the ages of man is very much a product of industrial thinking, it is still useful when tempered by an awareness that cultural evolution does not in fact take place, rung by rung, up a single ladder of development. In the technical language of anthropology, this model of change is called unilineal evolution. It requires that progress in technology and social organization be kept in step everywhere by means of short or long distance contacts with centers of innovation, and that any time lag is merely a function of the distance traveled by knowledge and skills.[30] A more sophisticated model, called multilineal evolution, allows for separate and parallel ladders of development. Local peoples change in response to local conditions. That the process may be alike in different parts of the world, even at widely different times, need not result from diffusion; given the universal ability of man to fit his technology to the prevailing habitat, and to organize his society so as to manage that technology, a similar environment will give rise to a similar line of development. Progress is repeatable. It requires no Egyptians crossing the Atlantic in papyrus boats to strike up a like civilization among the Incas of Peru; the Incas did it on their own, responding to a parallel need to adapt agriculture to a semi-arid land. In both cases the adaptive technology was large-scale irrigation, whose works were constructed by a labor force rallied to the task in each locality at a state level of organization.

Plausible as the multilineal theory may be, it is in part an overreaction to diffusionist theory. Like the unilineal theory, diffusionism has its historical context. It was born out of the colonial experience in which the industrial nations of Europe looked for markets and raw materials in "backward" parts of the world, at the same time intending to bring the blessings of civilization there. Diffusionism limits the rise of advanced cultures to a few places, whose distinctive features are then carried outward to less advanced areas. Normally the process of diffusion is accomplished by the direct movement of colonists. All culture change in the direction of progress, or as it may be, of regress, is the result of invasion, whether by advanced or backward migrants.[31] Stonehenge III, therefore, had to be built by a Mycenaean Greek, or someone else familiar with a great building tradition. Such has been the view of that monument by prehistorians for some twenty years. But now it appears to be the work of a native people themselves in command of a great building tradition. For all that, migration does in fact operate as an agent of social change; the *degree* to which it applies to Stonehenge is what fascinates and perplexes us.

At its extreme, diffusionist theory can plummet to the nadir of inanity. Around the turn of the century Grafton Eliot Smith named Egypt as the creator of all other civilizations, and of many additions to primitive cultures in between; for the burden of Egypt in civilizing the world had to be carried across many barren places. So it was with Atlantis, as given in 1882 by Ignatius Donnelly, the father of the modern cult of Atlantology. At least Eliot Smith started with a land known to archaeology, not an unknown continent sunk in the Atlantic ocean. By collecting culture traits from all over the world that had anything in common with anything in Egypt, Eliot Smith "proved" that Egypt was the source of them all. If agriculture, or weaving, or dyeing, or metallurgy appeared in the Americas, it had to come from Egypt; if circumcision, sailing, the sun cult, boomerangs, or phallic symbols were worldwide in distribution, they were distributed from Egypt. Everyone in his time believed Egypt to be the oldest civilization, so the rest was obvious.[32] Today we know better, that Egypt is not the oldest (Mesopotamia is), and that there is no one center for everything. Yet the spirit of Eliot Smith lives on in Thor Heyerdahl, who in *The Ra Expeditions* describes his two attempts to sail a papyrus boat from Africa to America. And if we substitute alien spacemen for Egyptians, it lives on for a gullible public in *Gods from Outer Space* by Erich von Däniken.

The idea of diffusion is not to be cast out, however, merely because we can rebut its monomaniacs. Some things *were* invented in only one place and one time. Witness the alphabet, devised by Phoenician traders to keep their accounts straight. They did better than the Mesopotamians with their cuneiform writing or the Egyptians with their sacred hieroglyphics, both of whom let their religious culture get ahead of their business culture, for which their priests had invented writing in the first place. All the same, the spread of a one-time invention will not account for those cases in which a novelty is absorbed by the host culture, yet is reworked in native terms. Archaeologist V. Gordon Childe won his reputation by thinking on this problem, in his attempt to unite evolution and diffusion within a single, coherent model; he saw the barbarian cultures of Europe developing in concert with that first civilized one in the Near East.

Thus, agriculture grew up with its first grain crops and barnyard animals on the hilly flanks of the Mesopotamian valley, later to feed an urban revolution in the marshes of the valley itself (which had to be drained if seed were to be planted, the reverse of the irrigation projects that had to be undertaken in Egypt and Peru). At the same time, villagers from the same Neolithic source expanded across Anatolia and the Balkans, transmitting agriculture to the Danubians who in turn carried it into western Europe. This is not exactly the case, seeing that the Old Europeans evolved in the Balkans a Neolithic culture of their own; and it was *their* example that was transmitted to the Danubians. Looking at it either way, however, no emissaries from the gardens of Mesopotamia are required, only that European agriculture springs from a common source or from a cluster of possibly related sources.

Likewise Stonehenge III had to be built by a people in contact with an outside tradition for massive building, if only indirectly. Since Mycenaean Greeks pushed their trade all across the Mediterranean, with middlemen linking it across the continent to Britain, Childe thought it must have been they who were responsible for passing on that tradition by way of a cultural bucket brigade, going hand in hand with the trade. But we know now that the culture to which Stonehenge III belongs began some five hundred years before the rise of Mycenae. Local people built it for reasons of their own out of their own skills, no matter how many traits Mycenae and Stonehenge have in common. And they *have* traits in common, many of them. The true explanation for this is that both have a common origin in the Indo-European heritage.

A better theory, the one used here, marries diffusion with evolution in a more subtle way. Several times we have remarked how cultures adjust themselves to their environments and develop internally. Those remarks come out of a theory of cultural ecology. Diffusing from another area, cultures can indeed intermix with indigenous peoples to form new entities. The process is far more complex than any of the older theories were ready to accommodate. For example, the spread of Indo-European languages into Europe occurred in several waves, not one, and they developed regionally after the initial spread. Nor is it necessary to have invaders or colonizers in order to have diffusion of an idea. Ideas often transcend the immediate culture complexes in which they first appear. The great anthropologist Alfred Kroeber recognized this long ago and labeled it *stimulus diffusion.*[33] Agriculture, for example, need not have been practiced only by one group of migrating peoples in Europe. When the Danubians approached northern Europe, to be specific, nearby Mesolithic peoples took up the idea of farming and adapted it to their own living habits. Most of their material culture remained the same, only they planted grain foods and husbanded animals as well as carrying on many of their former activities. In the same way, it is entirely possible that many henge monuments in northern Britain were built by people who may not have understood all the cosmological niceties of the early henges of southern Britain, but who understood the political idea of henges and built them accordingly. In the realm of ideas, religion is one of the great areas of stimulus diffusion. The spread of Christianity and its absorption into all manner of cultures is an outstanding example. When in the next chapter we trace the political history of Stonehenge, we speak of more than the evolution of social organization; the process of cultural evolution in our view subsumes all those other ones of adaptation, internal development, diffusion, migration, absorption, and blending.

3. Political History of Stonehenge

In all parts of western Europe, Britain included, the landscape is dotted with a class of prehistoric monuments called dolmens in French Brittany and *dysser* in Denmark. They are tombs built with large upright slabs of stone roofed over with an even larger slab, originally covered with earth. With examples of single standing stones (menhirs), long lines of standing stones (alignments), stone circles (henges), and grouped settings as at Stonehenge, they comprise what are known as megalithic monuments. A recalibration of the radiocarbon method of dating now establishes many of them to be older than the pyramids of Egypt, even older than the first cities of Mesopotamia, attesting that Europe owned a great building tradition not indebted, as once thought, to the Bronze Age civilizations of the Mediterranean.

Megalithic is not the name of an "age" as are the other -lithic words defined in the previous chapter; it merely denotes a structure of large stones. Megalithic structures by no means belong to a single stage of cultural evolution. They were built at first by Neolithic farmers who had blended with Mesolithic hunters, and later by Bronze Age peoples. Originating on the Continent, the tradition of building them was carried to Britain by nomadic farmers who there developed a novel class known as henge monuments.

Typical free-standing dolmen, from Wales. This is the central burial chamber of a megalithic tomb. Time and man have stripped it of its covering mound.

It was to the *dysser* and other megalithic monuments of his homeland that Olaus Wormius devoted a life of study, making him the father of prehistoric archaeology. His results, published in *Danicorum monumentorum* of 1643, he communicated to Walter Charleton, who from them correctly deduced the political nature of Stonehenge (see chap. 1). Dr. Worm, of course, had no way of knowing how old the objects of his study really were; he ascribed them to the Vikings. And so Dr. Charleton described Stonehenge as a place where a Viking chieftain crowned his success in vanquishing the England of King Alfred. But Dr. Worm wrote at a time when the very best of the Bible scholars, the Irish prelate James Ussher, had in 1650 dated the creation of heaven and earth at 4004 B.C., the initial entry of his *Annalium Pars Prior*. We in the twentieth century are privileged to see Stonehenge on the true time scale of prehistory.

In Table 2, the three main phases of Stonehenge are placed within a chronology that spans intervals of five hundred years each, from the Mesolithic hunters of Star Carr to Caesar's conquest—and, five hundred years later, to the conversion of Irish chieftains by St. Patrick in the fifth century A.D. and the recording by later monks of the last, best glimpse of an Indo-European warrior society we shall ever get to see. Not all the events listed in this table took place in the British Isles, however, for Stonehenge itself is not a local event merely. Everything that took place in Europe before Stonehenge, as outlined in chapter 2, is relevant. Cultural evolution is not a single process nor does it take place in geographical isolation. We have taken Stonehenge as a focus of interest for the whole movement of European prehistory, and indeed this book will serve as an introduction to that subject. All of that is prerequisite to understanding the evolution of Stonehenge society, and its changing monument, from a communal to a layered form. To trace that course of change, we must move through a tangled history of relations with the Continent and with yet more local entanglements, from the various non-Indo-European migrants to southern Britain, through the proto-Indo-Europeans we know as the Beaker folk, to the Indo-Europeans we know as the Wessex warriors. After that came the Celts, the high barbarians of Europe who are little more than Battle Axe people equipped with swords and chariots and wine flagons derived from an Iron Age empire, that of the Romans, themselves a civilization evolved from the same Indo-European heritage.

First Men in Britain

Who were the peoples that built the various Stonehenges and for what reasons were they built? Of late, much attention has been given to the astronomical aspects of the final structure, but that was not an end in itself. Stonehenge is a social question and in that it is far more interesting and closer to the primary interest of its builders. As we have said before, the question is not astronomy but cosmology, the parallelisms of heaven and earth. Cosmology is the expression of a whole people, not a product of scientific expertise. In order to examine the builders' evolving culture and its mythic pieties, we must turn back to the first men in Britain and their Continental origins.

	British Isles	W. Europe	E. & Central Europe	Aegean	Black Sea Steppes	Egypt & Mesopotamia	Caucasian Steppes and Anatolia	India
500	St. Patrick in Ireland							
	Roman conquest							
A.D. B.C.	Belgae	Caesar's conquest of Gaul						
500	La Tène	La Tène			Cimmerans-Scythians			
				Homer				
1000	Hallstatt	Hallstatt		end of Mycenae				
		Urnfield						
1500	Food Vessel			Tholos tombs		Hyksos Kassites		
	Late Wessex			Mycenaen shaft graves				Aryan invasion
				Minoan palaces				
2000	Stonehenge IIIa					1st Intermediate		
	Early Wessex						Hittites/Hurrians	
2500		Early Únětice			Kurgan IV	Step Pyramid		Indus Valley civilization
	Stonehenge II							
	Beakers	Beaker/Corded Ware						
		Beaker folk				Royal tombs of Ur		
		Vučedol						
3000	Stonehenge I					writing		
	Windmill Hill	Corded Ware/ Battle Axe				Sumer		
		TRB	Battle Axe people				Kuro-Araxes	
3500								
4000	Wessex farmers	Danubians			Kurgan I			
					domestication of the horse			
4500								
5000			Danubians					
			Copper					
7000			Old Europe					
8000	Star Carr	Mesolithic						

Table 2. Chronology of Stonehenge and related events.

The first members of *Homo sapiens* to inhabit Britain lived in a Paleolithic state of culture during the fourth and last phase of the Pleistocene geological epoch, or Ice Age, when that island was still connected to the Continent. The ice of the Ice Age in its glacial phases tied up enough of the world's oceanic waters to lower the sea level by hundreds of feet. Members of *Homo erectus*, identified in the cranial fragments of Swanscombe Man, lived in British caves at the start of the second glacial phase, but the intense cold evidently drove them out. The last phase of glacial movement did not advance the ice as far south as the others, and so permitted Upper Paleolithic men to hunt large, cold weather animals such as the woolly rhinoceros, mammoth, and reindeer which fed on the lush moss and tundra vegetation growing in the melt waters of southern Britain. When the ice sheet retreated north for the last time, rain no longer was tied up in snowfall packed into glaciers; the climate became warmer and moister, the ground wetter; together with marine transgressions caused by rising ocean levels, the coastal and riverine areas in northern latitudes turned quite marshy. With a rise in temperature tundra plants were replaced by a succession of forests, ultimately those of oak, elm, and beech. At the same time, most Pleistocene game animals became extinct, to be replaced as of 10,000 B.C. by the familiar fauna of the Holocene or Recent epoch. In British forests these smaller, more elusive animals included red deer, roe deer, elk, wild cattle, and wild pig. A new breed of skilled hunters moved in, a Mesolithic people, who also hunted water fowl with bow and arrow and took fish from streams and ponds with leisters and bark-floated nets. The famous site at Star Carr gives best evidence of these people over a long period of occupation and reoccupation. They traveled on inland waterways in dugout canoes, one aspect of their general mobility as hunter-fishers.

The arrival of Neolithic pioneers, after cutting a long swath across western Europe, disturbed the Mesolithic natives not one bit. In fact, they flourished all the more, having picked up a few Neolithic tricks from the newcomers, leading in time to a more vigorous and amalgamated state of culture we call Secondary Neolithic (vis-à-vis Primary Neolithic). This melded culture we shall identify in the next section with the Windmill Hill folk. The newcomers, who imported a Primary Neolithic culture, are known as the Wessex farmers. They at once proceeded to homestead the once forested but increasingly windswept grasslands of the Wessex down. From them the old hunter-fishers learned the Neolithic technologies of grain cultivation, animal husbandry, pottery making, and stone polishing, but not without giving up their mobility, shown in their persistent habit of making temporary campsites. As at Star Carr, these remained what they always had been, Maglemosian type platforms and jetties of felled timber laid down on boggy ground in marshy areas along rivers and around the coast.

But if the swidden method of farming borrowed by the Mesolithic old-timers remained primitive, the while they continued to hunt and fish, their habitual mobility gained them new rewards. Game trails and watercourses now served also as trade routes. Moving about unseen in the woodlands and backwaters, they came to deal with the Wessex farmers in natural foods such as dried fish, nuts, and herbs, and plant and animals products such as antlers, hides, and cordage. Most importantly, they satisfied the taste of the newcomers for stone axes made of exotic minerals; even Wales and Ireland supplied raw materials for these goods. Such a contribution to the trade should not surprise us, for Maglemosian hunters everywhere, in Britain as in Denmark, had long since devised a simple but effective axe head of knapped flint, suitable for hafting. The finished product was good enough to fell small trees used in the making of dwelling platforms. The borrowed technique of polishing compact stone made not only for an improved product, but for an export item in trade with the very farmers from whom the hunters had learned that improvement. Thus did a population of Mesolithic hunter-fishers, abiding in the presence of Neolithic settlers, expand their skills to the mastery of maritime travel across the Channel and the Irish Sea, and to the manufacture of polished stone axes. Factory sites at hundreds of different outcrops of distinctive rocks supplied the Wessex farmers with large numbers of axe heads rare and beautiful to them. More than that, trade, a means of interaction between these different peoples, had become a cause for their amalgamation. The outcome of that blending process was a state of culture we have designated above as Secondary Neolithic.

The outcome, however, seems to have been latent in preexisting habits of trade unusual for a Mesolithic state of culture. Why else does chert from Portland Island, Dorset, show up in campsites on the southwestern main? That island has nothing to recommend it as a habitat; it was poor in game and lacked beaches along which shellfish could be collected. We may conclude that chert was collected from there by one or more hunting bands and traded to others, possibly at joint campsites such as Starr Carr may have been, the largest one yet uncovered and which was occupied only for some time between January and April. Here is a precursor of those prolonged seasonal gatherings at the causewayed camps of the Secondary Neolithic period where stone axes and exotic raw materials for making them were traded among the Windmill Hill folk.[1]

Windmill Hill Folk and Stonehenge I

The Neolithic way of life itself was carried to Britain by swidden type migrants who crossed the English Channel in skin-shelled boats and coasted up to the Irish Sea. The dates for this are now known from a revised dating system to be as early as 4400-4300 B.C., almost a millennium earlier than the earliest previous estimates. The precise identity of the people and their continental provenance is a complex problem we cannot attempt to simplify here. It is sufficient to say that Neolithic life on the Continent, outside the cultural provinces of Old Europe, remained itinerant. Swidden folk traveled up and down the Atlantic seaboard from Spain to the Low Countries, mixing several Neolithic traditions and blending with Mesolithic folk as well. Those who came to Britain were of that eclectic variety.

These first farmers brought with them sheep and goats, Emmer wheat, and einkorn. Cattle and pigs they domesticated from wild forms browsing in forests yet to be destroyed. They settled at first on the chalk downs and sandy soils of southern and eastern England (with a branch moving to Ireland) where thin woodlands could easily be cleared and the light soils easily tilled with an antler pick, a wooden digging stick, or a shovel made from the shoulder blade of a cow. A few outlines of their flimsy wood and sod houses, both rectangular and round in plan, show that the settlement pattern consisted of individual households and their kitchen gardens, not villages. Still standing, however, are their earthen tombs or long barrows.

Such are the remains of the Wessex farmers. During the course of trade with them, the native hunter-fishers were so revitalized that they came to dominate the intruders and establish a whole new culture, what we have been calling Secondary Neolithic. We must not think of this as a

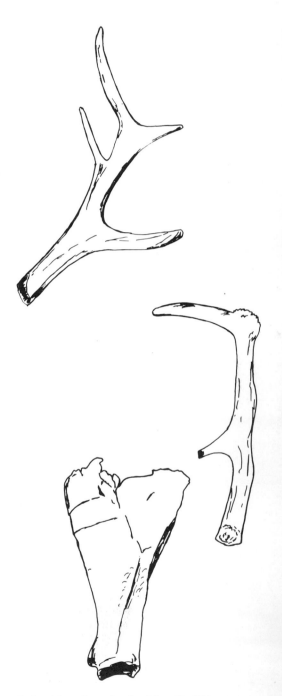

Antler picks and scapular shovel from Neolithic Britain.

debased version of "pure" or Primary Neolithic, although in the past many prehistorians took it to be so. That amalgam of cultures, blended together in the Secondary Neolithic, in reality produced a new and resurgent culture more fully adapted to the changing landscape of southern Britain than did either one on its own. The resulting monuments, at the hands of the Windmill Hill folk, were causewayed camps, henges (including Stonehenge I), and megalithic versions of the old style long barrows. On the Continent, like results obtained from the same process. The massive stone tombs or *dysser* built in Ole Worm's Denmark, for example, were also products of a resurgent Secondary Neolithic.

In northern Britain (Lancashire and Yorkshire), the Mesolithic tradition of the native hunters long continued to coexist side by side with the Neolithic one of the intrusive farmers. But in southern Britain and the midlands, the Mesolithic simply disappeared into a blend with the Wessex farmers with whom its hunter-fishers had traded for over a period of about a thousand years. By 3500 B.C., that long process of cultural melding gave rise to a Secondary Neolithic culture we call Windmill Hill after its first great monument, a causewayed camp atop Windmill Hill about eighteen miles from Stonehenge. Its distinctive feature is farming with a pastoral bias, given a landscape changed by the gradual opening up of pastureland.

What wind had begun by sweeping the Wessex downs of its cover of oak and beech, Windmill Hill farmers completed with their grazing animals and their tree-felling axes. But among these folk the axe had symbolic significance beyond the utilitarian, as indicated by the burial of axes having heads of sandstone and chalk too soft to cut anything. Noteworthy too are oversized axes made of precious stone; the walls of rock supporting the megalithic tombs in which they lie buried often are carved with the likeness of the same axes as are the stones of Stonehenge, later, inscribed with the carvings of bronze axes. Also found in some few instances are symbols of the Old European great goddess, owl-eyed figures with breasts or simply geometric lines indicating her eyes. The axe, symbol of foresters, is also *her* symbol.

None of these axes are battle axes. Neolithic life, on the whole, seems to have been peaceful. A gathering of people from their scattered households took place seasonally within ditched enclosures built atop low hills and knolls, such as the partially excavated one on Windmill Hill. These earthworks are circular or oval, with numerous causeways across the ditches, which themselves number from one to four in a concentric arrangement. In all these causewayed camps the ditch is outside the bank, as it is at Stonehenge. Under the banks or even between them are found remains of hutments, temporary dwellings of the excavators. Causewayed camps doubtless were corrals for the autumn roundup of cattle that pastured throughout the rest of the year in nearby forests (and probably destroyed them, too). This annual event among widely scattered homesteaders surely was the occasion for trade, both in cultic axes and real goods, the making of marriage alliances, and general festivities, not to say the banqueting on surplus cattle.[2] Even in those days cattle must have been a

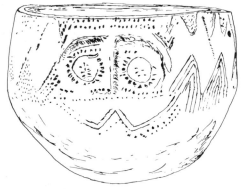

Pot from a megalithic tomb at Sving, Denmark. The eye motif may be of a piece with swirls and eyes found engraved on megalithic monuments in many parts of Atlantic Europe.

prime index of wealth. Perhaps also the celebrants of these carnivals were so organized by their attendance as to muster individual homesteads into tribal groups, the identity of each centered on its own causewayed camp. These tribes may then have raided for cattle among each other and suffered reprisals. This is a strong feature of the later heroic societies and there is no reason to doubt its beginning in the Neolithic. The presence of arrowheads at Windmill Hill may attest to hunting, a Mesolithic survival. On the other hand, they may point to intertribal warfare. At least one archaeologist is convinced that he has found evidence for territorial rivalry during this period in Wessex.[3] Herein we may find a political basis for causewayed camps such as the one at Windmill Hill; they were a rallying place for each tribe and thus symbolic of its collective wealth and glory. The ditched enclosure of Stonehenge I, built perhaps close to 3000 B.C., may have been a seasonal cattle pen and tribal center of the same sort.

Causewayed camps must have taken many years to construct, given small populations and the primitive tools at hand. One estimate gives one hundred thousand man hours to throw up the ditches at the Windmill Hill type-site, or put another way, one hundred men working ten hours a day for one hundred days. And that represents a whole tribe at work, collected seasonally for the purpose. But even the social units that comprised the tribe, each clan to its own task, constructed tombs that also took more than one season to complete and a considerable organization of labor. The unchambered long barrows of the Wessex farmers were elaborated by the Windmill Hill folk in both size and complexity, with the addition sometimes of burial chambers built with stone slabs or timber or both. The long barrow at Fussell's Lodge, less than ten miles south of Stonehenge, not only contained a mortuary house of solid logs at one end, but the whole enormous mound was dressed on the outside with a facade of the same construction. Each log was in fact a great tree trunk, some 13 feet in length, which when green must have weighed some 67 pounds per cubic foot for a total of about 2^{1}/3 tons. A labor force to handle that kind of material in quantity is a match for that required to haul and erect the bluestone pillars of Stonehenge II. As a matter of fact, timber and stone handling and working were interchangeable for the megalithic workmen of southern Britain, as attested by the composite character of some tombs and by the techniques of joinery applied to the sarsen stones of Stonehenge III, with their mortised lintels seated on tenons and tied together, tongue in groove.[4]

As we shall see, the kind of organization it takes to gather and direct labor for the construction of meeting places must lead to political change, to the evolution of a layered society out of Neolithic equality. The upshot is Bronze Age chieftainship; an aristocratic order is led by a solitary figure who openly commands labor for his own glory and that of his warrior followers and not that of the tribal community at large. Another transitional feature of Windmill Hill culture, similarly related and involving large expenditures of labor, is the construction of long barrows. They take on political significance in bridging the political distance between the Wessex farmers of old and the Wessex warriors of the future. For these

Plan of a long barrow in North Germany (after Ashbee, 1970).

long barrows are collective tombs, reflecting a communal ideology if no longer the social fact, insofar as they were directed to be built under the authority of religious chiefs who preached an ancient but passing ideal; whereas later the tombs of Bronze Age chiefdoms are single graves, reflecting the individuality of chiefs and their detribalized followers, warriors we shall be calling the heroes of heroic society. For an overview of this development, to be discussed from here on, see Table 3.

Time	Culture and Society	Political Order	Economy	Burial Type
		Aristocratic Chiefdoms		
Stonehenge III	Wessex Culture	big chiefs	pastoralism and	
(2000-1500 B.C.)	(Indo-European)	war bands	barley farming;	
Bronze Age	Heroic Society	shaman/priests	metal trade and	
		commoners	metal working	round barrows
				(single and
		Petty Chiefdoms		family burials)
Stonehenge II	Beaker Culture	little chiefs	barley farming	
(2600-2100 B.C.)	(Proto-Indo-European)	shaman/priests	and increased	
Early Bronze Age	Emergent Heroic Society	tribesmen	stockbreeding;	
			metal trade begins	
Stonehenge I	Windmill Hill Culture		mixed farming;	
(3500-2600 B.C.)	(Pre-Indo-European)		trade in stone axes	
Secondary Neolithic	Egalitarian Society	**Communal Chiefdoms**		
		clan heads		earthen long barrows
		shaman/priests		and megalithic tombs
	Wessex Farmers	tribesmen		(collective burials)
Primary Neolithic	(Non-Indo-European)		mixed farming;	
	Egalitarian Society		barter with	
			hunter/fishers	

Table 3. Political history of Stonehenge and its cultural context.

The long barrows, of course, also embody religious ideas, those connected with the afterlife. Both camps and barrows, however, indicate the real locus of interest of the people who built them, for both have proved more lasting than dwellings. More enduring than homes of the living are houses of the dead, the long barrows of chalk rubble, 100 to 300 feet long, often heaped around a rectangular mortuary house of wood. Like the Danubian longhouses they resemble, they are the "homes" of an extended family or clan. Interred in these burial chambers, or directly in an earthen mound when there is no mortuary house, are the remains of up to fifty individuals (though only about a half-dozen on average) of all ages and both sexes. The mound was thrown up last, after bodies had lain in the wooden house or were perhaps exposed in the open for some time. The custom of exposure, incidentally, is reminiscent of seventh millennium Anatolia and Jericho.

Within the old Wessex district (which embraces the present-day counties of Wiltshire and Dorset), are some 120 long barrows, all of Neolithic vintage. Among the most conspicuous is the tremendous barrow at Fussell's Lodge, where dead bodies were permitted to rot and the bones then piled up at one end of its wooden mortuary house. After a certain amount of accumulation in each instance, a decision was made to cover the charnel house with earth, forming a tumulus. One end of the barrow, where the bones reposed, was always piled higher than the other, and usually faced east, toward the rising sun. At ground level within these tumuli, pits were dug, similar to the Aubrey holes at Stonehenge, in which offerings of food or drink were placed. At some barrows a forecourt was delimited, the scene of ceremonies and feasting after the labor of earth heaping was finished, and that in itself may have taken more than one season of work. At one, outside of Wessex to the east—Skendleby in Lincolnshire—eight wooden posts were set up in the forecourt, perhaps to represent the eight bodies within. As we shall see later, such nonanthropomorphic studies of men may also be read into upright pillar stones or menhirs of the megalithic tradition placed inside henge monuments; they clearly embody funereal ideas. The very architecture of Stonehenge III, for example, exhibits carryovers from the construction of magalithic tombs, which occur to the west and north of the Stonehenge site.

In megalithic tombs, the wooden charnel house beneath their earthen covering is replaced with chambers built of huge upended boulders capped with massive slabs of undressed stone or sometimes with corbeled roofing. The grandest one in Wiltshire, West Kennet near Silbury Hill and Windmill Hill, shows evidence that its multiroomed tombs remained open for close to a thousand years, which makes a beginner of Westminster Abbey as a place of burial and worship.[5] All are continuous in design and distribution with megalithic tombs throughout western Europe, the dolmens, *dysser*, cromlechs, and giant's graves of local parlance and with as many local variants on the basic convention.

Tomb types are numerous, but for our purposes the following will suffice. Passage graves have a chamber and perhaps side chambers connected by a long passage to the outside of the covering mound. Gallery graves are simply long passages with occasional internal divisions formed by stone slabs, also with side chambers, under long mounds. The major passage graves are in the Boyne Valley in Ireland and are often constructed with a stone kerb and corbeled roofing. There are other variants, but these are the basic types.[6]

At one time archaeologists believed that megalithic tombs originated in Crete about 2500 B.C., which in turn were modeled after Near Eastern burial chambers hollowed from solid rock. The path of diffusion led to Europe after colonists leaving the Aegean brought a megalithic technology with them from their homeland. Carrying the cult of the Mother Goddess these "megalithic missionaries," as Childe called them, moved across the Mediterranean, stopped at Malta to build a series of splendid temples, thence on to Iberia. From there the new religion was carried up the Atlantic coast, through France and especially the Breton peninsula to Britain and Ireland at one turn and to the northern countries at another. Indications of the cult itself are the few carvings of female figures and more numerous eye symbols and curvilinear motifs that decorate the tombs. We now know that the Aegean diffusionist model is mostly wrong, though

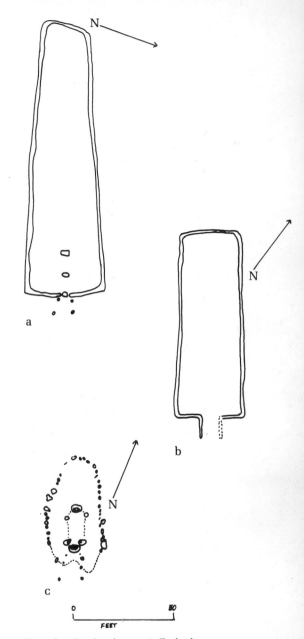

Plans of earthen long barrows in England:
a) Fussell's Lodge; b) Wor Barrow;
c) Wayland's Smithy (after Ashbee, 1970).

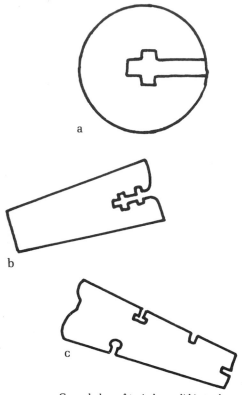

Ground-plans of typical megalithic tombs:
a) Passage Grave in a round barrow; b) Gallery
Grave in a long barrow; c) Severn-Cotswold
Gallery Grave.

not entirely discredited. From recalibrated dates, megaliths in Brittany date from well before 4000 B.C. and perhaps from the middle of the fifth millennium in Iberia! They are, in fact, the oldest massive stone buildings, the oldest stone architecture, in the world. The temples on Malta, for example, which may have some tenuous relationship to European megaliths, predate the oldest Pyramids of Egypt by 1000 years. The greatest megalithic graves of Brittany, Ireland, and the far-off Orkneys predate the Step Pyramid of Djoser, built ca. 2600 B.C., by at least half a millennium. Should we now reverse the arrows of cultural diffusion? The very thought would stun our teachers from whom we learned the doctrine of Light from the East. But why not? If they admit the later intrusion of northern barbarians into the Mediterranean, why not earlier the eastward flow of ideas from the west?

Instead of calling upon a wave of civilizing, tomb-building missionaries whose impulse begins in the Aegean, as out of Atlantis or Egypt for an older generation of strict diffusionists, we find the key to megalithic development in European inventiveness. We find no exception here to the complex forces of culture change we have described for European prehistory in general. A spontaneous variety of megalithic tombs is the natural result. To examine some of these varieties is to see the old familiar principles of local adaptation, migration, diffusion, and blending at work once again.

Take the Danish *langdysser*, for instance, that underneath their earthen mounds contain one or more stone-lined pits surrounded by a stone kerb, if not sometimes by a wooden charnel house. Similar passage graves are found among secondary Neolithic peoples in northern England, and they likely have some connection with Denmark, seeing that the interred pottery in both cases is of a type general to north European and Baltic distribution. Or again, take western Iberia, where group burials in the same kind of stone-slabbed cists are surrounded by no charnel house nor kerbing, but are simply covered by a mound of rocks. In Brittany, similar graves date from as early as 5000 B.C., surely not a borrowing from any civilized tradition of burial, none of which had yet come

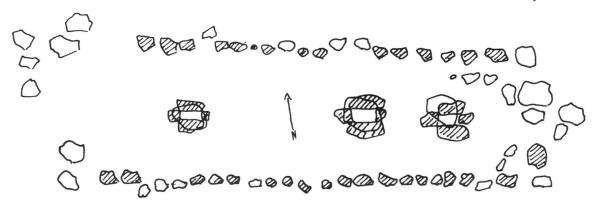

Plan of a *langdysse*, Denmark
(after Klindt-Jensen, 1957).

into existence. To come to the point, these pit burials, whatever the housing around them or the covering over them, belong to a Mesolithic burial technique. Childe himself noted that the distribution of megalithic tombs coincided with those regions where hunter-gathering traditions remained strongest. This tells us everything about conditions that foster Neolithic dispersion.

Swidden farmers moving along the Atlantic seaboard, noted earlier, mixed with native Mesolithic peoples just as did the Danubian pioneers, moving into western out of central Europe. It is here, in western Europe, along the littoral, that passage graves in all their regional variety developed out of a blending of Neolithic and Mesolithic traditions in all their cultural variety. The wooden mortuary house, where it appears, may very well be a northern derivative of the Danubian longhouse; the stone kerb may imitate the walls of that house in a new medium. These are Neolithic features in a megalithic medium. On the other hand, cist burials are Mesolithic in origin, again related to cremated burials in the Aubrey holes of Stonehenge I. And if we add the principle of local adaptation we find restraints imposed by the availability of construction material. The passage graves of western Britain occur where stones for building their chambered rooms occur. Earthen barrows are found in regions where stone is less abundant, but Windmill Hill pottery is found in both types. Both belong to the same megalithic tradition, giving it a social not a technological definition, insofar as organized labor is called for their construction. We have already denominated British henges, even when they lack stones, as megalithic monuments.[7]

Megalithic Tombs and Communal Society

In zones of western Europe ready for the introduction of farming and stock raising, thanks as much to the suitability of the habitat as to the native hunter-gatherers who welcomed the ingress of a Neolithic economy as an extension of their own, population density increased beyond any a Mesolithic economy ever sustained. The upshot of the Neolithic way of life, especially in the case of steady settlement, is more of it; the effect of man's control over the lives of plants and animals by way of domestication is to increase their numbers and density and thus to increase his own numbers and density. Rapidly. This leads to a competition for territory and its defense.

So much is indicated for the growth of Windmill Hill culture. In a demographic study of causewayed camps, Paul Ashbee of the University of East Anglia has divided up the arable land of Wiltshire (the home county of both Windmill Hill and Stonehenge) by the number of camps, concluding that each was the center of some twenty to thirty homesteads. Each of these comprised an extended kinship group of some kind. In addition to its membership in a camp, every stead or small group of steads had its long barrow, its membership in a mortuary society, as it were. A similar study has been carried out in the Orkneys, small, treeless islands off the northern coast of Scotland (famous for their well-preserved houses

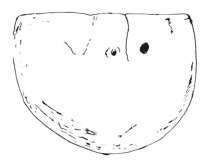

Windmill Hill pottery. Bag-shaped, these pots seem close in form to leather bags or wooden bowls and, therefore, typical of a pastoralist peoples living near to a wooded environment. The pots are simple in form, with little or no decoration.

and internal furnishings of stone). Here, too, the distribution of tombs coincides with distinct areas of arable land, albeit later in time.[8] The conclusion drawn in this case was that each tomb was the possession of an extended family (amounting to twenty or thirty individuals) or perhaps of a clan. The latter is more likely the case in Wiltshire, where the regional compartments of the land are larger. And with larger economic areas larger populations may be assumed, big enough to furnish labor for building causewayed camps. The role of camps in focusing regional interests is later transferred to henges (see Map 3).

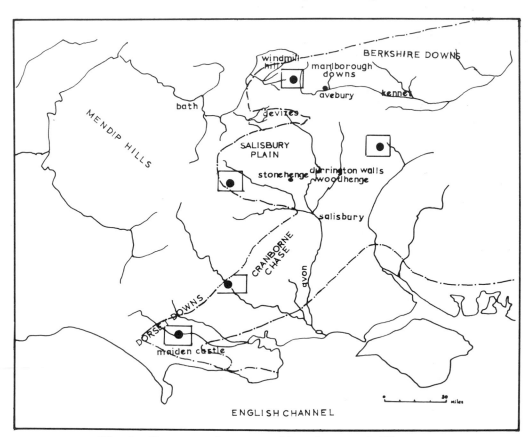

Map 3.   Causewayed camps and long barrows in Wessex.

It must not be imagined that these early tribal societies, for all the large amounts of labor they organized for the construction of tombs and earthworks, were themselves organized in any hierarchical way. Quite the contrary. Their megalithic tombs are not monuments to great chiefs, constructed by their followers, but the mortuary focus of small egalitarian communities. Each tomb served local residents, all of whom (except infants) would be buried there as death came.

The construction of great earthworks must have been related to the social system for building tombs. It worked like this, we would guess: When a family or clan decided it was time to close their ancestral funerary center (would that we could know if the exact timing of this decision was astronomically determined, for surely it would have been on the advice of a shaman/priest) neighboring families or clans were invited to participate in the work and enjoy a great feast. Cattle were slaughtered and gifts—sacred axes of precious stone would serve—were exchanged. Evidence of festive activities abound at tomb sites. It might also be remembered that the great long barrow at Fussell's Lodge took five thousand man hours to construct. Fifty people might work ten days for ten hours a day and that is not too long a time to hold a carnival. The greater the feast, the better the gifts, and the greater the prestige accruing to the gift givers.

Ethnologists identify such events as *potlatch* festivals, named after the practice among a confederation of American Indian tribes, the Kwakiutl, of the northwestern United States and British Columbia. Potlatching is the giving away of property, both real and cultic, at a public banquet whereby the host may lay claim to some rank or title. With the help of his family or his tribe, who provide goods for the giveaway, the host will invite other families or tribes to witness his claims in light of his genealogy, real and mythic, recited by his "potlatch secretary," a shaman. His claims are validated when the group receiving gifts returns them with interest, asking his people to accept them in the name of his new rank. Political leadership and generosity go hand in hand. One gives away gifts not only to get more wealth, but to win chiefly titles. For the other guests, the potlatch is a festive occasion, a time for entertainment and feasting.

In economic terms the potlatch, like the *kula* ring, is a ceremonial vehicle for the exchange of economic goods. The potlatching place is, for all its fun and games, a kind of market place. It serves the opportunity at first for the redistribution of surplus throughout regions of like produce, then between regions of disparate produce. Small-scale potlatching is a first step in the evolution toward exchange centers under the political control of chiefdoms. At the same time it is a means of keeping the peace, for things eventually will be repaid at a return engagement. All participants thus get obligated to each other. It is certainly a more peaceful way of exchanging wealth than the raiding and counterraiding of cattle, although participants at Windmill Hill and other causewayed camps may not have thought this the better way. Behind the valid economics of redistribution is a cultural variable, the chosen means of doing it. For the Windmill Hill folk it had to involve the honor of the group and probably also satisfy spirits of the dead.

But we have gotten ahead of our story. The Kwakiutl tribes are not egalitarian and the potlatch is held by aristocratic chiefs to validate hereditary positions, or to celebrate the taking of yet another genealogical honor. The chief is the Big Man of the potlatch, who thereby wins glory for himself in vying with lesser chiefs within a tribe or with big chiefs from another tribe. By contrast, the potlatching of stone axes at the tomb sites of Windmill Hill folk was held among members of an extended family or clan, and the occasion was closing the ancestral barrow by heaping up its earthen mound over the megalithic or wooden substructure. Later they would gather there for commemorative ceremonies, and these would serve group, not individual, interests.

The causewayed camps, much larger earthworks, must have been constructed at similar festivals, only on a tribal basis. That the homesteaders living around the camps were related seems obvious; intermarriage would doubtless have tied them together, defense and offense would have made that permanent. We now have tribes territorially organized with their locus on causewayed camps and within them individual clans and families vying for prestige in a generally informal way. In times of crisis, responsibility for direction would likely fall to perhaps collective leadership or to a Big Man of the leading potlatching family.

The internal organization of a simple tribal society is just that, simple. There are no formal political means for enforcing order or keeping down internal friction save the potlatch system, that is gift-giving, and related to that an informal ranking of social status. In normal times leadership of internal affairs will fall to a shaman/priest; heads of high status families will lead in times of external crisis. That territorial conflicts must have been fairly common among Neolithic and early Bronze Age cultures may be inferred from the pastoral side of their economies. Pastoralists need more territory than do cultivators. Since they wander over larger tracts of land they come into contact with other pastoralists and engage in raiding and skirmishes over grazing land. This kind of conflict is not always internecine, for to destroy the enemy is to destroy a potential source of wealth. Terror tactics are more in order here, a little judicious headhunting and cannibalism for example, behavior that intensifies with the rise of heroic warrior societies.

These war-making chiefdoms were victims of their own economic success. Growing wealthier with the increase of livestock, a pastoral tribe would need more space, or it would require a bigger potlatch to kill off and feast upon unwanted cattle. Since few animal bones remain at Windmill Hill encampments, it appears that among the early farmers of Britain expanding grazing land was the answer. As long as the population of humans and cattle remained small and localized, warfare was kept to a minimum. But when that stability was unbalanced by growth and expansion, social changes of great magnitude followed. In this case we have an excellent model for the change that took place.

The Rise of Chiefdoms

In a theoretical work on cultural evolution, Elman Service, Professor of Anthropology at the University of California at Santa Barbara, has described the organizing principles of chiefdoms and explained how they came about.[9] His general description well serves the political history of Stonehenge. In his view, political leadership evolves out of an egalitarian condition of family oriented life without private property or social classes: the near condition of Primary Neolithic Britain at the time of the Wessex farmers. The starting point is the egalitarian *societas*, whose evolutionary end product is the political state, or *civitas*. In between stands the

chiefdom. It is this order of things that we recognize in the societies of
barbarian Europe during its heroic age.

A chiefdom is based on kinship yet is not egalitarian; there is no formal government, yet the chief does exercise authority; there is no private
property nor specialized markets, yet the chief controls the redistribution
of wealth, insuring its unequal disposal; there are no social classes, yet real
differences in rank and status obtain. The political state differs from its
evolutionary precursor in that it exerts legal means of control. To maintain order, the state must interfere in the private relations of its compo-
nent groups or individual citizens. The state can grant and withhold in
relation to the perceived common good. At all times, though, it must hold
a monopoly on force. When that is combined with supernatural powers at
the call of bureaucrats trained by priests for this or that department of special service, we see the basis for Bronze Age kingdoms—Egypt or Akkad.
How very different from the proud, bragging warriors of the chiefdoms
in Celtic and Teutonic Europe. And yet these same barbarians became as
civilized as any ancient metropolite. Their transformation is the story of
the early Middle Ages; the semibarbarian, semi-Christian epic poetry of
the Germans, *Beowulf* in particular, speaks for that historical event.

But since the chiefs of heroic society are dynastic figures on the verge
of kingship, we must bear in mind that the chiefdom, as a political type
standing midway between tribe and state, may itself be subdivided into
evolutionary stages. Aristocratic chiefs do not arise directly out of a simple tribal order, in which no social organization exists apart from the life
of families, without a history of intermediate development. The starting
point is tribal, to be sure, but even egalitarian societies exalt individuals if
not offices. They follow ceremonial leaders, accept advice from wise men,
and believe in unequal access to supernatural power on the part of shamans. Out of this arises the communal chief, a theocratic leader who is
self-effacing insofar as his leadership is undertaken in the name of the
community, not himself. This is what we suspect to be the case among the
shaman/priests of the Windmill Hill culture who directed the building of
Stonehenge I. They are followed in time by a conquest leadership under
the Beaker warriors, whom we classify as petty chiefs, and who either
subsumed the old shamans or worked with them as coequals; it was they
who directed the building of Stonehenge II. Only with the advent of the
Wessex warriors, who built Stonehenge III, do we find evidence for leadership under aristocratic chiefs of the sort celebrated in epic literature.

The basis for social control in a chiefdom of whatever stage is leadership over a combination of religious and economic activities. The chief
stands at the center of an expanded territory whose ecological parts have
diversified and whose people have multiplied their divisions of labor. He
holds everything together by assigning regional products and individual
skills in the service of community projects that used to be undertaken
without the aid of chiefs, such as the long barrows of the Wessex farmers
and perhaps the first small encampments of the Windmill Hill folk. The
new economics of the wider social territory require the old pieties to keep
it one territory, and the first chiefs were probably theocratic. As Service

explains, chiefdoms arise in response to the growth of regional and occupational specialties, and the chief takes it upon himself to reallocate for common use one or both of these. "One (probably the more frequent) is the regional, or ecological, specialization of different residential groups; the other is the pooling of individual skills in large scale cooperative productive endeavors."[10] The latter, of course, will explain the building endeavors behind Stonehenge if not the causewayed camps. The former goes to the core of redistributional as against market economies.

As a growing Neolithic population filled up the available land in southern Britain, whether farmers expanding from the best to least endowed soils, or herders taking up more and more pastureland on the same basis, specialization was inevitable. If the economy was to remain intact, somebody would have to initiate exchange between the parts. But secular markets had not yet been invented. An extension of the old custom of potlatching would do the job, however, and that would be a Big Man's or a shaman's to undertake, making for overt leadership. And he would have to rally his duties around a center of attention already established as a ceremonial one in the bygone days of communal society when there were no chiefs other than communal chiefs.

The seasonal gatherings of the Windmill Hill folk at their causewayed camps, doubtless imbued with religious import like the fairs of Medieval Europe, are the first evidence in Britain of that kind of center (see Drawing 1). The deep flint mines of eastern England early on in the Neolithic attest to a specialized craft and an exchange system connected with it, all the more since the axes made from flint mined from these places had more than utilitarian interest. They might well have been cycled through a kind of *kula* ring, or given away at potlatch festivals. Special technologies that divide labor, such as mining and the manufacture of ceremonial axes, make for breakaway parts of society at the same time they invite chiefly integration. A social order that accommodates more than a collection of families all pursuing the same domestic tasks is a political order. For that, full-time craftsmen are not only possible but demanded. Hence, notes Service, "the rapid improvement of the products of craft specialization at the point of the rise of chiefdoms."[11]

Once the process of redistribution gets going under the guidance of a chief, it will pull in more peoples beyond his immediate tribal home (see Map 4). Greenstone axes passed down from northern Britain and Wales at the time when the first stones of Stonehenge were being erected may be an instance of this. But the process can start with casual trade between two neighboring economies. We already have seen how the Wessex farmers bartered with hunter-fishers in the forests all about them, with the unplanned result that a totally new culture replaced both partners to the process. Out of this amalgamated culture we know as Windmill Hill came the beginnings of a communal chiefdom that carried the process forward with a directive intelligence, leading in the end to that political amalgam we believe to be a tribal confederation centered upon Stonehenge III.

Chiefdoms at all stages are flexible enough to attract and add diverse peoples to their cause, that of expansion and confederation, a cause that

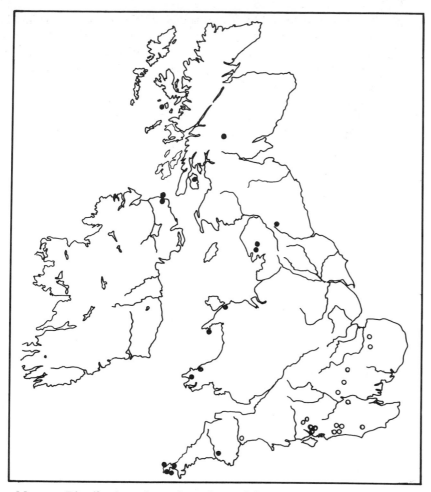

Size of dot indicates intensity of numbers.
● = axe factories
○ = flint mines

Map 4.   Distribution of axe factories and flint mines in Neolithic Britain.

may jell out of nonpolitical relations, as we have seen in the outcome of barter between the alien Wessex farmers and the native hunter-fishers. But chiefdoms are more likely to confederate with neighbors of similar language and culture because intermarriage, the blood pump of intertribal politics, is more likely to take place under these circumstances. This will be an important consideration when we come to explain how the invading Wessex warriors incorporated and enlarged upon their precursors, the Beaker folk; they are similar in language and culture because both peoples share a common Indo-European heritage. A spectacular example of tribal accretion known to recorded history, between the time of Caesar and Tacitus during the first century B.C., is the snowballing union of small Teutonic tribes led by local chiefs into one great agglomeration led by a high chief who became a king, his people a nation whose modern descendant is Germany. Political evolution of this kind can happen swiftly. For these German tribes it took little more than a century. Significantly they came to call their Teutonic union that of the alamans, meaning "all

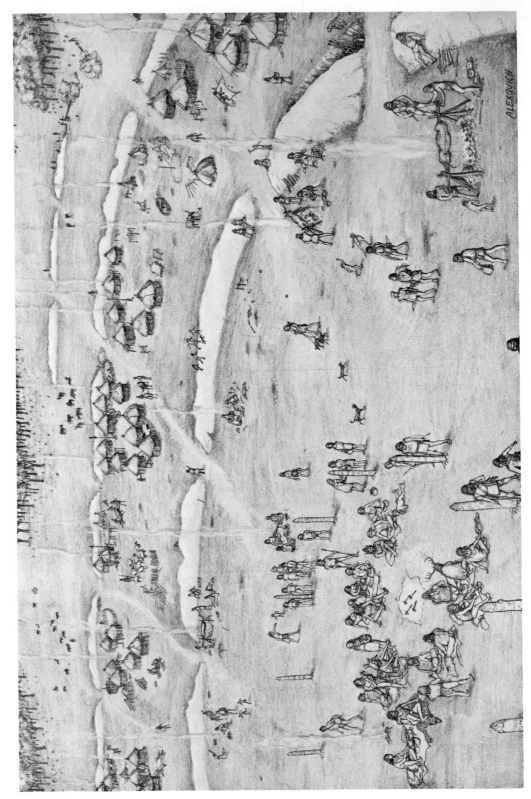

Drawing 1. A seasonal gathering at Windmill Hill. (David Alexovich)

58

men." Such is the upshot of a process that got started at Stonehenge but, for some reason, fell short, and its monument never completed.

Service's model of tribal accretion is by definition based on a social territory that covers different ecological zones, but his examples are drawn from sedentary peoples only. Will his model also accommodate mobile pastoralists and the hero-chiefs who built the final Stonehenge? We think so, yes. Herding peoples have always been symbiotic with farming folk; each depends on the other for the other's products. We have already seen that herding specialized out of Neolithic farming in various parts of Europe, only to be caught up in a redistributive system with people living the very sort of life from which they had liberated themselves. In many cases herders come to dominate the system and supply its leadership: cow chiefs lording it over cultivators. This power arrangement may evolve peacefully within the system when cow chiefs accumulate enough wealth in cattle to carry it off, or by conquest, a case of forced redistribution! A recent example of the latter are the Tuaregs, pastoralists who live in the Atlas Mountains of north Africa. They hold farming land in lowland areas, worked for them by captured slaves. Meanwhile they go about their ancient ways, tending goats and sheep in the mountains.

As chiefdoms evolve, however, they differ in the particulars of leadership. At the start, chiefs act merely as firsts among equals and only later do they become aristocratic hero-chiefs. The chiefdom in this its earliest stage is a communal chiefdom. Monuments are built in the name of the whole community, and social direction is given by shaman/priests or informally chosen leaders—again Big Men of the potlatch, but ones who have not yet acquired a hereditary position. The communal chiefdom appeared during the later Neolithic or Windmill Hill period in Britain, out of which evolved the heroic type with its dynastic chiefs. These came to eminence as successful war leaders or perhaps big-time potlatchers, the biggest of the Big Men. Perhaps they derived from priestly families, whose pedigree was ancient and unchallengeable.

The point, however, is that when the office of chief becomes a permanent family possession it no longer serves an equality of interests with the rest of the populace. The chief at once becomes a greater consumer and the sole benefactor of goods, services, and honors. He thus holds an elevated status, his prestige, in an interesting circular process, deriving from the fact that he *is* the redistributor. His office is hereditary, passing down from a god or a line of heroes. We might see these chiefs, in a way, as Big Men who give away gifts that cannot be returned in kind. Men of lesser status become obligated to him and form his body of followers, a detribalized gang or war band. The reverse is that since gifts cannot be returned in kind, the chief soon ceases to give out valuable objects but rather honors, such as the honor of membership in his exclusive war band. As the chief is under little obligation to give out his most precious material goods, he will accumulate more of them than anybody else. His main obligation will be to give out food and shelter to his followers and, of course, to render military service to the community. But he keeps the loot. When it is apportioned out it goes only to his immediate followers and will obligate them still further to him, as seen among the early German chiefdoms and celebrated in *Beowulf* by the phrase, "ring-giving Hrothgar." Heroic societies that exalt individual chiefs and warriors are the natural outcome of ritualized trade and potlatching.

Chiefdoms and Civilization

It is not possible to establish heroic chiefdoms in conditions of material poverty, specifically a lack of some valuable commodity a Big Man would desire to accumulate. Jadeite axes might have served in Neolithic Britain, but soon something more useful would appear: copper and gold, then bronze. The presence of these metals in continental Europe for more than a millennium before they reached Britain persuaded archaeologists to explain the rise of barbaric chiefdoms as a result of contact with or diffusion from a "superior" culture, a civilization.

This argument holds that the technological advance in metal working, after which the Bronze Age is named, was limited to a focus of development in the city-states of the Mediterranean. Kings there took in all valuables and then redistributed them, after keeping a share, to warriors, clients, and allies, by way of winning their support. The kept share determines the success of the kingdom; if it is too much support will fall away. So far, so good; this is exactly what chiefs did in Barbarian Europe. But the diffusionist argument goes on to claim that Near Eastern kingdoms are the model; that chiefdoms are a feeble imitation of the real thing, a mirror image of corporate civic society in which custom replaces formal laws, cults replace an organized priesthood, and war and piracy are a substitute for peaceful trade and commerce. All is brought forth by a barbarian lust for metals issuing from a distant source, and a derivative use of them for crude ornaments and weapons on the part of parvenue chiefs who are nothing more than copycat kings.

Applied to Kurgan pastoralists of the Ukrainian steppeland the argument may have some validity. But it does not account for one vital point: no social system will be imitated unless internal conditions are ready for it. Even so, there is no evidence that it was the rising urbanism of Mesopotamia that influenced the Kurgan folk; therefore, they must have developed chiefdoms outside this possible sphere of cultural diffusion. In fact, they already had copper from the Old Europeans in the Balkans and bronze from the Transcaucasian peoples of the Kuro-Araxes culture; the import of metals from these two areas must have reinforced a social process already in motion. As we have seen in chapter 2, these same two areas developed metallurgy on their own, perhaps even to supply the very craftsmen that were attracted to ply their skills in Mesopotamia!

Because all cultures fall into a pattern, integrated by a unified world view, and are not randomly patched together, one that borrows from another will admit traits that fit and screen out the rest. Here again is the story of those German tribes on the borders of the Roman Empire who confederated themselves under a high chief as the Alamanni. The chiefs who for over a century pursued this ambition did so in cooperation with the Romans, serving them as *foederati* in exchange for Roman military gear such as regulation belt buckles. But these metal objects were not used to dress up army uniforms—the German warriors were heroes of individual combat, not soldiers—but as valuables for redistribution. The chiefs who acquired them in the name of a military alliance, as the Romans perceived it, rather played with them in the same old giveaway game of potlatching. Just as Big Men of the potlatch built up chiefdoms on the basis of redistributing bronze axes and other metal goods, which they gained through control over ritualized trade, *kula* style, so the high chief of the Alamanni lorded it over lesser chiefs with control over a source of Roman belt buckles gained by way of a so-called military alliance. The buckles he perceived as just another metal commodity serving the politics of chieftainship, not military hardware in the service of an allied army extending the reach of Roman legions. No doubt every German chief who contracted with a Roman governor for such a deal saw in the latter just another big chief, whose quartermaster supplies made him a worthwhile trading partner in the business of enlarging a native chiefdom, and not as an agent securing the former's participation in the politics of an Iron Age empire. So, too, at an earlier time were the Celts of southern France receptive to silver coins passed to them from nearby Greek colonies; these were acquired, however, not as units of commercial exchange but as giveaway objects. The new input of metal into the native system of potlatching made for the confederation of smaller chiefdoms into larger ones, aristocratic chiefs, more inequality, and deracinated war bands. Money was not money for the Celts, but only another commodity that intensified the existing pattern of culture and its political thrust.

Similarly, the Windmill Hill folk of southern Britain already were moving toward the politics of chieftainship on the basis of a cultic trade in greenstone axes by the time a number of Beaker migrants carried bronze axes with them from the Continent. The result was a stimulus for the evolution of native chiefdoms from a communal type to one less egalitarian but not yet aristocratic, a type we call a petty chiefdom. The principle at work here is the acceleration by outside contact of an ongoing trend, and its monument is Stonehenge II. As such, it must have been constructed by much the same sort of organization, controlled by a shaman/priest, that earlier built megalithic tombs and even the causewayed camps. The mobilization of labor in almost all primitive societies is associated with a religious object. Even if secular chiefs can organize their people to build large monuments, they will have to do so with the help of a shaman/priest group, for there are few symbolic structures built without a supernatural/mythological idea underlying them. We can speculate, then, that Windmill Hill society was directed by sacerdotal ministers in charge of communal chiefdoms before it evolved heroic chiefs. The presence of religious leaders from the earliest period of Neolithic colonization by the Wessex farmers, and maybe even before among the Mesolithic natives, is attested by evidence for the continuity of customs and belief-systems that underlie the causewayed camps and their related structures, the henge monuments. With the rise of heroic chiefs, priests will render services to them, will celebrate their deeds, recite their genealogies, will in short give sanction to a new social order. They will help erect a work of megalithic architecture in the name of that new order whose design will body forth all the basic values of the old, of which they are the keepers and conservators.

Beaker Folk and Stonehenge II

The Windmill Hill period lasted in Britain until the middle of the third millennium, at which point small nomadic bands of pastoralists arrived from the Continent (see Map 5). These are the Beaker folk, so called after a characteristic drinking cup (for beer, probably) found with their burials everywhere. These are not the communal graves of the Neolithic, however, but single inhumations, often with the skull trephined, under small round barrows. The normal grave goods include the ubiquitous beaker, flint arrowheads of a distinctive type, archers' wrist guards, tool kits for leather working, and conical buttons made of amber, jet, or shale. Traveling in the company of the Beaker folk were smiths; for also included in the burial inventory of Beaker graves are open and bivalve molds for the casting of bronze axes, daggers, and awls.

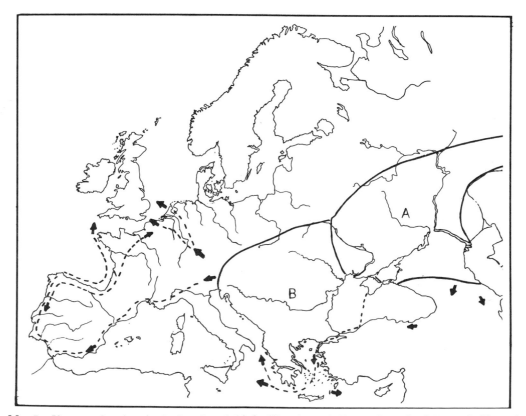

Map 5.   Kurgan migrations in the fourth and third millennia B.C. A. Kurgan homeland; B. area infiltrated in fourth millennium. Arrows show migrations routes; western arrows show Beaker migrations.

Because the Beaker folk often represent a physical type—round headed and stocky—different from the older Neolithic populations among whom they came to settle and dominate, they are thought to have had one place of origin.[12] From that center, wherever it was, they seem to have radiated out in roving bands, driving their cattle, trading, and even conquering, over much of western Europe. We now know that the problem of Beaker origins is far more complex than once believed; archaeologists have not been able to fully trace the migration routes and as yet no homeland is agreed upon. The problem is of some interest in a study of Stonehenge, and it may be stated briefly.

Complicating the question is the fact that more than one type of diagnostic pottery exists. Beaker folk moved so rapidly, in small groups, that they quickly merged with local peoples, everywhere producing variant types of the same basic vessel. Therefore, after perhaps one or two generations in one part of Europe whether Spain, southern France, or the Rhineland, the original Beaker tradition got modified over and over again. So far as the Beakers who entered Britain are concerned, it is sufficient to say their immediate point of takeoff was from among one or more of these modified groups. But the remoter question is still of interest.

An older opinion holds that Beaker folk began their career in the Iberian peninsula, after suffering the decline there of a mission to deliver tin and copper for the workshops of Bronze Age cities in the Aegean; and that these prospectors then migrated out of their base of operations, a walled township surrounded by some hundred passage graves at Los Millares in southeast Spain. Unhappily, the Beaker physical type is not represented in Millaran graves before the appearance of their distinctive culture.

The Beakers were prospectors, all right, but not in the employ of any civic society; that's the old diffusionist theory again, arrows of Light from the East penetrating the darkness of barbarian Europe. Barbarians themselves, they mined and smithed and adventured in their own employ. In a divergent opinion, to which we subscribe, Beaker origins may be placed in central Europe, in the region of the Vučedol culture, named after its type site in Croatia to the south of the Hungarian plain, which is a former province of Old Europe. Here, on the mountain slopes of the eastern Alps, embedded with ores of tin and copper, dwelled a number of peoples who, like those of the Kuro-Araxes culture in the Caucasus Mountains, smelted nuggets of metal from nearby mines and got rich by trading out finished goods of their own invention (in substance if not in form). Smiths in both cultures had learnt to smelt copper, and then went on to alloy copper first with arsenic and then with tin, making bronze. It was they who invented the very substance of the Bronze Age, not craftsmen in the city-states of the Mediterranean after which the "age" is named. Civilization at first was but a centripetal force, a cultural whirlpool, drawing in the barbarian know-how of making bronze (and other technologies) for its own peculiarities of urban growth. Thus again are the arrows of diffusion reversed! Meanwhile, poor relatives of the Vučedol metallurgists, shepherds living in foothills around the Hungarian plain, took up the same tech-

Arrowheads from a Beaker burial. Beaker folk were archers and these barb-and-tang arrowheads are the standard for their culture.

Material from a Beaker burial: beaker, dagger, wrist-guard and button. Wrist-guards, often made of schist or slate, are common in Beaker graves and attest to their archery. Buttons, made of various materials, were the most common clothes fastener. Beaker folk made woolen cloth, some having been found in graves.

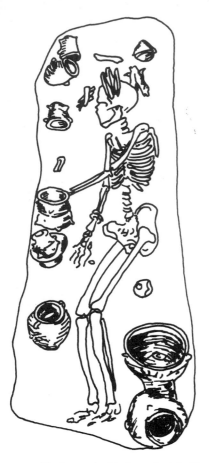

Single-grave burial of a man buried with copper bracelets, rings, stone daggers and celts. Early Bronze Age (Tiszapolgar Culture), Hungary (after Kalicz, *The Clay Gods*).

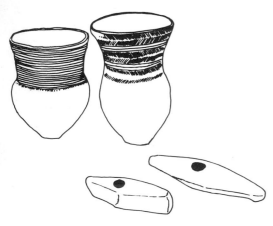

Single-grave material from Denmark: Corded Ware and Battle Axes.

nology for *their* own purposes, to go adventuring and conquering with it. This took place sometime between 3000 and 2500 B.C., and marks the beginning of Beaker radiation. One of the groups entering Britain encountered another pastoral culture to the north of the Beaker homeland, that of the Battle Axe people, who are descendants of warlike Kurgan herdsmen come out of the eastern steppelands. In full they are termed the Battle Axe/Corded Ware people, the latter part named after a long necked, cord marked vessel. It is one of the many local modifications of the basic Beaker style.

Since much of the argument about Beaker identity reduces to a question about variant pottery styles, it is far more sensible to widen the focus of attention and examine the cultural generalities with which they are associated. Beaker vessels of whatever type were manufactured as a special class of mortuary furniture, whose burial place is normally a single inhumation, with perhaps a few family members added later. All Beaker groups were users of bronze or employed smiths and bore weapons: daggers and axes. They were nomadic warriors, probably leading their own small families as they traveled to new lands and new opportunities. Moving in among the Windmill Hill peoples of Britain in about 2200 B.C., perhaps earlier, they no doubt impressed the natives with the magical power of their technology, and its fire-produced metal may have suggested equally the magical power of the sun. The petty chiefdoms they established must have come out of an idea strengthened by their mixing with related pastoralists, the Battle Axe people. There is good evidence that Kurgan herdsmen had long since domesticated the horse.[13] The implications are that in the Battle Axe/Corded Ware and Beaker cultures we have the beginnings of a horse-riding aristocracy.

Beaker occupation of Britain is constantly being clarified in the light of new research. Recent findings show a variety of Beaker vessels distributed within Britain itself, as on the Continent. Some, with Atlantic coast affinities, are found along the western coasts of the island. Others of the Beaker/Battle Axe mix are found concentrated within a sixty-mile radius of Stonehenge.[14] In their maritime distribution, Beakers bear evidence of intermixture with a megalithic folk, whose tombs sometimes include Beaker as well as native burials. Or so it is in the Scilly Isles where Beaker people seem to have settled down in small groups, side by side with local inhabitants. A rare settlement of that sort has been uncovered at Easton Down in Wiltshire. It consists of a small house whose foundations, ten by five feet, were dug into the ground and surrounded by a light hurdled fence and small circular storage or refuse pits. There is also a dog burial that harks back to a feature reminiscent of the Kurgan people far off in eastern Europe. Botanical remains from this site show that the family living here cultivated cereal crops, with barley accounting for 80 percent of the total. Barley grew well in the dry soils of the sub-Boreal period and it was to be the chief grain of the Bronze Age in Britain.[15] Its presence earlier tells us that the Beakers did indeed drink beer from their characteristic vessels. At the same time cattle are present and so are pigs, a sure sign of sedentary life because pigs cannot be driven in herds like cattle from one place to another.

The total picture is of a Beaker people given to the practice of mixed farming in company with an indigenous population doing the same. The fact that the Beaker newcomers were interested in the religious cults of their hosts is evidenced by their additions to Stonehenge I, their raising of the bluestones on that site. Being metallurgists they would have been welcomed as awe inspiring, honored guests of the local shamanistic/priestly leadership, the chiefs of a communal society. Beaker control of metal goods, for which they traded as far away as the Boyne Valley in Ireland, would have been a source of envy by these chiefs. Perhaps at once Beaker settlers married into chiefly families. If so, the double circle of bluestones may represent marriage alliances (see Drawing 2). Or perhaps they simply took over by dint of their obvious supernatural powers (not by the power of their weapons alone since stone weapons are every bit as capable of doing injury as copper or bronze, and the Beaker immigrants did not arrive in numbers sufficient to overcome an established population *vis a fronte*).[16] However they did it, the Beaker folk reinforced a local trend in the evolution of chieftainship, and made metal its new focus of interest. The necessity to trade far and wide for metal and to raid for it, to collect and distribute it among followers, led to a more overt leadership. Whether Beaker folk arrived with a warrior chief in the van or not, they soon raised a new and militant level of chieftainship on the basis of the old. Their metal daggers and axes, though doubtless imbued with mystical significance, were used not for ritual purposes but for war and conquest, or the threat of it. Cultic significance, however, still attached to *stone* axes and their raw materials.

Beaker interest in glamorous minerals took monumental expression in the erection of Stonehenge II, which is no longer visible as a unit, but which can be reconstructed from the so-called Q and R holes at the center of the enclosure. The holes once held a double circle of some sixty undressed bluestones, each weighing upwards of four tons. Two extra pairs were raised inside the circle in alignment with the Avenue, also a construction of this period. The double circle, seventy-four and eighty-six feet in diameter respectively, was only three quarters completed; the unfinished western quadrant is even devoid of stone holes. One theory for the abandonment of this project has it that shipment of the required number of stones from Pembrokeshire was stopped. But the bluestones are now known to be local. More likely the project was abandoned for a new plan, Stonehenge III, decided by yet another influx of newcomers.[17]

Battle Axe People and the Heroic Tradition

So far our discussion has turned on the peoples who built the first two phases of Stonehenge. The third, the standing structure, belongs to a heroic, warrior-led society, one of several scattered in time and space across Europe, from the Ukraine down to Greece and Italy, across the north European plain and into Britain. Entering Greece these warriors are the ancestral Mycenaeans; entering central and northern Europe they are the Battle-Axe/Corded Ware folk. The origin of these groups is to be found in the steppe country of southern Russia among the Kurgan peoples.

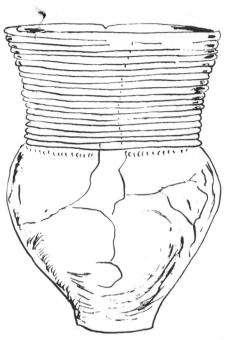

Corded Beaker (after J.F.S. Stone, 1960).

Drawing 2.   A Beaker wedding at Stonehenge II. (David Alexovich)

There is every reason to believe that the homeland of the Indo-Europeans, who are the authors of what heroic literature is left us, is rooted here. The first pulsing of movement by many Indo-European groups out of that heartland begins in the fifth millennium. Some move west, some east as far as India and China. To set them in perspective we must turn now to the first of the nomadic warriors—the Kurgan chiefs.

Kurgan people, as noted before, are so named after their burial mounds.[18] Their distinctive traditions arose on the eastern edge of the Old European cultural domain, in the general region of the north Pontic steppe lands, sometime during the fifth millennium. By the middle of the fourth millennium they are a horse breeding, mainly pastoral people organized in militarized chiefdoms. During the previous centuries they had traded with metal working Transcaucasian peoples to the south of them and were thus in contact with the inhabitants of northern Mesopotamia. Access to metals clearly enhanced the development of chiefdoms, proof of which is found in the richly furnished graves of Kurgan chiefs. Following the Caspian Sea coast and down into the Caucasus, Kurgan graves grow in number and wealth. One at Stepanakert contains thirty-six skeletons, human sacrifices, on a platform above a central grave, in which is buried a male with a bronze dagger and stone mace-head.[19] He is one of many chieftains buried there. None at this early period are well equipped with metal goods, however, but enough to show that bronze was important to high status.

Certainly human sacrifice bespeaks powerful and probably god-related chiefs, a political conception best illustrated by the stunningly rich graves—royal tombs, no less—at Maikop north of the Caucasus Mountains on the Black Sea coast and related tombs on the Pontic coast of Anatolia (Alaca Hüyük and Horoztepe). With the new dating system, these tombs probably belong to the middle of the third millennium, thus to the latest phase of Kurgan culture (Kurgan IV). The Maikop tomb was constructed as a multiroomed, underground mortuary house of limestone with wooden posts holding up a wooden roof. The main chamber held brilliantly wrought vessels of gold and silver engraved with animal figures. Bronze weapons of both local and Mesopotamian type appear as well. The bodies, one male and two female, each in a separate chamber, were covered with red ochre, a feature of Paleolithic antiquity. Other goods deposited in Kurgan tombs were woven fabrics, wagons, or sometimes just the wheels, which were solid, not yet spoked. The wagons are thought to be derived over some distance from northern Mesopotamia, certainly not from the intermediate mountain country where they would be unfeasible for transportation. That wheels, and their implications for the domesticated horse used as a draft animal, are found in the sepulchres of great Kurgan chiefs allows us to visualize a scene characteristic of later steppe-nomad peoples, in which the chief's goods were carried in wagons, drawn at the forefront of his tribe as it migrated.[20]

Mesopotamian connections are also evident in axe types, pottery, metal vessels, and jewelry. One feature of late Kurgan culture, however, is paralleled in only one instance; and that is large-scale human sacrifice,

Metal vase and implements from the Maikop tombs.

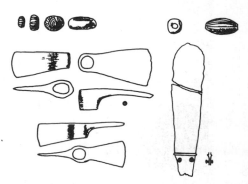

Grave goods from a chief's burial at Maikop: copper, turquoise and carnelian beads; copper axes and a dagger blade (after Gimbutas, after Childe and Hancar).

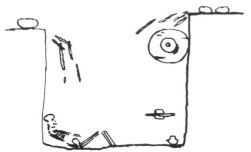

Chariot burial from the South Russian steppe lands. This is an early version of a grave type common to many later Indo-European peoples, those with warrior chiefs. Chariot graves have been found as far east as China and in the West are perhaps best known in Celtic La Tène culture (sideview after Piggott, 1965).

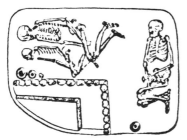

Early Indo-European burial, Catacomb Culture of the southern Russian steppe area. This kind of grave has been found as far south as Palestine and is a marker of the spread of Indo-European peoples. The tradition is the beginning of single-grave rites in all of Europe.

which is known in no other of the great cities of ancient Sumer but in Ur, excavated during the 1920s and '30s. The royal tombs of Ur are chambered palaces wherein kings and queens were interred together with their treasures and their slain courtiers, amounting to as many as sixty individuals.[21] A clue to the meaning of this may be found in literary traditions about an ancient semidivine king of Uruk (thirty-five miles southwest of Ur) named Gilgamesh who became a chthonic or underworld god after his death. Surely the courtiers and retainers who allowed themselves to be slain in the grave of their dead king must have believed him to be on the way to godhood, a state they would share with him in the afterlife by virtue of accompanying him in death. Is there a connection between the royal tombs of the Kurgan people and Ur? Massive human sacrifice is known only in Egypt in the western world, and even there not nearly on a par with Ur or the Kurgan tomb at Stepanakert. Chambered tombs that place the main occupant in a separate room is another parallel feature.

Once it would have been obvious that barbarian chiefs imitated the practice of civilized kings. Now the arrows of diffusion seem to point the other way, for the royal tombs of Ur date to about 2800 B.C. while those in the Caucasus begin at a date closer to 3500 B.C. Were the kings buried at Ur party to a Kurgan dynasty? Was Gilgamesh himself, though from a city in which no such tombs have been found, descended from a Kurgan chief? If either case were true, Ur or Uruk, it would provide the first example of a barbarian dynasty ruling a civilized people.

Meanwhile, Kurgan people expanded into the Old European areas beginning about 3700 B.C. All over the Balkans and down into Greece, Old European towns began to defend their settlements with walls and bastions. Currently there is a debate whether this represents home-grown chiefdoms in Old Europe or the influence of Kurgan folk. It seems likely that the latter possibility comes closer to the truth. Attesting the presence of Kurgan migrants are single barrow burials containing supine skeletons with the legs contracted, bronze daggers of triangular shape with midribs for strength (very much like later Mycenaean types), bronze axes with drooping blades, cord-decorated pottery, evidence of horse burials (from the teeth, frequently), occasional dog burials, and human sacrifice. In the European graves, sacrifice often is of a woman to accompany a man, and in a subservient position. This looks like *suttee*, a custom still practiced in India in the last century.[22]

No less than the Danubians, an earlier population on the move, Kurgan migrants mixed with indigenous peoples to form new cultural blends. This happened from Greece to Italy in southern Europe just as it did in central Europe where incoming Kurgan warriors acted to intensify metallurgy among Old Europeans there to produce the Vučedol people, who in turn may have been progenitors of the Beakers.

Within several hundred years mixed Kurgan peoples were to be found all over Europe, their warrior culture dominant in many parts of the continent. Their northern extensions are the Battle Axe/Corded Ware peoples. Peoples, in the plural, is an appropriate word because their culture really incorporates a loose aggregation of ethnic groups ranged across the north European plain, each with a different ceramic tradition, but within a similar life style. Be it noted, however that the Battle Axe peoples, unlike their Kurgan cousins living closer to Caucasian metal working centers, carried stone not metal weapons until they met with Beaker folk who provided the latter. But stone axes remained cultural heirlooms.

In life style these Battle Axe folk were all stockbreeders and hunters as well as hoe farmers; they interred their dead of high status in wooden mortuary houses under barrows, complete with a type of human sacrifice we know as *suttee*; their grave goods include cord-impressed drinking cups, used either for taking beer or perhaps *koumiss*, that beverage of fermented milk preferred on the steppes; and the weapons from which the culture itself takes its more romantic name, battle axes. These battle axes are beautifully cut works of stone, pecked and polished in exact imitation of copper axes cast by the original Kurgan folk to the east, imitated down to the last detail of their drooping blades and casting seams. Despite their name, however, these stone weapons of the Battle Axe folk show no sign of ever having been used for bashing and killing. Perhaps the practical ones were discarded after combat, dead warriors buried only with ceremonial ones imbued with religious significance. Ample folklore retained in the surviving epic literature demonstrates this to be the case.

By 3000 B.C., the Battle Axe peoples had spread to western Europe and formed regional variants on their basic culture from Denmark to Central Europe. The classic example of Battle Axe/Corded Ware culture in central Europe is the Saxo-Thuringian, whose cemeteries are quite distinctive, made up of both barrows and flat graves with particular concentration in the uplands, hence pastoral lands. Their grave goods are all that one would expect to find among a Battle Axe people, save for a number of metal artifacts, specifically copper rings, double-spiral ornaments of Eastern origin, and Kurgan-style pins for fastening cloaks. The double spirals are of particular interest in that they typify a standard Bronze Age motif that is likely related to the sun cult. Sometimes skulls are trephined in the Beaker manner (and here might possibly be seen some relationship to the later skull cult of the Celts, who decapitated their enemies and displayed the crania as trophies about their forts). In some few cases the dead were cremated. From this point on a small number of cremations occur among all Battle Axe populations and their descendants. Perhaps they were confined to a special class, shamans we could guess, priests of the fire-related cult of the sun. Based on the evidence of mortuary houses, Battle Axe/Corded Ware peoples lived in porched houses of the megaron type, precisely the same type built by their relatives in Greece. In the eastern portions of the Saxo-Thuringian culture the ritual internment of horses, cattle, and pigs is common.[23] The last, pigs, are obviously important to the economy just as they would be in later epic poetry. Their presence shows that a horse-breeding people had become somewhat forest adapted. The pattern depicted here, petty chiefs governing over small clearings in the forests of eastern Europe, is one that recurs all over Europe up to and through the Middle Ages.[24]

In about 2500-2200 B.C., Corded Ware/Beaker groups composed of this and other mixtures crossed the Channel to settle in among the old farming folk there, but not without taking over the local leadership, for the

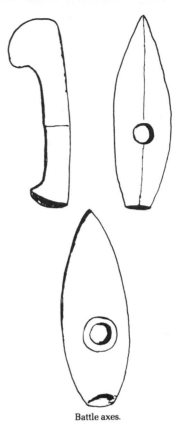

Battle axes.

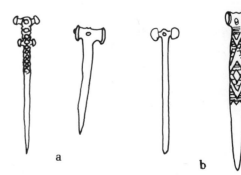

Bone and copper pins: a) Battle Axe culture (Poland); b) Kurgan graves, southern Russia. The hammer-headed pin is one of the indicators of Kurgan cultural influences. It originates in that culture and accompanied Kurgan peoples everywhere (after Gimbutas, 1956).

a   b

communal tombs once built at the direction of Windmill Hill religious chiefs are replaced by graves built at the direction of Beaker warrior chiefs. Other Battle Axe peoples moved to Britain at a later time. Departing from the Rhineland they found on Salisbury plain a number of petty Beaker chiefdoms not dissimilar to their own, and with which they merged. The mixture of the two traditions, plus its acquired roots in ancient British ways, plus the continuing evolution of chieftainship, plus ongoing connections with Brittany and the Rhineland in search of precious metals—out of this nexus of gathering culture change will arise the Wessex culture, whose aristocratic chiefs built Stonehenge III. To understand them better we must once again turn to continental Europe, where an equally rich culture antecedent and parallel to Wessex is well known to archaeologists.

The Únětice Chiefdoms

In central Europe the tradition we have identified as the Battle Axe/ Corded Ware culture evolved during the early Bronze Age in much the same way as did its extension in Wessex. By the time Battle Axe culture gives rise to aristocratic chiefdoms it is called Únětice after its type site, a cemetery near Prague, in Czechoslovakia. It begins sometime in the early part of the third millennium and includes in its early phases elements of its parental cultures, including that of Old Europe. In chronology and development it runs parallel to the Mycenaean Greeks, albeit in a somewhat "barbarized" form owing to its distance from the more civilized Mediterranean basin. It is a society headed by wealthy chieftains, as known from their status burials beneath single-grave barrows of great bulk. In several phases over the course of some five-hundred years, Únětice reached its classical period in the latter part of the third millennium B.C. Bronze objects proliferated in both numbers and quality, thus marking the full flowering of the European Bronze Age. Weapons are particularly prominent, highly decorated, and well-made, including richly ornamented daggers with bone and amber inlaid hilts.[25] Also evidence for chieftains are the number of ornaments once attached to their bodies or clothing— bracelets, coiled armbands, necklaces made in the shape of the ubiquitous spiral, and amber imported from the Baltic (the latter two items both perhaps part of the sun cult). All were made by specialist craftsmen who grew in proficiency as time went on. The area covered by Únětice culture includes the important copper and tin-bearing regions of central Europe, long vital to the enrichment of surrounding peoples by way of trade.

For a time it was thought that the Únětice culture was heavily influenced by developing centers in the Argolid of Greece, that it rose in direct response to Mycenaean trading expeditions. We now know the chronology of this putative contact to be entirely wrong and that both cultures are roughly parallel in time. Nor do we need any longer to postulate external contact for the rise of warrior chiefs; barbarians were quite capable of organizing chiefdoms on their own. Únětice culture arose as the result of a union of warrior herdsmen, ultimately derived from the steppes of south-

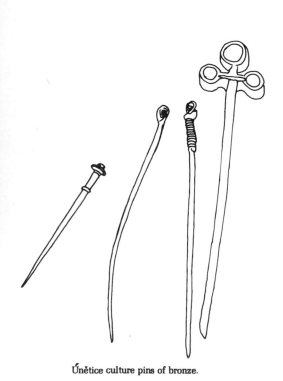

Únětice culture pins of bronze.

ern Russia, and the Neolithic settlers of Old Europe in its Danubian province. The model for this union of contrasting ecologies is, once again, redistribution centers taken over by Big Men of the potlatch. The proof is in the type of settlement the Únětice warriors made for themselves, fortified hilltops, where an abundance of weapons is a reminder that craft specialists once worked there under the control of big chiefs.[26]

Concomitant with all this is a division of labor between pastoral and agricultural specialists. Each hilltop fort controlled diverse lands worked in different ways by herders and farmers, though wealth obviously was reckoned in cattle and horses as well as in bronze and gold. The chief's stronghold was an economic center, but not a marketing center of the sort we associate with civic society. Chiefs bartered only with their fellows, usually for precious materials; and in this way, from tribe to tribe, hand to hand, amber passed down from the Baltic and ended up in Greece. In reverse, faïence beads of molded glass passed from the Mediterranean into central Europe (though it is now commonly accepted that most beads were made locally). There is thus no evidence that Únětice chiefs answered to the example of incipient Mycenaeans. Nor is it likely that the direct trade normally postulated as a stimulus ever existed. In its place was a series of local exchanges by barter or perhaps reciprocal gifts in the manner of the *kula* ring, gifts exchanged in the name of political alliances for the purpose of confederation and the enlargement of the most dynamic chiefdoms. The fact is, Mycenae and Únětice (and Wessex for that matter) are similar and parallel because they grew out of the same evolutionary process rooted in the same cultural origins. Únětice hilltop forts are the northern version of Mycenaean "cities," which are not cities at all but the homes of big chiefs and their redistribution centers.

Mycenaean cities are not true urban centers because they did not function within a market economy; no redistribution system does.[27] The system functions for the sake of social hierarchy, not free trade. It is, in short, a caste system, arranged for the benefit of the upper ranks exclusively. Mycenaean palace culture, with its civilized features including a written language borrowed from the Minoans, an Old European people located on the island of Crete, is just that and nothing more. When it is nothing more than the apex of a potlatching system, palace culture is a very fragile thing, unlike its integration within the marketing system of the much later cities of Classical Greece. Any upset in the balance of chiefly face-offs, adverse change of climate upsetting harvests or disease among cattle and sheep for example, will quickly ruin the system and bring down its dynastic chief and his warrior nobility. If not open revolt against this privileged caste especially when a body of armed freemen exists, as it obviously did, then simple abandonment of the center will suffice for ruination. Remaining only will be the subsistence farmers, eking out their living in the same old Neolithic way. There will be fewer of them, but they tend to remain, even in the shadows of fallen palace architecture. This is exactly what happened to Mycenae in due course and, to cite another example far away in the New World, to the great Mayan civilization.

Most of the material remains of the Únětice culture have been recovered from its cemeteries. These speak of an aristocratic society and they also tell of dynastic chiefs or clan heads. Graves tend to be grouped together with something like twenty burials in each group. Most are not contemporaneous, and there is no question of massive sacrifice. But there are frequent double graves, man and woman, suggesting the ritual of *suttee*. This burial system is perfectly analogous to the famous shaft graves of Mycenae, those princely tombs discovered in the nineteenth century by Schliemann which still evoke our wonder that barbarians could be so splendid. If the Únětice graves contain hereditary chieftains, even of a lesser sort, they must have followed one another for several generations in a line of succession.[28] Since this does seem to be the case, one may easily postulate the appearance of chiefly dynasties, the very organization described in eyewitness accounts by visitors from Greece and Rome to barbarian Europe, and in its surviving epic poetry. Únětice surely anticipates the heroic society of the historically known Celts and Germans, who in turn are the same kind of people who inhabit Homer's *Iliad*.

It does not strain the evidence in the least to put forward the Únětice warriors (together with their counterparts in Wessex) as early Celts. It is not only their chiefdoms, organized from their centers on fortified hilltops, that suggest this continuity, but some few other features as well. By the time Únětice culture expands to reach central Germany, burial mounds have enlarged to become great royal tumuli; kings, no longer small tribal chiefs, are buried in them. In this funereal pomp they are true precursors of the historical Celts. Their iconography includes pigs and cattle and the ubiquitous horse, just as celebrated in the Irish epics (although the chariots mentioned in these epics had not yet appeared). Neck rings of bronze, those torcs beloved by the Celtic warrior, are found in the thousands everywhere. We might reiterate the phrase "ring-giving Hrothgar" from *Beowulf* as a distinct memory of this symbol of status, gifts from a king to his followers and allies. At one site in Czechoslovakia a wood-lined well was sunk into a thermal spring in much the same fashion as the sacred wells and ritual shafts of the Druids.[29] Trephined skulls are common, and the circular pieces of bone so removed were often made into amulets. Here is a direct development from Beaker practice that terminates in the later Celtic cult of the human skull. All these traits, and more, indicate the strong likelihood that Celtic origins lie here in the Erzeberge Mountains of central Europe and, once again, are derived ultimately from the Indo-European homeland to the east.

As the warrior chieftains of Únětice moved ever westward, they in time came into contact with the chiefs of southern Britain. There were sound economic reasons for continued movement. One of them was simply a rise in population to the point where, in the perception of the chiefs, more land was needed to maintain their expansive way of life. Based on later models, Vikings for example, it is safe to say that any migration will have been led by the younger sons or other relatives of an aristocratic family.

An equally compelling reason for movement turns on the demands of early metal prospecting. The earliest bronze objects in the Únětice series, it can be demonstrated, are made of local copper and tin, but as time went on sources were sought further and further to the west. It is entirely likely that Únětice contact with Wessex came about by way of a mission to search for and exploit British metal resources in gold, copper, and especially tin. Tin is much more scarce than copper, and besides, the two are not often found together; therefore the addition of considerable tin to a bronze alloy will almost necessarily imply trade or barter. It is likely that smiths were itinerant in the early days of bronze making because only that way could they acquire the crucial raw material; they had no big chiefs to secure it for them from an abundant source. The Beaker folk are the case *par excellence*. Their alloys were mainly arsenical at first; tin they discovered later, probably because of its close appearance to forms of arsenic. When something like 12 percent tin is found in bronze compounds there can be certainty of either trade for it or the presence of local tin deposits. What kept prospectors on the move is the fact that the mineral usually was available to them only as small, scattered surface finds, where a few walnut-sized lumps of cassiterite (tin oxide) had been washed out of its natural beds by the action of running water in ancient streams later become defunct—in dry surface deposits known as tin streams. Independent smiths would thus move from region to region, picking up tin as they found it, making bronze as they went. Or else their chief, if in the employ of such, would barter with locals to do the scavenging instead.[30] Either way, the process is carried out by a small group of people accustomed to mobility. We prepare no surprise, then, when we suggest that Únětice interest in Britain focused upon a highly unusual concentration of rich tin streams located in Cornwall. The implications of this for chieftainship among the biggest men of the potlatch circuit is obvious.

Wessex Warriors and Stonehenge III

The Wessex culture was named by Stuart Piggott from evidence gathered from the most richly furnished round barrows in that region, which in all number more than six-thousand.[31] Its chiefs replaced or subordinated those of the resident Beaker folk. Beaker vessels (thought to have held drink for the dead) are missing from the richest of these graves, and in their place are the so-called food vessels derived from local Neolithic prototypes and "incense cups" used in some now forgotten ritual. These latter are tiny pots whose outside surface is covered with grape-like knobs between which air holes have been drilled. It seems as if these little pots were designed not only to contain some burning substance but to protect from the heat the hands that held them. If they are called "incense cups" it is only because archaeologists are in the habit of classifying every artifact of which they are ignorant as some kind of "ceremonial object." We hazard the guess that they were used for sniffing hemp, as we know Viking berserkers did. Our Indo-European ancestors, it would appear, were "pot" smokers.

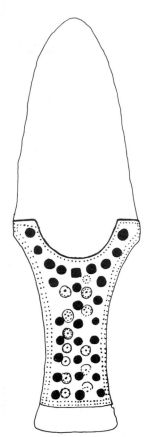

Bronze dagger, Wessex culture, from Milston, Wiltshire.

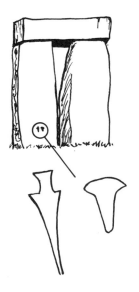

Still favored in the Wessex culture is the battle axe, as it was to remain well into historical times. Many of these are of stone, some of bronze made in Ireland, while others, flange axes, are of Únětice make. Bronze daggers, as many as six or seven in one grave, are of both Únětice and Breton derivation. The former are ovoid in shape with thick mid-ribs and three rivets to fasten the hilt. It is of an almost standard west European design and, like those in the early Bronze Age, not dissimilar to Mycenaean types. Some of the daggers are decorated with tiny gold pins in the haft, another European Mycenaean design feature they hold in common. Interesting local products include miniature, bronze-bladed versions of the metal-shafted halberds typical of the Únětice homeland. Interesting, too, is the supposed sceptre of office inlaid with zig-zag bone mounts found in the warrior-chieftain's tumulus known as Bush Barrow.[32] It was thought to match one from the shaft-graves of Mycenae, but a new interpretation of the object makes it unlikely to have been a sceptre at all.[33] The gold work is justly famous. Gold plaques decorated with lozenge designs and probably meant to be sewn on clothing are among the best known Wessex treasures. Surely the most beautiful one, however, is a gold cup from Rillaton in the vicinity of the fabulous tin streams of Cornwall. Like many of these others, it once was thought to have come directly from the hands of some craftsman in the Mediterranean by way of Mycenaean trade, but closer examination reveals that it is really a Beaker vessel carried out in new material. British craftsmen learned well from the Únětice neighbors on the Continent how to work gold, and produced nothing but the best for their chiefs. And as we have seen, not even the Únětice culture was a product of Mycenaean influence.

Why anybody ever should have thought otherwise can be explained by a chronological error which has to do with the standing trilithons of Stonehenge. Carved on the inner surface of sarsen stone number 53 is what seems to be the life-size representation of the square-hilted, diamond-bladed dagger emblematic of Mycenaean royalty, the same buried in the shaft graves of Mycenae about 1500 B.C. Because of weathering, the faint outlines of this dagger on the stone were not discovered until 1953, when just the right shadow caught it in relief for just the right observer on the spot. Since then the many greasy hands of passing tourists have made it visible from two chains and twelve links away to any observer on the western side of the embankment, from which it may have been meant to be seen by tribal spectators to a chiefly gathering if, as we may speculate, the intaglio had once been hammer filled with some soft gleaming metal such as copper or gold. All power to the sun chief! All reflective metal to his glory! All solar mirrors gleaming in his name! But all speculation aside, this dagger carving and others like it now inspected have no association with the Argolid, given recalibration of Carbon-14 dates from the site to about 2100 B.C., perhaps half a century before the rise to power of the Mycenaean Greeks.[34]

This date is not the only one figured for the Wessex culture, but it is the decisive one. Based on comparative grounds Wessex is seen to have run parallel to and then have superseded the Beaker cultures of Britain at

Plate 3.   Dagger and axe carvings on stone no. 53 (the second impost from the right). (Hans Schaal)

one end of a time scale starting at about 2090 B.C. At the other end, recalibration of the last of the Wessex barrows, or what we presume to be the
last of them, yields a new Carbon-14 date of about 1500 B.C. Taken together, the flush of Wessex culture seems to have spanned a period of
some five-hundred years, that is, preceding Mycenae and overlapping it.
That we must conclude if the Mycenaean dates are correct. They run from
about 1600 B.C. for the shaft graves, through the beehive shaped tholos
tombs of megalithic construction (with strong hints of civilized influence
from West Asia), to eventual collapse in the century before 1100 B.C. But
even if Wessex did begin some hundreds of years before any Mycenaeans
reasonably could be expected to have arrived in Britain, that is, before
they themselves were raised up as a distinctive culture, could they not
have influenced the *late* phase? Perhaps through trade expeditions for tin
in Cornwall? This line of reasoning would place the "golden age" of Wessex culture, when the richest artifacts from the most diverse origins ap-

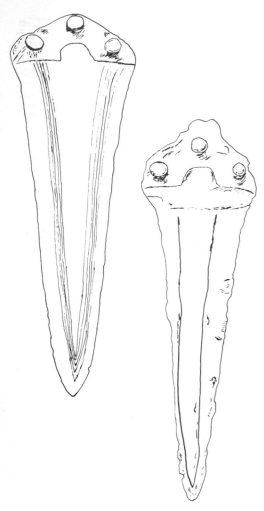

Dagger blades, Wessex Culture. These three-riveted blades were once thought to have Mycenaean origin. With the revolution in dating, such weapons may now be seen to have been part of a generalized type found throughout Europe in the Bronze Age.

pear, within a relatively short period of time. But those who actually argue the case for a short chronology rather concentrate it on the early phase! While there is as yet no complete catalogue of Wessex grave furniture, it is safe to say that the Mycenaean argument is largely ephemeral.[35] How much more reasonable to suggest Únětice connections, whether as conquerors, traders, or colonists, and the local use of exotic material for the glory of native chiefs. The matter of Wessex culture is, as Colin Renfrew says, a problem of social evolution above all else. It has more to do with the rise of chiefdoms than with the diffusion of "civilization."

It is not that Mycenaeans could not have got to Britain at some time, that is always possible. After all, the time of warrior heroes celebrated by Homer is also the time of Mycenaean trade and exploration, should we take Homer to be more Bronze Age than he really is. It would seem that the truly Bronze Age myths of the voyages of the Argo in search of the Golden Fleece and the Theseus myth are more to the point. Nevertheless, some like to think that the Laistrygonian episode in the *Odyssey* is a dim recollection of northern trading expeditions. Homer describes that land as a place where "the paths of day and night are close together," i.e., a northern latitude where midsummer days are very long. Hesiod, roughly contemporary with Homer, also speaks of the Laistrygonian capital city as Telepylus, the "Distant Gate," as the place where Night and Day come together. J. V. Luce thinks this place might be the furthest known part of the ancient world, beyond the Pillars of Heracles to the west or northwest.[36] Most significantly, however, it was described as a gate through which the sun-god passed before "returning to the east." All of this has more religious meaning than geographical, that is, the west is an eponymous place and signifies death. Laistrygonia is merely a distant land in myth, not reality.

Be that as it may, Mycenaean recollections in the *Odyssey* are very slim indeed; though in the *Iliad*, the earlier work, they are more numerous and specific.[37] There is no reason to suppose knowledge of northwestern Europe to be necessarily Mycenaean since by the time the Homeric epics were set down in their roughly present form the Greeks had occupied southern France and traded in Spain (and thus probably Britain in competition with the Phoenicians) for more than a century. The dagger carvings, so dimly seen, far more likely belong to the axe head carvings on the trilithons of Stonehenge. The "Mycenaean" dagger might just as easily be an Únětice weapon, and rather than ask its provenance we should inquire as to what it means. Might it testify to the interest of Wessex chieftains in bronze weapons, especially one of greater value for having been imported? Or might it be of a piece with the Indo-European warrior god who figures so prominently in rock carvings all over Europe from Italy to southern Sweden?

In some ways, Wessex, Únětice, and the Mycenaean "civilization" are more alike than are Mycenae and the centers of high civilization upon which it is supposedly modeled. The original centers of Bronze Age civilization revolved around cities; Mycenae around court life. The hill-top city of Mycenae is not a true city, but a fortified palace estate built around the king's court or megaron. Court-centered life in its early stages is the very opposite of corporate civic life. Where the Wessex chieftains held court is not identifiable in the archaeological record, but urbanism is clearly lacking. In any event, the warrior graves of Wessex and the shaft-graves of Mycenae are alike in that they provide the dead with an excess of weapons, numerous daggers and war axes in the former, as many or more daggers and swords in the latter. The pride of Mycenaean kings and Wessex chieftains alike demanded a show of costly weapons of war, to be exchanged as "presents" in the ceremonial niceties of trade among aristocratic equals, or to be won in that meritorious thievery of loot and conquest that makes a king's gift kingly in the poetry of Homer.

The society represented by the Wessex barrows is that of warrior chiefdoms. That settlement sites are yet to be discovered is perhaps indicative of constant land use during the intervening centuries and perhaps of a more pastoral element at the time. It would not be unreasonable to suppose, however, that tillage survived in the Wessex region as it did to the north where the allied Food Vessel peoples carried on in pretty much the same old Neolithic way. Wessex chiefdoms were built on Beaker patterns of organization. In perhaps the same manner that Beaker folk impacted the developing communal chiefdoms of Neolithic Britain, so the new Wessex chiefs were influenced by the fully developed barbarian cultures of Únětician Europe. If not that, they learned and borrowed from the Continent to reinforce their own evolving aristocracy.

The very eclectic nature of Wessex grave goods seems to indicate that. Within a few centuries, Wessex craftsmen sought raw materials elsewhere, mainly Ireland and Cornwall, and had developed their own style of craft techniques. Because no chiefly centers of Wessex culture have yet been discovered, neither have centers of craft specialization. Yet Wessex chiefs were able to mobilize manpower to construct the last phase of Stonehenge and to subsidize their metal workers. The meaning of such a seeming paradox may be resolved by observing that Wessex lies at the fringe of the Únětician culture center, that it is a local variant of an almost standard type of European chiefdom. Its craftsmen, then, do not cluster at a court but are scattered around the countryside and are probably itinerant.[38] The kind of social control possible in Mycenaean Greece or on the Continent is not at all that of Wessex. Smiths still likely had an aura of religious mystery about them, and served their aristocratic patrons at the same time they retained their mobility. It is the lower orders, tillers of the soil and husbandmen if they can ever be identified, who would have been subject to chiefly control. They were the real builders of Stonehenge III.

Stonehenge III is apparently the product of three separate operations (see Table 4). The first, Stonehenge IIIa, is the most impressive. The double circle of bluestones was removed to make way for the erection of the five sarsen trilithons, the sarsen ring, the Four Stations, and the Slaughter Stone. The Slaughter Stone now lies recumbent, parallel to the axis, just inside of the embankment to the visitor's right as he looks out upon the Avenue from the center. Originally it stood upright at that place, one of an intended pair framing the causeway, although its fellow was never

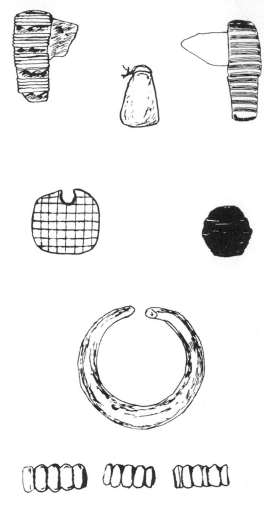

Faïence beads and jewelry, Wessex culture. Wessex ornaments are made of jet, shell, ground stone, gold and faïence. The last is a bead of vitreous material and it was upon these objects that theories of diffusion from the Near East were based. The kind of bead shown here, segmented, is well known in the eastern Mediterranean. In fact, molds for a very similar type have been found in the ruins of Tell-el-Amarna in Egypt dating to the 14th century B.C. Diffusionist theory held that Mycenaean traders obtained the beads from Egypt and traded them to the barbarian Wessex peoples in exchange for raw metals, many of which were supposed to have come from Ireland. Recent scientific work on the British beads, however, tends to show that the overwhelming majority were made locally. The rest, and the form itself, may be accounted for by local trade of items passed on hand to hand across central Europe or up from the Mediterranean seaboard.

Phase	Architecture
IIIc	bluestone circle bluestone horseshoe Altar Stone
IIIb	Z and Y holes
IIIa	trilithons Sarsen ring Station Stones Slaughter Stone bluestones removed

Table 4. Phases of Stonehenge III.

erected. The Four Stations form a rectangle with stone holes 92 and 94 (in twin mounds) and Sarsens 91 and 93, which features are placed against the bank. The mounds cover a number of the Aubrey holes, putting them beyond the reach of any counting stones Hawkins may want moved about for the reckoning of lunar eclipses. The Four Stations themselves, however, may have some astronomical significance, or at the least some geometrical significance. The line between Stations 93 and 91 cuts the line between 94 and 92 at the center of Stonehenge. The sarsen blocks are invariably said to be derived from Marlborough Downs, twenty miles away over hill and dale to the north, and much ingenuity has been spent in covering that distance by means of log rollers or sleds, on snow or ice, or even by telekinesis. But Edward H. Stone argued very persuasively in 1924 that the sarsen stones were native to Salisbury Plain.[39] Stonehenge evidently was built where the stones were.

But Stonehenge IIIa was never completed. Standing, fallen, or ruined are the complete set of stones for the five trilithons. Missing from the sarsen ring are twenty-three or twenty-four of its thirty lintels and six of its uprights. None of the missing stones have been found anywhere in the region.

Sometime later—how much later is uncertain—the double ring of sixty Z and Y holes around the outside of the incomplete sarsen ring were dug to accommodate the bluestones set aside from the dismantling of Stonehenge II. That activity comprises Stonehenge IIIb. Excavation shows that these holes never held stones or ever were refilled.

Still later, Stonehenge reached its final phase of reconstruction. The sixty bluestones from Stonehenge II were now reset within the sarsen circle to form the present bluestone circle, and nineteen dressed bluestones were set within the embrace of the great trilithons in a horseshoe surrounding the Altar Stone, also put up at this time. This is Stonehenge IIIc, a poor juxtaposition of leftover bluestones and the magnificent sarsen structure with which they have no architectural connection and which the master builder left unfinished.

A distant echo of the continuing use of Stonehenge into the Iron Age perhaps may be heard in the account of a fourth century B.C. Greek his-

Plate 4.   View of Stonehenge from the Avenue, looking across the recumbant Slaughter Stone (no. 95) which lies just inside the causeway. (Hans Schaal)

torian, Hecateus of Abdera. He wrote a book on *The Hyperboreans* ("the beyond-the-north-wind people"), now lost, but which is quoted by a later Greek historian, Diodorus Siculus, a contemporary of Julius Caesar who flourished around 50 B.C. The fragment of Hecateus quoted by Diodorus includes a passage that describes an island opposite to the land of the Celts in Gaul, where the inhabitants worship Apollo, the sun god. A sacred enclosure is dedicated to him, as well as a circular temple, where priests of the god "constantly chant hymns and tune lyres."[40] The island is probably Britain, the enclosure the earthen bank at Stonehenge, and the temple the sarsen structure within. The chanting and lyre playing may be a garbled interpretation of the sound of priests instructing their pupils to the rhythm of a musical instrument. An oral literature requires memorization of an immense body of traditional lore, which is best assimilated when reduced to verse. The traditional methods of Japanese carpentry and other skills, for example, were conveyed to apprentices in that very way. A Druidic school where apprentice priests learned their versified lessons would thus sound like a choir of religious worshippers to a civil-

Plate 5.   In the foreground are three bluestone pillars (numbers 68, 69 and 70, reading from the left), which were removed from Stonehenge II and here re-erected as part of Stonehenge IIIc. The ones shown are arranged within the hoseshoe array of trilithons, of which imposts numbers 37 and 38 appear in the background to the right. To the left is the heel of the hoseshoe and its one standing impost, stone no. 56. (Hans Schaal)

ized observer whose own learning tradition was literary. As a matter of fact, Julius Caesar, who spent nine years in Gaul, describes the Druids there as spending as many as twenty years memorizing poetry, and said this system of training had originated in Britain, where the truly diligent student traveled for the most advanced lessons.[41] Stonehenge, however, may no longer have been an active center of chieftainship by Caesar's time.

At all events, the end of Stonehenge surely came about after its reinvestment during the Roman conquest by a Druid-led rebellion associated, perhaps, with the reconstruction of Stonehenge IIIc. The Druids at that time, we know, made their temples in wooded groves; and the Romans made every attempt to cut these down. The Romans, usually tolerant of native religions within the imperial ambit, took exception to Druidism and pursued it ruthlessly to extinction. Why? It is said the Romans would tolerate any religion other than their own so long as it did not call for human sacrifice. But this is not good enough. The Romans were attracted to Britain, mainly, for its grain production. Salisbury Plain was taken over as an Imperial Estate and administered from Old Sarum nearby, not alone to feed the army of occupation but to supply the more important European garrisons.

In the midst of these great wheatfields stood Stonehenge, appropriated by Druids as a gathering place for rebel elements everywhere.[42] Stukeley may have been right! At least for Stonehenge IIIc. But that is the end of Stonehenge as a living monument, not its beginning, which we now will recount in detail.

A British Druid as visualized by Stukeley.

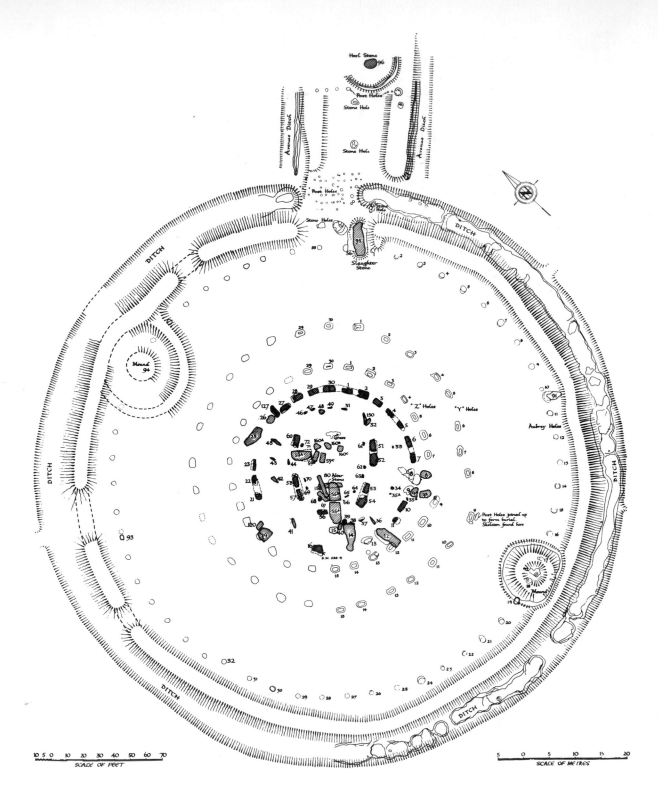

Official groundplan of Stonehenge, courtesy Department of Environment. The stone numbers used in the text refer to those on the plan. Permission by HMSO, Crown copyright.

4. The Stones of Stonehenge

After the Tower of London, Stonehenge is today the biggest tourist attraction in all of Britain. Its popularity began in the middle of the eighteenth century with the publication of Stukeley's book associating it with the Druids. When in 1918 the owner of Stonehenge gave it over to the state, the transfer was accompanied by rituals enacted by those latter-day Druids who still parade about the place in white sheets whenever they are called by the midsummer equinox to do their duty by a sunrise ceremony. This will be less easy to conduct, now that the site has been roped off by the British government's Department of Environment, in order to protect the monument from further vandalism. For thirty-five centuries the relentless pressure of high winds has scoured out soft spots in the stones and even pushed some of them over. But the rapid process of erosion under the pressure of tourism is even more severe, for visitors from the very start have taken a fancy to bringing little chips of Stonehenge home with them. In Stukeley's time, souvenir dealers sold hammers for the purpose.

For all its ruination Stonehenge still stands magnificent, despite the fact it never was completed. Were the visitor allowed to cross the ropes and enter the monument to see it as we last saw it, he would see a tumble of fallen stones, others standing in irregular fashion, all within a worn down earthwork.

Plate 6.   Wind erosion on the backside of one of the trilithon uprights, stone no. 52. (Hans Schaal)

Architectural Remains

Let the visitor enter the monument from the northeast along its proper entranceway, the Avenue, and not the official path set forth by the tourist guidebook. He will first step across a causeway 35 feet wide bridging a circular ditch and bank. The ditch is unevenly excavated, a quarry for the embankment, which is 320 feet in diameter and weathered down from 6 to about 2 feet in height. Walking into the enclosure, the visitor next will step across the ring of 56 chalk-filled Aubrey holes which form a circle 288 feet in diameter. As he marches toward the array of massive stones at the center of the monument, he will pass through an archway framed by two uprights, stones number 30 (to the right) and number 1 (to the left), and a lintel stone, number 101. These numbers are the ones assigned by Flinders Petrie, the great Egyptologist, in the course of his survey of Stonehenge in 1880,[1] the same that appear in the fold-out map to the official guidebook written by R. S. Newall.[2]

The archway just mentioned is part of the least ruined section of the sarsen ring (three continuous lintels in place) whose original plan called for 30 such portals. Immediately inside the sarsen ring are the ruins of the bluestone ring, a circular arrangement of solitary pillars, many of which are decapitated, fallen, or missing. And then, the visitor may enter and be embraced by the broken arms of the great horseshoe array of trilithons (named by William Stukeley), within which more bluestones repeat the horseshoe plan.

If the visitor will now step to the focal center of the horseshoe he will find a recumbent slab on the ground, stone number 80, the so-called Altar Stone. This is covered by the fallen remains of the largest of the five trilithons at the heel of the horseshoe; otherwise one could stand on it and look back upon the Avenue (flanked by running embankments with their ditches on the outside), from a perfect vantage point to observe the axis or central line around which Stonehenge is built. But standing in front of the Altar Stone will do as well. Looking down the Avenue a short distance beyond the causeway, the observer will see a massive upright stone, number 96, leaning badly and terribly weathered, the so-called Heel Stone. A line drawn from the Heel Stone to the observer at the Altar Stone roughly forms the axis of Stonehenge—roughly because the Heel Stone is somewhat offset from the center line of the Avenue.

Plate 7. The tumble of stones fallen amidst the standing ones at the center of Stonehenge. To the left is the heel of the trilithon array marked by its solitary impost, stone no. 56 (with tenon on top). (Hans Schaal)

Plate 8.   The official path leading into Stonehenge, from the north. The
Avenue enters from the northeast. (Hans Schaal)

Plate 9.   A closer view from down the path. (Hans Schaal)

Plate 10. Impost no. 56 at the heel of the trilithon array is framed between uprights numbered 30 and 1 (reading from the left) in the sarsen ring along Stonehenge's true axis. (Hans Schaal)

Plate 11. A section of the bluestone ring, arranged directly inside the sarsen ring, of which uprights numbered 1 and 30 (left to right) appear at the center. (Hans Schaal)

Plate 12.   The axis of Stonehenge as viewed slightly off center from behind trilithon impost no. 56 and over its fallen twin, stone no. 55. (Hans Schaal)

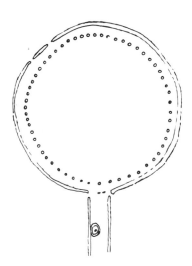

Ground plan, Stonehenge I.

But almost everything the observer sees built around this axis was not present in the first phase of construction, which took place during the Secondary Neolithic (Windmill Hill culture). Stonehenge I consisted only of the circular bank and ditch, the 56 Aubrey holes, and the Heel Stone. Post holes in the causeway probably supported a gate but there is no indication that any structure ever stood at the center of the enclosure, the point from which the embankment and the ring of Aubrey holes would have been circumscribed. Stonehenge I is not unique; it resembles a number of other henge monuments distributed from Cornwall to the Orkney islands. A *henge* is a circular enclosure with a single avenue leading into it, a class of monument coined after the name of Stonehenge itself. The second element of this word is thought to have come from an Old English verb, *hengen*, to hang, in this case lintels resting on pillars. But more likely it is a corruption of Old English *Stan-hrycg*, meaning "stoneridge," or, stones on the ridge. At any rate, the causeways of all the henge monuments point in different directions. Some of the later ones seem to have a sunward orientation, though only Stonehenge is significantly oriented to the rising sun at midsummer.

The Aubrey holes, six feet in diameter and four feet deep, are similar to holes for offerings to the dead excavated in the floors of the so-called long barrows, those Neolithic burial mounds situated in the Stonehenge region and elsewhere. Were they also repositories for offerings? For stone or wooden uprights? No one knows. It is clear, however, that they were refilled soon after digging, thirty-five of them later reopened for the deposit of cremated human remains, perhaps tied up in leather bags fastened with bone pins in Windmill Hill fashion, together with grave goods such as flint tools, pottery, mace heads, and axe heads of Cornish stone. The purpose of Stonehenge I can never be known with certainty, although in chapter 3 we have presented a reasonable theory. The Aubrey holes, which Hawkins wants to see as positions for the movement of counting stones in a digital computer, were in existence long before the rest of the structure he connects with them was built. What is more, his solar observatory, which takes the Heel Stone as the foresight, is aligned with a back sight, the Altar Stone, formerly upright but which was not erected until the advent of Stonehenge IIIc, a last touch added to the final phase of construction.

Perhaps the most puzzling feature associated with Stonehenge I is the Greater Cursus, named by Stukeley, a long straight earthwork over 100 yards wide and more than 3000 yards long, bounded on either side by a bank and a ditch, and which passes 800 yards to the north of Stonehenge. A smaller cursus lies to the northwest. These two earthworks are not unique in Britain, some twenty have been discovered, but are unique to that island. Nor is the Greater Cursus the longest such monument to be found; that honor goes to the Dorset Cursus at Cranborne Chase, which runs some six and a quarter miles in length. Others have been found in East Anglia, the Midlands, and, more recently, underneath a later henge at Thornborough in Yorkshire. The Greater Cursus at Stonehenge resembles a narrow version of a racecourse built for chariots by the Romans, and before them by the classical Greeks, and before them by the Mycenaeans, as Homer and graphic evidence relate; which is why Stukeley, with his classical learning, named the structure a Cursus. Furthermore, it is ideally suited as a racetrack, running as it does into a vale from two hills on which spectators could have followed every yard of the action (see Drawing 3).

In Homer, racing is associated with funeral games held in the honor of dead heroes and kings. The games consist of five events: 1) chariot racing, 2) boxing, 3) wrestling, 4) footracing, and 5) fighting in armor.[3] Stonehenge I was built somewhere around 3000 B.C., that is, at the very least a thousand years before the advent of Mycenaean culture. If funeral games were played in Neolithic Britain, they could not have imitated those of a Bronze Age civilization; rather, they are the distant precursors of those games which still live in at least the ideal of the modern Olympic games. To date, archaeology has not provided a definite explanation for cursus monuments. They may have been processional ways, antedating the Avenues at Stonehenge and Avebury, or even cattle pens. It is tempting, however, to see funerary games, footraces probably, perhaps even some ritual

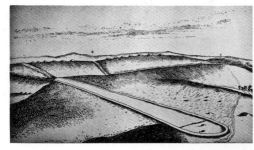

The Greater Cursus drawn by William Stukeley.

Drawing 3.   A funeral game at the Greater Cursus (Stonehenge III). (David Alexovich)

games with bulls as in Minoan Crete, as the real purpose. Such games could not have included chariot racing, however. Chariots are a Bronze Age invention and the horses of Neolithic Britain were wild ones hunted for game or sport. With the rise of heroic society in Britain, horses may have been domesticated for riding. Horse-drawn chariots did not enter Britain until the seventh century B.C. Even if the Cursus was not used for games, it surely was used for elaborate ceremonies, probably funerary in nature. That much is clear from the great cemetery in which Stonehenge is located (see Map 6).

Whatever the exact nature of the events at these places, they very likely occurred as seasonal celebrations. We have already suggested that megalithic tombs and large earthworks were constructed at seasonal gatherings of a tribal people otherwise dispersed in clan estates or family homesteads. So, too, was Stonehenge itself. Recent excavations of the Avenue and the main ditch, with an eye to comparisons with the stone-lined West Kennet Avenue, show them both to have been built in straight sections that angle somewhat to each other.[4] This evidence corroborates the idea that all these features were constructed over a period of time, not all at once. Each season, during the annual tribal gatherings, a section of ditch would be dug. At other times, parts of the stone structure might be put up. All of these actions were part of an age-old event. Perhaps it was the autumn cattle roundup, or celebration of the vernal equinox and the coming growing season, or even the summer solstice. To quote the Avenue's excavator, George Smith: "There seems to be a frequent association between Late Neolithic henge monuments and rivers, whether by proximity or by connecting avenues. There can be little doubt that the Stonehenge Avenue was of a ceremonial nature and as such provided a formal approach to Stonehenge itself."[5]

Yet over the long centuries of occupation by different peoples, the site retained a continuity of purpose. The Avenue (as well as the West Kennet Avenue) was constructed during phase II of Stonehenge, the Beaker period. The main ditch, built exactly the same seasonal way and lined up with the already existing Avenue, was dug during phase III, that of Wessex culture. Therefore, working backwards, we may see the Cursus as a ceremonial place belonging to the Neolithic phase of Stonehenge I. The Windmill Hill people who made use of it may have competed with each other at their annual gatherings, giving way to another kind of ceremony

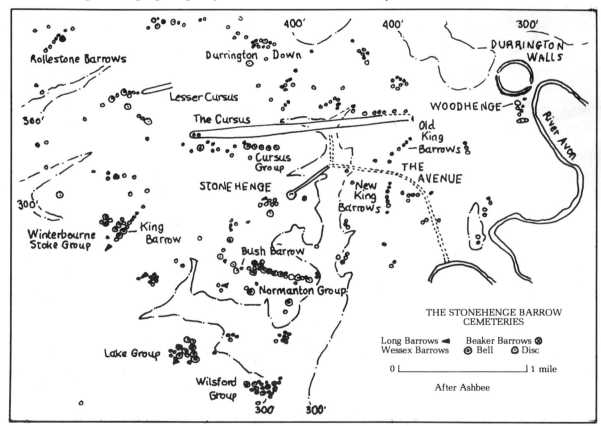

Map 6.   The Stonehenge region.

in which chiefs of the Beaker folk took center stage. We may suppose these chieftains to have traveled by boat up the River Avon, landed at the river end of the Avenue, and then proceeded up to the site of Stonehenge. Perhaps they competed in duels of mock combat in the manner now familiar from Indo-European epic literature. Last, the Wessex chiefs would have used the same processional way, only this led to a more impressive monument that was Stonehenge III. The seasonal festivals would live on into historical times, perhaps little changed. One example will suffice. In Celtic times, which extend into the full light of history, different tribal groups assembled to celebrate the beginning of the harvest season. The place of meeting was always on a hilltop which overlooked a landscape of growing corn, pasturing flocks, and thick standing woodlands.[6] From Windmill Hill to Celtic Britain, millennia of continuity obtained among a whole series of farming and herding peoples in sharing that vista.

Shaping the Stones

There is nothing in the manual labor required for the building of any phase of Stonehenge that could not be accomplished by a Neolithic technology. The bluestones of Stonehenge II were set up in circles of unhewn boulders; later, after the sarsens of Stonehenge IIIa were put up the bluestones were reerected as obelisks, dressed to shape by the Neolithic technique of bashing and abrading with stone mauls. The most unusual feature of Stonehenge is the presence of stones that have indeed been shaped; no other megalithic site in prehistoric Europe can boast them. For some time it was thought to be a distinctive architectural feature which had to have been carried out by a master builder from a superior culture, i.e. a Mycenaean. Now that that connection has been broken, the nearest parallel is the extraordinary temples of Malta. Apart from the use of lintels in the sarsen structures, which might just as well have derived from domestic architecture, and a few religious motifs, there is no tangible relationship between the two areas. Stonehenge might well have been planned by a master designer, but two other things may have as much bearing on the style as a newly conceived design. These are cultural continuities and the nature of the stone itself. Perhaps a single architect took both aspects into account and fused them in a novel way; if he did, his ideas were taken up by succeeding builders and then, finally, lost.

All the same, the technique of bashing and abrading applied to the bluestones was used only for spot finishing in the case of the sarsen stones. They are too hard to yield much to the maul. Sarsen stone ranks 7 out of 10 on the Mohs' scale of hardness, a measurement of the surface resistance to abrasion. Steel ranks 6.7 on the same scale. Sarsen is as hard as quartz and harder than steel. It is not easily pulverized under the blows of a hammer stone, which can remove only 6 cubic inches per hour. This is not the way the biggest upright of the biggest trilithon, 50 tons in weight, 29 feet 8 inches high and 2 feet 8 inches thick, was shaped. The method of working sarsen follows from certain characteristics of its original formation.

Sarsen boulder at Avebury. (Hans Schaal)

Plate 13.   Sarsen boulders in a circular array at Avebury. (Hans Schaal)

Man became man during the Pleistocene; we today are men of the Holocene, the two epochs comprising the Quarternary period. The sarsen stones were formed during the Eocene epoch of the Tertiary period, about 60 million years ago, some few million years after the evolution of the first mammals; sarsens are the remains, in the form of boulders, of a sand bed that once covered a layer of chalk. The chalk formation once rested on the bottom of the sea, which towards the end of the Secondary period rose to become the floor of shallow, littoral waters silted over with sand. Another rise during the Eocene epoch, and the chalk with its superimposed sand beds was exposed as dry land. Some of the sand hardened while looser portions of it were carried away by weathering, leaving sarsen boulders lying on the chalk. Yet another geologic upheaval raised the denuded chalk layer hundreds of feet above the sea, resulting in the present chalk areas of Salisbury Plain and Marlborough Downs on which rest boulder-sized relics of the ancient sand beds. The sarsen structure of Stonehenge III was built from these same boulders, once scattered around the site.[7]

Local, too, were the bluestones (spotted dolerite) comprising the second Stonehenge. These long have been observed to be petrologically related to formations on Mt. Presely in Pembrokeshire, southern Wales. Bluestones, therefore, had to have been brought from that source, perhaps in a climax to the long history of trade with Lancashire and Wales for jadeite axes. Was old Geoffrey of Monmouth relaying a garbled version of this ancient trade when he spoke of Merlin (a Druid after all) bringing the stones to Wessex? Or was he the first geologist of the Middle Ages? Neither, actually, because it has now been demonstrated that the bluestones were to be found on the plain itself. They were dumped there at the tail end of a newly discovered glacial moraine during the last retreat of the ice.[8]

Plate 14.   Another boulder at Avebury. (Hans Schaal)

Sarsen boulders retain the stratification of the sand bedding in which they were formed, and thus they split readily and evenly in planes parallel to the strata. They were formed either at the top or the bottom of the original sand beds, so that when fractured at right angles to the bed, a well shaped rectangular block is separated from the parent body, one face flat, the other rough. If the boulder occupied the entire thickness of the sand stratum, then its two original faces would be flat and parallel. These are the two types of sarsen boulders that once lay on Salisbury Plain, unlike the irregular, shapeless boulders—formed wholly within the middle of

Plate 15.   Tabular sarsen at Stonehenge, standing in the sarsen ring, stone no. 16. (Hans Schaal)

the sand bed at its thickest—that characterize the so-called greywethers of Marlborough Downs.

The greywethers of Marlborough Downs have been exploited in modern times for building stone with the help of steel chisels and sledge hammers. But this method of working sarsen stone was not available to a stone age technology. Therefore, the stones of Stonehenge could not have been taken from Marlborough Downs as erroneously proposed by almost all authorities. To be sure, the stones of Avebury derive from that source, but these are uncut boulders, unlike the rectangular slabs of Stonehenge. It seems obvious that the building of the sarsen structure at Stonehenge was suggested by the proximity of suitable material consisting of large tabular blocks up to 30 feet long. The sarsen boulders of Salisbury Plain were never as plentiful as the profusion of greywethers which still litter Marlborough Downs, but they were of the right kind, and Walter Charleton in his day noticed not a few still lying about. Only one or two big slabs remain today. Even the small boulders, rejects and leavings from the Stonehenge project, have been used up for various other purposes over the centuries.

The sarsen uprights at Stonehenge were fractured from tabular slabs that in their natural state suggested the imposts for which they were used. The front and back of the uprights thus display the upper and lower surfaces of the parental slab, or, in the case of boulders split lengthwise in order to obtain the width required, an original face and a fractured face.

The method of cleaving the stones of Stonehenge was deduced by E. H. Stone from his experience as an engineer with the government of India during the British raj. Stone concluded that a technique once used by the subjects of the Nizam in Hyderabad for the quarrying of stratified granite would have worked on the stratified sandstone of Salisbury Plain.

> In the neighborhood of the city of Hyderabad there occurs in several places a formation of stratified granite (or "gneiss") which can be separated into layers of varying thickness.
>
> To obtain stone for building purposes a layer of this granite is split up by native quarrymen, in a very simple manner, by the use of spherical masses or "mauls" of granite. These mauls are precisely similar to the largest mauls found in the excavations at Stonehenge.
>
> A number of men stand in line across the layer in the direction in which the slab is to be split. Each man has a maul which he holds between his two hands above his head. At a signal from the foreman each man dashes down his maul simultaneously on the granite layer, which is thereby split across with a fairly even fracture.
>
> The pieces thus obtained are long blocks similar in size and shape to the sarsen stones of the outer circle at Stonehenge. These blocks are afterwards broken across into pieces of suitable size for building purposes.[9]

In a way, this method of knocking out whole blocks of sarsen rock is reminiscent of the Paleolithic technique of stone knapping, or what was probably more apparent to the builders, the grainy texture of their raw material reminded them of wood. Like wood split into boards, the boulders once fractured were ready for use with little further preparation. The Neolithic technique of pecking and bashing was limited to dressing minor

Plate 16. In the background a tabular slab in the sarsen ring at Stonehenge (the inner face of stone no. 16), and in the middle ground the bigger slab that forms impost no. 56 at the heel of the horseshoe array of trilithons. In the fore-ground is the shaped bluestone. (Hans Schaal)

irregularities on the flat sides of the uprights (which were faced toward the center of the structure) and to seating the lintels. Otherwise, the imposts were erected very much as found naturally in tabular slabs three to four feet wide, or they were split to size from thicker slabs, while the lintels were taken from smaller slabs. The cavities present in the sandstone today are the long-term results of its uneven concretion when formed during Eocene times, subjected to uneven weathering (they certainly were not prepared, as Hawkins has suggested, for the convenience of some prehistoric astronomer that he might insert his head, the better to improve a celestial alignment).

The mortise-and-tenon jointing between impost and lintel is a carpenter's device translated into dry masonry. In the sarsen ring each upright is topped with two tenons (shaped by abrading down the stone around them), that fit pecked-out mortises in the underside of the lintels. The ends of the lintels fit together with a tongue-and-groove joint, another woodworking formality. The great lintel atop each trilithon is seated on a single tenon protruding from each impost, the very same structure to be found in the archway of the Lion Gate at Mycenae. The similarity manifestly owes to a common Indo-European heritage of carpentry and not diffusion from Mycenae, because the Lion Gate is somewhat later than Stonehenge IIIa. Stonehenge is really a wooden henge monument carried out in a different medium, the readily available stone. The long barrows of Neolithic times were earth and wood versions of passage graves (or vice versa) built in areas where wood (or stone) was more readily available, but Stonehenge IIIa was built at a time when the Wessex plain may not yet have been completely denuded of its forest cover. If so, then it was meant to be a more permanent structure for social or political reasons, else wood would have served as it did elsewhere. The shape of Stonehenge was, therefore, culturally dictated even if it had been planned in the mind of a master architect. It was built within an old carpentry tradition; it was built of rectangular sarsen stone, and thus looks the way it does only because that material accorded with familiar techniques of construction for a familiar purpose.

Raising the Stones

Not only is sarsen stone very hard, it is very dense and heavy, 154 pounds per cubic foot. The uprights of the sarsen ring average 26 tons in weight, the lintels $6^{3}/_{4}$ tons. The trilithons are bigger and heavier, but the mode of erection must have been the same, calling only for more ropes and more men. Given a concentration of sarsen boulders near the site, the chief engineering problem was setting them up, not transporting them.

The first of the sarsen structures to be erected had to be the array of trilithons, followed by the sarsen ring. Otherwise the latter would have interfered with raising the former. A circle for the sarsen ring would have been described by a cord $48^{1}/_{2}$ feet long, attached to a round stake at the center, the same method used for describing the circumference of the more distant embankment. Indeed, at a few henge sites the stake hole at

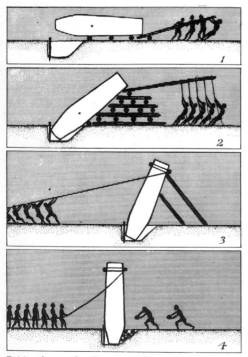

Raising the uprights. Drawing courtesy of Her Majesty's Stationery Office. Crown Copyright.

the center of their earthworks has been found. In locating positions for the uprights of the sarsen ring, the circle would be divided into thirty equal parts as measured at intervals of 10½ feet between the stones, as they vary in width, averaging seven feet. In other words, the spacing between the stones was made equidistant, not their center lines. Because the uprights vary also in thickness, the circle defined the position for their inner faces, not the center of the pits in which they were placed. As obtained from the quarry, the stones were flat and smooth on one side and rough on the other, or sometimes relatively flat and smooth on both sides. The smoother side was the side placed against the inscribed circle, facing inward.

Transport over the short distance to the building site was more likely to have been undertaken with sleds or greased tracks than with rollers. Any unevenness in the surface of the ground would tilt the rollers slightly in different angles, distributing the weight of the burden unevenly, making for excessive friction if not actual breakage of the rollers. What is more, even if the ground surface were perfectly level and smooth, if it were not also perfectly hard and unyielding, the log rollers would not roll. It is a picturesque method of moving heavy stones, but wholly impractical.

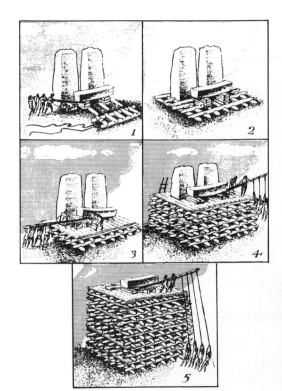

Raising the lintels. Drawings courtesy of Her Majesty's Stationery Office. Crown copyright.

Sledges were commonly used to transport large stones in Egypt. There is strong evidence that friction was reduced by pouring water in front of the sledges.[10] This may have been done at Stonehenge, if grease was not used. Experiments conducted by R. J. C. Atkinson, the foremost authority on Stonehenge, with sledges that were not lubricated suggest that some 16 men would be required to haul a ton of stone, hence the largest bluestones would have used 110 men. The largest sarsen would have required 880 men to haul it only 1 kilometer per day! The rest of the evidence about the construction seems to indicate nothing like these numbers of laborers were ever employed at any one time and this in itself suggests an immediate origin for the great sarsens. That being the case, it is equally likely that the stones were levered to the construction site. This was the method demonstrated on Easter Island by Thor Heyerdahl.[11] Nor, as we shall see, does the levering technique require nearly so much labor as hauling.

Apart from depositing the uprights of the sarsen ring at their proper stations, the first task was digging the foundation pits to the right depth, so as to accommodate the variable length of the stones, when erected to a uniform height of 14 feet. The side of the pit into which the stone would be lowered was ramped at an angle of 45 degrees. The wall of the pit opposite the ramp was lined with heavy stakes, protection against the rubble-making effects of the stone as its toe was lowered. Gravity would settle the stone onto the ramp at a 45 degree angle once its center of gravity was pushed to the edge. The work of raising the stone all the way up was probably made easier with the help of a pair of shear-legs located on the other side of the foundation pit. In experiments with scale models, E. H. Stone lashed a cross-bar to the underside of the top of the stone to be raised. From each end of this cross-bar ropes were strung to a correspond-

Drawing 4. Raising the impost of a trilithon. (David Alexovich)

100

ing cross-bar at the top of the shear legs at a height calculated to give the most leverage, that is, where the pull of the ropes is at right angles to the plane of the stone. The stone is then raised by another set of ropes pulled from the top of the shear legs (see Drawing 4). Stone estimated that a 26 ton impost could be pulled upright in this manner with a force of $4^{1}/_{2}$ tons exerted by 180 men, each hauling on the ropes with the pull of 56 pounds.[12]

E. H. Stone raised the lintels in his scale model experiments with boarding ramps. There is, however, no evidence of a major digging effort to pile earth that high. Atkinson does not think this was the way the job was done and he describes a method using levers and a timber crib. The lintel is first levered up a foot or two on temporary supports, then the first floor of the crib is placed under and around it. Each floor is composed of a set of planked-over beams. The stone is levered up, floor by floor of timber running at right angles to each other. Experiments show that levering the stone up level by level with a four foot bar would take only about seven men. At the top level, the lintel is levered sideways into position. A similar method, with stone cribs, was used on Easter Island to raise "topknots" weighing up to 20 tons onto the heads of giant statues.[13]

One of the most fascinating results to have come out of these and other experimental studies of ancient construction techniques is that much less manpower is required than might be thought. The experiments on Easter Island, for example, show that a team of 12 men can lever a 25 ton stone statue in place within 18 days.[14] Given that kind of evidence Stonehenge need not have taken vast hordes of labor or even sustained lengths of time to construct. As with the other monuments of early Britain it could have been done on a seasonal basis. This would be entirely consistent with the obvious astronomical features of the structure and the political ones proposed here. That is, Stonehenge was the meeting place of regional tribes at seasons of religious importance. These were also the seasons during which Stonehenge was under construction. It was done in short bursts over a very long time, perhaps decades, even a century or so, and by only a relatively few people. It was apparently the center for an important chiefdom whose leadership may have dominated tribal alliances within its region of influence for the period of time during which the monument was abuilding. That it was never finished may well speak of an equally unfinished political structure that failed with the unstable fortunes of all tribal hegemonies. They must expand forever—or die. That much is clear from the earliest historical accounts of the barbarian peoples of Europe. It is obvious, too, from the epic tales that go back even further. Once again, Stonehenge is a monument stable only in its material features; the ideas that it represents have slipped into the river of unwritten history, and vanished.

Sepulchral Continuities

It is often said that Stonehenge is a megalithic monument unique to barbarian Europe for its architraves. The temples of Malta and monu-

Trilithon entrance to passage grave, La Houge, Jersey.

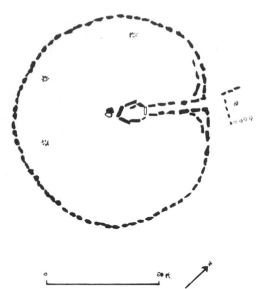

Ground plan of passage grave at Bryn Celli Ddu, Anglesey, Wales. This is a classic grave of its type. Note that a decorated stone has been found in the central burial pit and an ox burial appears at the entrance.

ments in Iberia antedate the last phase of Stonehenge by perhaps a millennium at the earliest. Nor can its singularity be upheld when viewed in light of internal evidence. Sir Arthur Evans long ago derived the architecture of Stonehenge from that of megalithic tombs.

> As I have elsewhere endeavored to point out, this original sepulchral connection of Megalithic Circles is of primary importance in its bearing on their origin. It enables us in fact to trace the embryology of these greater monuments to the smaller and simpler circles that actually mark the limits of the primitive grave-mound. The three component parts of the most characteristic of the Megalithic Circle, the circle itself, the stone avenue opening from it, and the cist or dolmen contained by it, are all of them mere amplifications of the simplest sepulchral forms. The Circle is an enlarged version of the ring of stones placed round the grave mound; the Dolmen represents the cist within it; the avenue is merely the continuation of the underground gallery. The only difference lies in the greater size of the stones in the Megalithic Circles, and that in this case they are no longer covered by or in juxtaposition with the earth mound, but have become free-standing. . . .
>
> And in Stonehenge itself we have to deal with a monument which, though of a more complicated arrangement and displaying greater technical skill, must still be regarded as belonging to the same general class as the simpler forms already alluded to. . . . The triliths are indeed a new feature in connection with the stone circle, but . . . are themselves only the perpetuation of a part of the sepulchral structure, the actual gateway of the subterranean chamber, which remains a ritual survival when . . . the galleried chamber to which it led has itself been modified away.[15]

It does not follow that Stonehenge must be connected exclusively with a funeral cult. The sepulchral design features could just as well provide a sanctified setting for tribal politics, as Christian churches do for the coronation of kings and queens. Religion evolves as well as politics, one with the other. Thus a monument belonging to an originally sepulchral class may no longer be associated with remains of the dead but come to represent the war and treaty making powers of aristocratic chieftainship, evolved from the tomb-building leadership of communal chieftains.

At Stonehenge, the most impressive features are its five great trilithons. Structures exactly like them, only smaller, occur inside both round and long barrows as transept entrances, that is, as gateways to subterranean burial chambers leading off from the main gallery. In some round barrows, the whole nexus of chambers is encircled by a ring of upright stones, the inner peristaliths. Equivalent to inner peristaliths at Stonehenge are the uprights of the bluestone ring encircling the trilithons. Inside the horseshoe ring of trilithons are a number of bluestone menhirs representing the symbolic effigies of the dead, or dolmen idols, that are found standing free in the central chamber of some tombs, as in the long barrow at Skendleby, Lincolnshire. Outside all complete barrows are two arcs of stones curving away from the entrance, the outer peristaliths. The equivalents to outer peristaliths at Stonehenge have been curved back on themselves to form the sarsen ring, whose lintels probably symbolize the roofing of stone slabs that under barrows support the earthen mound

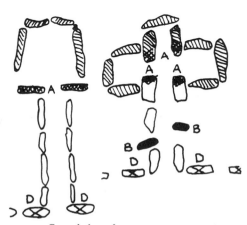

Ground plans of passage grave compared with that of Stonehenge. (Continued on page 103.)

above. Even the Heel and Slaughter stones will fit the sepulchral tradition if they are allowed to have had fellows by their sides, making for two pairs of large stones framing the Avenue and leading directly to the portal framed by stones 1 and 30 of the sarsen ring. These three pairs are equivalent to the several pairs of large stones set at right angles to the walls of the main gallery in almost all chambered barrows, long or round.[16]

So much for architectural continuity with sepultures in the design of Stonehenge III. It was no doubt preceded by a wooden structure of similar form considering the techniques of carpentry used, which may have been transferred from the construction of wooden chambers once underlying some barrows, but now rotted away.

As for a functional continuity with gravesites we can only guess. Evidently the ceremonies of ancestor worship conducted seasonally in the forecourts of megalithic tombs so grew in prominence that a larger arena was required to accommodate them, yet retain sepulchral associations. This change in venue surely involved a political change as well.

All ceremonies of ancestor worship known to anthropology serve a political function in that they rehearse the membership of persons in social groups united in a claim to special advantages. The most famous example comes from the clan states of late Bronze Age China, when the business of state was a family business whose principle of organization was ancestor worship. The business of each state, named after its ruling family, was conducted in its ancestral hall and arsenal, where a ranking of the tablets of the deceased on the altar extended the hierarchical organization of living clan members, the politically active males. The degree to which members participated in the rituals of ancestor worship were determined by rank, as calculated by degree of kinship with the clan head. Ritual prerogatives served as a formal reminder of one's position within the group as a policy making body seeking to secure advantages for the state against rival states, over and above commoners who were not even privileged to bear family names.

With the rise of imperial China, which organized all the clan states as provinces within a unified political entity, only the emperor was permitted to conduct ancestral worship as a ceremony of state, while the prominent families of the realm practiced ancestral rites for the sake of domestic organization merely.

Chinese civilization takes us a long way from primitive society, but its religion of ancestor worship, domestic and imperial, may nonetheless be seen as a complex development evolving out of a Neolithic cult of the dead. When the prehistoric Chinese made their transition from a Mesolithic economy of hunting and gathering to a Neolithic one of plant and animal domestication, the new economy as elsewhere was capable of sustaining a larger and denser population, although the size of each village settlement was limited. With the expansion of numbers, new villages formed by fission from old ones grown to capacity, but we know from archaeology that daughter villages remained in touch with each other for the conduct of burial rites held in common. Neighboring villages shared the same cemetery where funerals and no doubt seasonal rites

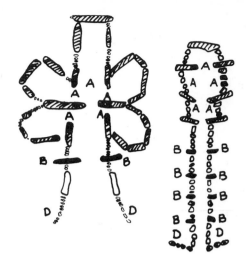

A — Transept Entrance
A — ditto
Walls of Transept
Walls of Passage
Stones at Right-
  angles to Passage
C — Inner Peristaliths
D — Outer ditto

Comparison. (Continued on page 104.)

Comparison of ground plans of passage graves with Stonehenge continued from pages 102 and 103. (R.S. Newell, 1929. With permission.)

were carried out under the leadership of shamans or priests. Their special residences or meeting halls are probably to be identified with a long house differing from the ordinary dwellings that comprised each village. Certainly their ceremonial headdress is represented in decorations on mortuary pottery buried with the dead, as distinctive as Beaker pottery manufactured for the same purpose.[17]

It is not difficult to imagine that as the original Neolithic colony in Britain grew in population, new communities would bud off from older ones when the local carrying capacity of the land was reached, and that the daughter communities would maintain kinship ties by sharing a collective tomb. A cult of the dead conducted at the entranceways of these tombs would serve to rehearse these ties under shamanistic leadership. As population grew in density and social organization in complexity, so too would the ties between communities grow more complicated until, perhaps, the old kinship connections came to be less important than rivalries in need of adjustment in some political forum. The need would have become even more pressing after the Beaker and later the Wessex warriors settled in.

Stonehenge, as a meeting place for these conflicting interests, would then require funereal associations in its architecture if it were to win religious prestige for its enlarged political purpose. Indeed, it is located in the midst of a vast cemetery whose sanctity was kept active with burials continuously from Neolithic times until the migration of Iron Age Celts. The Stonehenge cemetery is, in fact, just one of four others like it in southern Britain, though it is the largest. The others are at Lambourn on Berkshire Downs, at Avebury on Marlborough Downs, at Oakley Down at Cranborne Chase on Dorset, and at Dorchester, also in Dorset.[18] Evidence from the one at Stonehenge shows that not all those buried there, however, were natives of the immediate locality.

After all, the place is not laid out like Arlington National Cemetery, with row upon row of graves, with now and then a distinctive one, where are gathered together the patriots of a single nation within a single resting place. At Stonehenge, the graves are clustered in distinctive little groups here and there, representing (we think) tribal worthies from different social territories. The fact, if it is so, that different regions *are* represented in one place suggests a political interest on the part of Stonehenge chieftains in a kind of intertribal hegemony that stopped short of national confederation.

Let us suppose this to be the case, that each funerary cluster does indeed signify the burial of persons from tribal areas from beyond the immediate Stonehenge region, as well as from within it. Given the idea, there is some evidence to support it, and not alone at Stonehenge. On the Ridgeway, a long chalk ridge in southern Dorset, both round and long barrows are set on high ground above bottom lands and stream valleys (perhaps so they could be seen above the treetops of a land still forested except for windblown highpoints). This is an area also rich in henge monuments, those gathering places of the Windmill Hill people who came together in them each autumn to slaughter surplus cattle, feast, trade axes, and do their tribal business. Both long and round barrows are located in the vicinity, the former belonging to the older Windmill Hill people, the latter to Beaker invaders. Each of the long barrows, as we have noted elsewhere, is a collective tomb containing the remains of an extended family or clan, the homesteading units of the Windmill Hillers. Surrounding each one of these solitary long barrows are a group of Beaker round barrows. To that extent, the newcomers followed the burial practices of the natives, choosing to locate their cemeteries at the same old sacred megalithic places.[19] More than that. On the Continent, the round barrows of the Beaker folk mostly contain single inhumations. But examination of a number of round barrows in Wessex and the high chalk wolds of Yorkshire show that round barrows there contain multiple burials more often than not.[20] Altogether, this evidence of sepulchral continuity between Windmill Hill and Beaker graves must demonstrate also a political continuity with the old established social territories into which the newcomers settled, and which they came to dominate. Something of the ancient beliefs proved congenial to them because they did indeed add new monuments to the old places, notably the stones of Stonehenge II, which are the very mark of Beaker domination.

Thus does the evolution of chieftainship in Britain move with an underlying current of cultural commonality that sweeps differing peoples along in one confluent tradition, with change taking place within that tradition, until it is revitalized and changed yet again by a merger with still other newcomers, the Wessex warriors. They in time raised a number of petty chiefdoms to the level of a dynastic confederation, and made the center of their drive for hegemony at Stonehenge, but not without carrying forward the symbols of an old megalithic order that would give the new aristocratic order its sanctity. Priests with memories of traditional British ways would see to that, conserving old religious values the while serving new political ones. It is they who would keep the prestige of the Stonehenge cemetery. We cannot even guess at the political geography behind the rights of each chieftain and his line to partake of that prestige in adding his round barrow to others grouped around this or that ancient long barrow.[21] But that Stonehenge was a place where such rights between local chiefs were debated, to the greater glory of an over chief, there can be no doubt.

While it is true that the quality of leadership at Stonehenge changed over time, from communal to hierarchical, a persistent belief system underpinned all phases of its construction and the tombs nearby. The architecture itself provides all sorts of clues to matters not only political and social but religious as well. All aspects fit together in one coherent whole. For instance, it is clear that the early collective tombs, counting both long barrows and passage graves, imitate the long houses of the Danubians whose unit of domestic life was the extended family. By contrast, the mortuary houses of later times in which heroic chiefs were buried individually may imitate the smaller houses of the Kurgan peoples, or Beaker

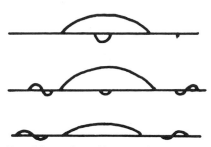

Typical forms of round barrows of the Bronze Age: a) Bowl barrow; b) Bell barrow with outer bank; c) Disc barrow. These and other minor forms are common in England and in Wessex cemetery groups.

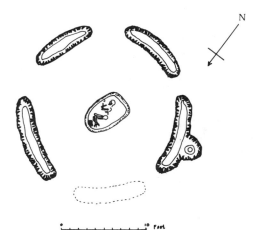

Beaker burial at Stockbridge Down, Hampshire (after J.F.S. Stone, 1960).

folk, whose unit of domestic life was the nuclear family. Yet the construction of both types appears to be animated by a similar world view, and this is worth some discussion.

What megalithic tombs seem to have in common, apart from stone construction, is some astronomical bearing, specifically with the sun. The entranceways of British and Breton passage graves most often face eastward, as do the higher ends of the long barrows where the burials are deposited. This orientation no doubt implies some belief in rebirth and an afterlife dependent on the daily rising of the sun, or, perhaps, a seasonal one. The whole nexus of belief and tomb architecture has roots as ancient as Mesolithic culture, with Neolithic additions. Mesolithic burial practices all over West Asia and Europe evince the same concern for orientation.[22] Since megalithic tombs seem to have developed in part from a west European type of cist grave covered over by a mound and surrounded by a stone kerb, there is reason to suppose a continuity of religious belief that extends back as far as the beginnings of stone funerary monuments. The additional idea of stone circles, of which henge monuments are an expression, is a contribution of the north British Secondary Neolithic, a fusion of Mesolithic and Neolithic cultures. Some round barrows are encircled with a ring of menhirs or, what amounts to a functional equivalent, wooden posts. Most impressive is one of the oldest of all megalithic tombs in the British Isles, the tremendous New Grange in the Boyne Valley in Ireland. The mound is surrounded by a ring of 8-foot menhirs that measures 340 feet in diameter and is thought to be contemporary with the tomb itself. Since New Grange probably dates from the middle of the fourth millennium, the tradition of stone circles combined with an orientational feature is of itself quite ancient, a tradition that survives as late as the middle of the second millennium when Stonehenge IIIa was built.

The other basic influence in the development of megalithic tomb architecture is Neolithic. If we may assume an Old European culture center for the European Neolithic, slow and complicated a process as the dispersal was, then a considerable body of religious beliefs must have accompanied it. The "great goddess" thesis already has been mentioned in chapter 2 and is widely accepted by competent authorities. Two of the main representations of that fertility goddess, apart from female figurines, are the spiral meander and the eye motif. The first is impressed in pottery diagnostic of the first Neolithic migrants to cross central Europe, the Danubian pioneers. Later the spiral meander is found inscribed on stone surfaces all over Europe, from the temples of Malta to the tombs at New Grange. What it means exactly is open to interpretation. Professor Gimbutas, who recently has elucidated a number of Old European cultic symbols, thinks it may have several associations, among them water, a primordial life force.[23] It may also symbolize the snake which, in turn, is frequently a decorative feature of solar discs. The snake and sun combination is ancient and widespread with a range from Europe to China. Not only is it old but it has had a long life, for in German mythology a snake curls about the roots of a cosmic tree to which all levels of heaven and earth are anchored. At all events, we have reason to grant the snake a symbolic value in Old European thought for eternal rebirth (and perhaps wisdom with that), hence a solar connection.

Just as widespread in ultramontane Europe and the Mediterranean is the eye motif. According to O. G. S. Crawford, who studied it some years ago, the so-called eyes are the eyes of the Great Goddess.[24] This may be so, but not apart from any solar connotations because the same double whorls incised on megalithic monuments serve also to mark the sun itself. Most likely (we believe) the eye motif dates no earlier than the Bronze Age, that is, later than the time of the megalithic tomb construction.[25] The inscriptions are the work, in short, of graffiti artists, the same who might spray the name of Norman Mailer on the home of William Shakespeare. As such the graffiti demonstrate, in yet another way, a continuity of interest in those religious ideas for which the great monuments of the old ones served as a constant reminder. The new wave of Beaker immigrants and others, coming upon a landscape already sacralized by the building achievements of a previous wave of Neolithic peoples, could not fail to have willingly grafted themselves upon the deep roots struck down by their ancient predecessors. As elsewhere in Europe, so it was at Stonehenge II and Stonehenge III, a reverence for an established past of communal life and at the same time a push toward inequality: a progress toward aristocratic chiefdoms conned in the reflection of a rear-view mirror.

But the sun is not the only astronomical object to have fascinated the old ones; the debate about the possibility of lunar calculations at Stonehenge reminds us of that. An interest in the moon appears to have moved Neolithic peoples everywhere in Western Asia and Europe to have symbolized it. The symbolism is reified in a bewildering variety of deities, but always it devolves upon the fertility cycle. As with many religious ideas conceived in primitive society, this one is based on practical observation and need. Neolithic farmers were indeed aware that cycles of the moon had something to do with planting and the proper time thereunto. But helpful shamans in time would have taken the simple observations of a farmers' astronomy and turned lunar phases and eclipses into mysteries, and mysteries into cults. Eventually, religious practice would have achieved a greater cultural value than the practical ideas it once supported.

Among Old Europeans and their descendants the moon takes on darker cultic aspects. While it may be symbolized by a cosmic egg, the germ from which all life grows, it most often is associated with a cult of the bull and a different mode of fertility. The bull cult is almost universal among agrarian peoples in Europe following the advent of the earliest Neolithic villages there. And that cult has to do with blood sacrifice, for it is only bull's blood that will serve to fertilize the earth. That gory aspect of the fertility goddess may be remembered in Greek mythology in the personage of Artemis (the Roman Diana), the moon goddess who also was a huntress, that is, she who kills animals. Artemis is but one of many such deities who preside over the sacrificial doings necessary to the fertility cycle. The most notorious of these is the Anatolian goddess, Cybele, whose

a

b

Decorated stones from megalithic tombs:
a) New Grange, Ireland; b) Gavr'innis, Brittany.
The swirling and eye motifs are typical of
megalithic art and are often though to represent
a female fertility deity. The axes carved on the
Breton example serve to highlight the cultic
importance of the trade in greenstone axes.

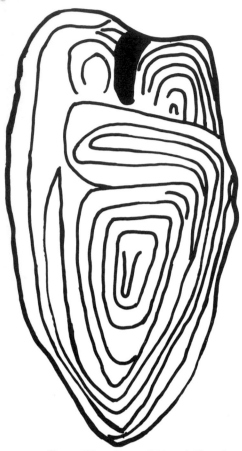

Eye motif from the megalithic tomb, Knowth West, Ireland.

cult demanded human as well as bull's blood. The Indo-European goddesses Brigit (Ireland), Freyja (Germany), and Kali (India) seem to share in this demand. If Artemis imposed on her people in the same way perhaps she can be connected to the orgies permitted by another fertility goddess, Demeter, at whose festivals crazed women, *maenads*, were wont to tear sacrificial animals to pieces with their bare hands. The male side of this among the Greeks is Dionysius who may represent the bull-god in person, the great fertilizer himself.[26]

But what has infusion of the soil with animal fluids, blood and sperm, to do with making crops grow? Why invoke human fertility to promote that of plants? The answer is not ignorance of biology, even though this may be the case. The cause-and-effect relationship between sex and procreation did not interest the ancients as much as did an aspect of social organization and its cosmic rationale. What is really mythologized is the sexual division of labor. Animals are active, and men either hunt them or husband them; plants are passive, and women either collect or cultivate them. It was the men who cared for barnyard animals in Neolithic mixed economies or for herd animals in pastoral economies, just as it was men who pursued game animals in the Mesolithic. If there was any understanding of reproduction it was limited to the sex life of animals on the part of male hunters or herders. For example, living hunters know that game animals are befuddled and easier to kill during the rutting season, and that celibacy keeps them more alert than their prey; stockbreeders know enough about the life cycle of their cattle to intervene, for the purpose of securing a supply of milk, by killing off most of the male offspring. It is doubtful if Neolithic gardeners, who were women, knew as much about the sex life of plants; nobody did until the advent of scientific botany. That is why agricultural rituals, such as those of ancient Greece, emphasize animal sexuality and include goat horns, cloven hoofs, and tails as symbols, even when these rituals are in the charge of female shamans or priestesses. The symbolism of plant fertility is carried over by analogy from the animal world, which is a male domain. Men dominate the activity of animals, women work the gardens. Men take women in marriage who, as a rule, have babies. Because this activity takes on symbolic meaning in primitive mythology, Carleton Coon has remarked, "copulation and cultivation are equivalent and linked."[27] Therefore, the most important thing that a man does to a woman makes the garden gorw. No cleavage between sex and agriculture exists, as in modern thinking, nor between animals and plants. They are two sides of the same coin, a metaphor that works even to the extent that coins possess a principal inscription on the obverse, a "head" that wags the "tail" on the reverse. Likewise, the practical zoology of the male domain provides the mythology for the less understood botany of the female domain, especially as this is carried forward by female shamans in the Neolithic.

Because female shamans do indeed come to prominence during the Neolithic in Europe, in association with the cult of the great goddess, some social theorists have argued that the agricultural townships of Old Europe and Minoan Crete were governed by them. This gynocratic world is summarized by the poet Robert Graves in his work of imaginative reconstruction, *The White Goddess,* which he later reworked into a novel of utopian fantasy, where the idea belongs, in *Seven Days in New Crete.* The idea of matriarchy is contradicted by at least two facts. First, even male shamans in any but the communal chiefdoms served only to give religious backing to political leaders, as did the priests of Egypt to the pharaohs, who never assumed that leadership directly for themselves; and the same must be the case with priestesses. Secondly, it is not true that with the advent of the Neolithic the economic role of women increased much over that in the Mesolithic, just because garden work became their work. The switch from hunting to planting therefore called for no switch from patriarchal to matriarchal authority. Women did nearly *all* the food getting *all* the time whatever the economy, hunting or planting. In the Kalahari desert where one third of the world's last hunters live, the male Bushman brings in only 37 percent of the camp's caloric intake from game animals, and that on a highly irregular basis, while the female brings home fully 63 percent from her foraging, day after day. Anthropologists are beginning to think this was the normal situation as well for hunting peoples in the past.[28] Clearly the woman's association with plant life always was important to the human economy, not just in Neolithic times. What is more, fertility magic for the political purposes of a matriarchy would require that its cultivators know as much about the sex life of plants as do hunters and herders about animals, a dubious assumption as we have seen.

The fact of the matter is that the sexual division of labor did not change with the change from food collection to food production. The basic change occurred during the human revolution, with the evolution from animal behavior to cultural behavior, when the two sexes no longer collected wild vegetable foods each on their own; the males pioneered meat getting and the females kept on with plant collecting. After that, males stuck by their animals, whether by hunting or herding, and the females by their plants as ever, whether by collecting or cultivating. At the same time, the Mesolithic hunter was not indifferent to plant life insofar as it related to the feeding habits of the game animals he sought to kill. As well as their life cycles he knew their habitats, and he followed them as they moved seasonally from place to place. Sometimes the animals might gather at water holes where they might be run down easier than in woodland. At other times, he might burn patches out of the forests, the better to provide his prey with open grassland to graze upon, and making it easier to hunt. It is obvious that Mesolithic peoples were familiar with the value of the different kinds of plants on which both they and their game animals fed.[29]

No doubt all these different resources were explained in a symbolic way; shamans would have summoned up deities both of the hunt and of growing plants. We may suppose that the tutelary gods of the hunt were masculine and those of the fertile earth feminine, they being modeled after the sexual division of labor among human kind. But since game animals fed on plants as well as did their hunters, it is not unreasonable to suppose that male gods were dominant in the Mesolithic cosmos. Their earthly representatives, the shamans, may have verified this and female shamans, if they existed as they seem to have done even at Dolní Věstonice, would have been subservient to their male counterparts. By way of historical continuity, among other reasons given above, the very same idea would pass into all the pastoral societies of Europe. When Indo-Europeans, themselves evolved directly out of Mesolithic culture, thought of female deities it thus was in terms of an earthly mother fertilized by and under the ultimate power of a masculine sky god.

This brings us back, after some divarication, to Neolithic lunar cults. Whatever the specific content of the belief, the moon has always a feminine aspect, the most common form of which is in astrology. Since in the next section we are going to examine Stonehenge from an astronomical point of view, it would not be amiss to note that astrology is probably the oldest form of organized astronomical study and that signs of the zodiac pervade the art of prehistoric Europe throughout.[30] Astrology postulates a whole cosmological system and is necessarily related to any monument built when its principles were dominant. It is just possible that the swirling designs on Danubian pottery, to say nothing of the pan-Mediterranean spiral motif, may represent a lunar rather than a solar aspect. At any rate, the cult of the fertility goddess, which is universal in Neolithic Europe, will call for a large measure of moon worship. The associated body of beliefs will, furthermore, remain as an underlying theme in later idea systems for it will continue to possess relevance for agriculture. From the start, the metal-using peoples of Europe may have centered their beliefs on the sun, but the moon would remain as a vital substratum.

The great tombs of Neolithic Europe, then, grew out of a mixture of Mesolithic and Neolithic ideas about death and life after death. While it is difficult to interpret the exact beliefs from the type of interment, it is evident that the idea of the afterlife is both chthonic and sun related. The passage graves are dark underground houses where rituals to ancestral spirits were carried out. At New Grange this took the form of offerings burnt on special flat stones which are surrounded on all sides by engravings of swirling sun, blood, or water signs. The afterlife itself might have been lived in the dark gloom of the underworld for at least part of the year. Some early epic literature postulates such a depressing fate; for example, *Gilgamesh* and the *Odyssey*. But this may be a Near Eastern tradition and a relatively recent one at that.[31]

Not all life in the underworld, however, is dark and empty. In Irish mythology the passage graves, called *Síd*, are the homes of the fairy folk who live in almost exactly the same way as their earthly counterparts, except that they have magical capabilities. Until very recently peasants in many parts of Eastern Europe believed that the dead lived a full and complete life directly underground just as they had when they inhabited the surface. It may be argued that these are merely later folk traditions invented to explain burial mounds long after the fact, but it is just possible they are far older. Consider the Greek myth of Persephone, the daughter of the fertility goddess who spent half the year underground with Hades,

god of death, and the other half with the sunlit seasons of spring and summer. Here is a clear connection between the cult of the underworld and
the life of the natural world; that is doubtless why the entrances of passage graves face the rising sun. But the return of life hoped for thereby is
not the notion of a purely agrarian ritual, for hunting peoples also shared
it if they did not help originate it.

The tombs themselves are mainly houses for the dead modeled after
those of the living (just as in Egypt and Mesopotamia). As time went on
they became something more: religious specialists made them houses of
ancestor worship. Clan and family organization would have been reinforced by these beliefs. But it is also likely that the great graves were made
symbolic of the cosmos itself. If the dead live on underground then the
roof of the barrow is the vault of the underworld sky. In exactly the same
way, the lintels of Stonehenge carry out this theme. But instead of slabs
covering the roof of the underworld they are roof lintels raised up on
symbolic pillars of the heavenly sky. Thus do they partake in the idea of a
cosmological whole on yet another level of a three-layered system as
follows:

Sky (cosmos and its gods above)
Earth (life here and now)
Underworld (afterlife down below)

This is an Indo-European concept (down to its triplism), seen for example
in German mythology with its Valhalla, Middle Earth, and roots of the
great tree Yggdrasill.[32] Whatever the politics of Stonehenge, it must embody the general, three-fold plan of this ancient mythos.

The funerary traditions of single-grave peoples, among Beaker folk
and the Kurgan-derived warriors, also manifest a distinct and readable
symbolism. As might be expected a good portion of the iconography is devoted to weaponry, in particular the battle-axe, dagger, and halberd. The
objects themselves are commonly found in warrior graves, but representations of them have been found carved on rocks in the northern Italian
Alps region (the famous Val Camonica), later in southern Sweden and
throughout the Bronze Age on monuments all over Europe. Not only are
weapons a common motif but also four-wheeled wagons, necklaces or
torcs, belts, stags, horses, and sun symbols. Sometimes a semianthropo-
morphic figure is seen with weapons, a belt, a torc, and sun signs. Professor Gimbutas thinks this is the earliest representation of the Indo-European warrior god, and that is likely, given its obvious Kurgan/Battle Axe
contexts.[33] Both the dagger and axe carried deep religious meaning.
Weapons of the warrior caste, those symbols of its separateness and
power, must always have had sacred meanings. If nothing else, the process by which they were made was magical and, since fire-forged, related
to the sun. So powerful was the magic in the object itself that it was worshipped by peoples well into historical times. Herodotus tells us the
Scythians worshipped a sacred dagger and the Saxons are said to have
been named for their own special weapon, the *seax*.

The axe is perhaps the preeminent utilitarian object imbued with
magical properties. Animism, the spiritualization of inanimate objects, is

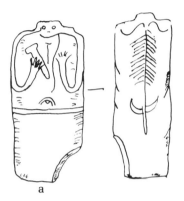

a

b

a) Anthropomorphic stone stele from Kurgan
grave, southern Russia; b) stele from Sion at
Petit Chasseur, Switzerland showing a belt,
dagger, double spiral and necklace (after
Gimbutas, 1970 and Gimbutas, 1973).

a well-known feature of primitive religions. No doubt it was the objects of greatest use to the early peoples of Europe that were thus animated. When codified into a set of religious symbols, that is, with identifiable gods, the object representing a god is endowed with that deity's spiritual force. The copper double axe is a prevalent symbol in the Old European cultures, culminating in the double-bitted *labrys* of Minoan Crete. There it is almost invariably associated with the sacred bull, itself a powerful fertility symbol. The double axe in this context may well represent the fertility goddess herself.[34] All of this, of course, is reinforced by the magic of the smith's art.

In northern Europe the axe was equally important, only these were made not of copper but of polished stone. We already have seen how special greenstone axes were traded in many parts of Europe; in Britain they were passed from centers in Lancashire and north Wales to other parts of the island. It is also interesting that such objects tend to cluster at henge monuments giving evidence of a seasonal religious festival. While the battle axe is a familiar cultic object, that probably of a warrior culture, the symbolic axe long had preceded its appearance as a weapon. It is probably fair to say that the polished-stone axe is a forest-adapted item. In the beginning it was a tool carried by the Danubians who used it to clear settlements in which they practiced swidden; no longer Mesolithic hunters at home in the forest they now attacked with a Neolithic technology, perhaps they found it a dark, mysterious place. This new perception of the forest environment entered the mythology of all northern peoples, in which tree symbolism is a dominant motif. For example, the Milky Way is regarded as a giant tree on which the whole cosmos is centered. Cult centers of Indo-European gods associated with axes were located in forested groves made holy by their immanence. Farther afield in Mesopotamia, the Gilgamesh epic tells us that the hero Enkidu dies as a result of striking the door of a great forest with his bronze axe. Whatever the exact meaning of that episode is, the symbolism is evident.

Battle axes long have had specific gods attributed to them in mythology and folklore, for example, the Indo-European god of thunder who is, at the same time, a warrior. He is known by many names: Thor, Donar, Jupiter, Tauranos, the Celtic Zeus, and perhaps even the weather god of the Hittites, Teshub. The famous hammer of Thor, called Mjollnir, representing the destructive power of the heavens, thunder and lightning, clearly is a mythic transformation of the battle axe.[35] The original symbol remained unchanged in the Baltic region where Lithuanian folklore down to the nineteenth century held that such axes symbolized the thunder god Perkunas.[36] At the same time, the symbol itself was widely held to be a protective device against evil and misfortune well into the Middle Ages. These features are an interesting remembrance of the role of warriors as both destroyers and protectors of society. Furthermore, the axe is closely linked to the sun. In the words of H. R. E. Davidson, in her book on the *Gods and Myths of Northern Europe*:

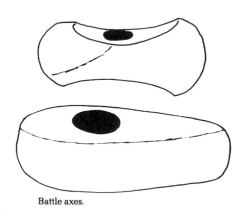
Battle axes.

> There may be some connexion between it [the hammer symbol] and the sun-wheel, well known from the Bronze Age, or it may have arisen from the use of the hammer or axe to represent thunder,

which was accompanied by fire from heaven. Thor was the sender of
lightning and the god who dealt out both sunshine and rain to men.[37]

The sun motif is found concomitant with the rise of single-grave cultures
belonging to the whole Battle Axe/Corded Ware complex. That motif is, of
course, much older than that amalgam of cultures, but is apparently a
dominating object of their religious attention. It is also quite plainly associated with the rise of metallurgy. Hence there is no reason to postulate
Mycenaeans inscribing axes and daggers on the trilithons of Stonehenge.
They are the emblems of the native warriors who built it. Indeed, this is
the historical fact intimated in legendary material transmitted by Geoffrey of Monmouth, who invoked Merlin's magic in building Stonehenge—for Merlin's older self is none other than Celtic Zeus.[38]

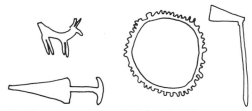

Axe, dagger, sun and stag symbols from the Val
Camonica, Italy. Early Bronze Age.

All the religious ideas outlined above may be deduced from the
Corded Ware barrows in which they inhere: ideas about the cosmos and,
very likely, an afterlife. Quite apart from the burial furniture (weapons,
personal adornments, and vessels containing food and drink), evidence
comes from the very disposition of the bodies themselves, whether extended or flexed. These two modes of inhumation seem to denote two different ideas about the cosmos, related, but with perhaps different roots.

The first Kurgan peoples who entered western Europe placed the
dead on their backs in either an extended position or with the legs tightly
contracted to the chest. The customary body orientation was either in a
north–south or a east–west direction. In later Kurgan burials the body
lies either on the right or left side with the legs flexed, so that they are at
right angles to the body, and the hands brought up to the face. Extended
burials lingered in the south Russian "homeland" and were always to be
found among pastoral peoples further to the east (such as the Pazyryk
burials of the Scythians). When extended burials reappear in central and
western Europe we may suppose a recurrent steppe influence, mostly in
the form of dominant chieftains.

These extended burials betray a polar orientation that can be related
to historical cultures of the far north, studied by modern ethnographers,
from the Lapps of Finland to the Samoyed of Siberia. Among these and
other Ural-Altaic pastoralists, myth has it that the universe revolves
around a column or pillar fixed to polaris. From the hub of the heavenly
world it passes down through the navel of the mundane world into the
depths of the underworld. This pillar, running through the *axis mundi*,
thus registers all three layers of the cosmos. Siberian shamans who teach
this doctrine also teach that the main support at the center of every tepee-
shaped dwelling tent is an analog of this. When performing rites of
divination for his clients a shaman will go into a trance and climb up the
tent pole to the "sky," where the pole sticks out of the smokehole, and
send his spirit flying about the universe; returning, he reports what he has
seen of the earth from his supernatural vantage and makes his prognosti-
cation.[39] The idea of a sacred pillar around which the heavens revolve
is not confined to Ural-Altaic steppe peoples, though it may be pastoralist in origin, but is embedded in many Indo-European mythologies as
well. If the idea is shifted to a forest environment, the pole becomes a

great tree; such is the Germanic conception of Yggdrasill around which the whole cosmos is likewise layered.[40] Indeed, trees may themselves be symbols of the whole cosmos, groves of trees—circles, really—in particular. In the absence of trees, stone stelae would serve as well. The idea of the circle might easily represent the movement of the cosmos around a pivotal center. Thus, too, battle axes and the gods they represent will always have tree associations beyond their utility in timber-felling. It should be observed here that some barrows in southern Britain once held a timber post running through their middles, or have been surmounted by a standing stone. Their original shape, then, would have resembled that of a conical tent.[41] Silbury Hill, whether or not it proves to be a huge barrow, still holds that shape despite severe weathering.

The second tradition, that of flexed burials, is by far the main western one. Specific rites vary among different peoples throughout Europe from the late Neolithic until the end of the Bronze Age when cremation, associated with urnfield burials, becomes the rule with a suddenness that should remind us that the ancients were no more slaves to custom than are we. Memories of the old ways have persisted in mythology, however, and that is why, despite change, it is possible with the aid of archaeology to reconstruct not only the artifacts of the past but its mentifacts and sociofacts as well.

At all events, the variety of flexed burials in western Europe can be explained by the fact that migratory Kurgan herders mixed with other folk, commingling their burial rituals. The result left to us is a bewildering variety of grave orientations. Most confusing is the evidence left behind by the Beaker peoples because of the unusual nature of their movements, which were swift and extensive yet they allowed for local melding. For all that a general pattern may be discerned behind the specific differences. With one or two known exceptions, male corpses are oriented differently than females. For example, Battle Axe/Corded Ware peoples of central Europe placed women on their left sides with their heads pointing east (facing south) and men on their right sides with heads pointing west (also facing south).[42] Among the first Beakers who migrated to Britain the rites of burial mainly had men lying on their left sides, heads to the north and thus facing east. Women faced in the opposite direction. On the whole, this pattern obtains in the Wessex cemeteries around Stonehenge.

A consistent difference between male and female graves is not the only common theme. The eastward orientation of some burials may be a carryover from Neolithic sun and fertility cults; these would have the portals of communal tombs, both earthen and megalithic, face into the rising sun. Beaker graves somehow accord with this, with a belief in an afterlife symbolized by the eastern sun, at the same time they maintain the older polar orientation. The south-facing Battle Axe burials do indeed carry out such a theme, which Ferguson, citing Plutarch, put this way:

> Whilst looking southward, the motion we make [in turning to the right] accompanies the apparent path of the sun in the heavens; and in completing the circuit, whilst facing the north, our motion corresponds to the sun's returning progress under the horizon.[43]

So it is that the north means the sun's death, especially in winter when the sun is low on the southern horizon, and the south the sun-side. The east is the beginning of life and the west its demise.

Consonant with these burial practices is the directionality of deities in Indo-European mythology; Goddesses face east while warrior gods look to the west.[44] Freyja, the Germanic fertility goddess, is described in some sources as looking to the east. So does the early Germanic goddess Nerthus who, as Tacitus tells us, was worshipped in groves of trees and swamps. Fertility deities always are related to the rising sun and thus to the spring and summer. By contrast, the lands of death are supposed to lie in the west. When males lie on their right sides, then, they lie on their weapon-wielding arms and at the same time face the setting sun. Perhaps they will live on in some warrior heaven. Or perhaps their warlike pro-clivities will be put to rest. German and Celtic warriors go to the west upon death, often by ship. That imagery ties up with the sun cult through-out European prehistory; Bronze Age rock carvings frequently combine ships and sun symbols. It is of further interest that some barrows in Eng-land have yielded coffins made of hollowed-out logs and made in the shape of canoes.[45] Yet the main orientation of Beaker graves is along a north-east axis and is perhaps navigational in content.

In just the same way that cardinal directions have cosmic signifi-cance, handedness—right and left—is important. It is a human trait to gauge the world in terms of the individual, to see what is external as ex-tensions of ourselves. So Robert Hertz would say:

> The relation uniting the right to the east or south and the left to the
> north or west is even more constant and direct, to the extent that in
> many languages the same word denotes the sides of the body and the
> cardinal points. . . . Right and left extend beyond the limits of our
> body to embrace the universe.[46]

In this conception, the left hand is associated with death and the under-world, the right hand with the sky and the upper world. Sufficient to say, throughout antiquity females were assigned functions of the left hand and males the right. And why not, since among Indo-Europeans the right hand held the weapons and forged the tools and ornaments that made a warrior what he was. Hippocrates, in thinking that the human uterus had two chambers, the right for the male fetus and the left for the female, advanced a very ancient concept.[47] And that concept may be evidenced in Battle Axe graves.

Can we go further to say that the connection of the left hand with women and death is a remembrance of the Neolithic fertility goddess, herself representing life and death together? In all folk traditions the left hand is "sinister." To turn to the left has always been bad luck. In England it is called "withershins," in Ireland *deiseal.* Turning oneself to the right meant not merely luck but reverence for the gods. So Athenaeus claimed of the Celts that "They worship the Gods, turning round to the right."[48] This is valid only if one begins by facing the east and turning to the south, following, once again, the course of the sun. To turn to the left means to describe the death of the sun in the north. This is a principle evident in those earthen long barrows and Megalithic tombs which face the rising sun. It is also evident in many of the single-grave traditions. Altogether

Votive boat, gallo-Roman Period, Blessey, France.

this idea represents a primitive world-view in which a certain dualism is a compelling feature: light and dark, life and death, male and female, left and right.

We should not be surprised to find that polar oriented burials carry out the same theme. If we picture the length of a burial mound oriented along a north-south axis to intersect with an upright post in its middle, running from polaris to the underworld, then a body heading north also observes a polar axis. The corpse lies in his mortuary house in which a center pole represents the *axis mundi*, turning along both vertical and horizontal planes. The burial mound is itself a circle representing the circling of the stars around the cosmic tree. Into the afterlife the deceased takes his weapons, those items likely to mark his status in life. Indeed, his mortuary house very likely models the very house in which he lived, thus linking the two worlds of life and death. When the weapons buried are daggers they represent a warrior god and his particular sun cult. When they are axes they represent a thundering deity, he who is tutelary of trees and male fertility. Thus the right hand, in which these items are held, is to the east when the body is extended looking north.

A particularly well-known illustration is the "royal" grave at Leubingen, Germany.[49] Dating to the later Bronze Age, this tomb contains an older man lying in extended position with his head to the south. Across his body lies a young woman, extended, looking towards the west. On the man's right hand (the east side) are ornaments of gold, daggers, axes, halberds, and a battle-axe. On the west side of the tomb is a pot surrounded by a stone circle modeled after a hearth. The directional aspects of the grave are apparent: the symbols of power are on the right-hand side while the symbols of domesticity, women's things, are on the left. The woman's position might be interpreted as having an eastward orientation, but that is not likely. She looks to the west, the deathlands, because she is meant to accompany the male to that place where she will serve his bodily needs. Here, incidentally, is a clear case of *suttee*, a well-known Indo-European custom.

On the whole it is not amiss to adjudge the main stream of Beaker graves as falling within this pattern. To be sure, they carry a mixture of traditions. But the fact that males have their heads to the north, face east, and have their right hands free can easily be interpreted as some version of the old Kurgan northward-looking burial rite. That females are generally buried in their own special disc barrows[50] and have their heads to the south and look to the west may be reminiscent of the great goddess, that Neolithic fertility deity who at once represents life (the south) and death (the west).

At the same time there is a long history of cremation which eventually supersedes inhumation altogether in the next phase of the Bronze Age. Close analysis of the whole inventory of Wessex graves, to say nothing of the various European series, would be instructive if ever carried out. Cremations predate these and so must be in some way related to the same practice on the Continent. In Únĕtice cemeteries a certain percentage of cremations always coexists with inhumations. This has been explained as

Chief's burial from Leubingen, Germany (Tumulus Culture). The major figure is an older man, the skeleton placed across his body is that of a young woman, a clear indication of *suttee*. The man is buried with the symbols of his power: battle axe, daggers, chisels and jewelry; the woman has her cooking pot so as better to serve her lord in the next life (after Piggott, 1965).

a rite with feminine connotations,[51] but more likely it is the practice of a special group in these societies, shamans or smiths. Rather than look for the gradual infiltration of a new custom, it would make better sense to assume an ongoing history of cremations among a minority, for this would help explain the apparent continuity of ideas from one period to the next. That is, if cremations were confined to shaman/priests, these intellectual specialists would also conserve and carry forward ancient beliefs and probably a conception of the universe built up over many centuries. When a fresh monument was built under a new chieftainship, it had to take shape as the end product of a long history of religious thought; in itself it embodied the accumulation of several traditions carried by the adepts in religion who directed its construction under their political superiors. That would account for the cosmology implicit in the final Stonehenge which looks back to the world view of tomb-building, communal chieftains even as it was erected in the name of triumphant aristocratic chieftains.

Whatever the exact mixture of new and old ideas, new and old cultures, the sun remained iconic among early Bronze Age peoples throughout Europe, of which the Wessex warriors are a part. The presence of amber discs in their barrows attests to the solar magic of these discs. And in the Indo-European world, the sun is everywhere of a piece with its warrior god. Heroes of Indo-European epic literature, the Irish Cuchullain a prime example, are said verily to shine in their glory. Even in regions strongly influenced by West Asian traditions the warrior god and the sun are closely linked, hence the cult of Mithra the Anatolian warrior god who is at once the incarnation of light itself. Sun symbolism is old, older than the Indo-European warrior chiefs who adopted it, and with them it takes on a new meaning. That new meaning we may expect to find attached to the ruins of Stonehenge.

Astronomy and Stonehenge

Some nine hundred megalithic circles—henge monuments—have been found all over the British Isles[52] (see Map 7). Not all are of the same date, like the phases of Stonehenge itself, therefore not all may have served the same purpose. Nor are they of the same shape, for not all are true circles. At one time the untrue ones were thought to be accidental results of faulty surveying. But now, Alexander Thom and Aubrey Burl have given these mathematical and astronomical meaning.[53] Thom has further postulated that all were designed with reference to a single measure, the "megalithic yard" averaging 2.72 English feet (1.66 meters), allowing for slight local variations. The measure at Stonehenge, for example, is taken to be 2.71 English feet.[54] On this point Burl disagrees, claiming that 66 percent of the circles he investigated bear no relationship to that proposed measure.

Both, however, agree that whatever the shape of the circles they were laid out with precision. Of them, 600 are true circles, 150 flattened circles, 100 ellipses, and 50 egg-shaped. According to Burl these types can be arranged chronologically, and he gives these B.C. dates for building periods: (A) 3300–2700 for true circles, the only type connected with Windmill Hill pottery and, significantly, with jadeite axes; (B) 2700–2050 during which true circles predominated, especially large ones associated in some places with Beaker pottery; and (C) 2050–1600 during which smaller and variant types of circles were constructed.[55]

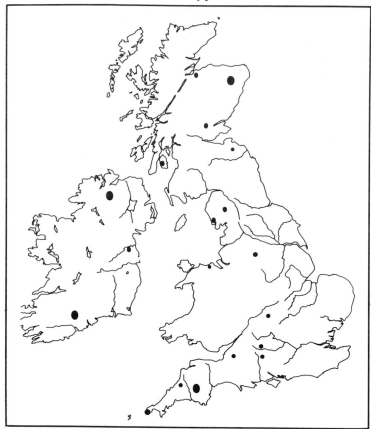

Map 7.   Stone circles and henge monuments in the British Isles.

But *are* these evolutionary types? It is doubtful and other theories are current. One has it that untrue circles of one shape or another were designed to calibrate their axial orientation toward the helical rising of this or that star, the target itself a matter of debate.[56] If not that complex a matter, then perhaps like the passage graves they were simply oriented toward the east, in the general direction of the rising sun. Neither speculation can be verified and besides, there is an easier explanation based on building techniques. Let us suppose that each circle of whatever shape was plotted from the end of a rope tied to a post at the center. Indeed, post holes that would have served as a pivotal point for such a purpose have been found at the center of a number of henge monuments.[57] Any project to build a ring of standing stones would have its four cardinal points marked from the start, the rest of the circumference filled in afterward. This sequence of activity most likely was carried out on a seasonal basis at periodic social gatherings. We are fairly sure this is the case with the surrounding ditches and banks of some henges, as with those of causewayed camps, because they clearly were laid out in a number of straight sections; each section must have been assigned to a team of diggers until the whole system was joined in a full circle. This may have been done at once, but more likely it was done intermittently over a period of yearly festivals, one section after another. Given a social interpretation of megalithic circles, their departure from the true is as understandable as their exact mathematical shape is irrelevant. Nor do the axial lines of untrue circles consistently point eastward or toward any stellar object.[58]

Again, there is room to question Thom's theory of a uniform measure; his megalithic yard may have been a man's pace, hence approximate.[59] Pacing was the standard well into the Middle Ages. The megalithic yard cannot be identified so long as its exact value depends on finding a point central to a surrounding ditch of irregular segments or to a ring of roughly dug holes and standing stones. For all circles lacking a central post hole, from which the circumference was described by rope and peg, that point is impossible to fix by derivation. And once the idea of a precise measuring system is found wanting, some of the alignments plotted by modern astronomers must also be suspect. But we do not preclude an interest in mensuration and perhaps "pure" mathematics on the part of prehistoric peoples.

It is possible that the many stone circles of variant shape, especially those in remote regions of northwestern Britain and Scotland, are imitations of earlier and larger ones. True circles are demonstrably the largest in diameter and are set with the largest stones while later ones, notably ellipses, are smaller on both counts. Distribution is interesting also. Large, true circles are found throughout the British Isles but with a concentration of the largest ones in southwestern Britain, the area where the tradition of building henge monuments began. Untrue circles of various shapes are found mainly in the northern and western highland regions in Lancashire, Scotland, and Ireland. Given Burl's chronology, at least two reasons for their construction may be adduced. Either the later ones are smaller because they were exercises in pure mathematics or experiments in astronomical observation and need not have been very large, or else they were built by petty highland chiefs who could not muster the manpower to build large ones let alone understand their original, esoteric purpose. If the latter, as we shall see, the earliest circles were above all tribal monuments expressing the sway of developing chiefdoms, a political evolution that commenced and carried furthest in southwestern Britain before the building tradition itself came to an end there. While other smaller chiefdoms arose elsewhere later in time, and note that the difference between phases A and C is more than a thousand years, only the basic idea of a circle as the symbol of chiefly authority would have diffused. The later ones in the highlands, therefore, were built in disregard of the original refinements, astronomical or whatever, now developed over the course of centuries beyond the reach of imitation in all respects. And because the highland cultures remained peripheral to the more rapidly changing lowland cultures, northern chiefdoms also retained the building

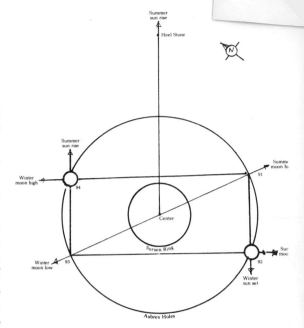

Some alignments related to the Station Stones as indicated by Gerald Hawkins (1965). Only stones 91 and 93 still stand. The missing ones, 92 and 94, once were seated atop two mounds located athwart the ring of Aubrey holes, covering at least eight of them. Therefore the Aubrey holes (Stonehenge I) never could have worked as an integral part of a "Neolithic computer," together with the sarsen ring (Stonehenge IIIa), for the prediction of eclipses as Hawkins would have them do. Note again the conflation of building periods, as if the monument were built at one time for one purpose.

As for the Station Stones, the very symmetry of their placement, the geometry of the whole layout, in fact, goes against the assymetry of the actual heavens in a scientific astronomy but does accord with a religious cosmology. Indeed, the Four Stations probably are memorials to surveyors' marks used to recalculate the axis and center of the sarsen structure within, just as it in turn is probably a memorial (among other things) to the practice of an earlier farmers' or navigators' astronomy. The fact that the new axis does not coincide with that of the earlier Avenue, nor the new center with that of the circular embankment and ring of Aubrey holes, once again indicates a fresh purpose and a new building period, yet continuous with the older ones.

tradition much longer. On the other hand, it is always possible that these late types belong to a distinct regional culture that pioneered a wholly new reason for henge building. This might be the case for the ellipses grouped in northern Scotland. If nothing else, however, all henges are the material expression of chiefly power.

Plate 17.   Stone circle in Northern Britain. (Hans Schaal)

In light of the foregoing, there is indeed some astronomical significance to Stonehenge; it is the degree and exactitude that is in doubt. Using a computer to work out positions of sun, moon, and stars as they would have been arrayed in 1500 B.C., Gerald Hawkins in *Stonehenge Decoded* concludes that Stonehenge was a giant observatory of celestial phenomena and a predictor of lunar eclipses.[60] All of this is far away and beyond the simple observation of solstices and equinoxes, that is, times when the sun reaches its northern, southern, and midway points on the horizon during its yearly journey. The movements of the moon are more complicated because its extreme northern and southern positions shift from year to year in the so-called Metonic cycle of approximately nineteen years. This was known to Babylonian and Chinese astronomers but probably not until the fourth century B.C. Hawkins thinks that the four Station Stones were set up as a rectangle to mark the extremes of the solar and lunar settings when sighted along diagonals running through a supposed geometrical center of the monument. The five trilithons were meant to frame the setting and rising sun and moon at their extreme positions. If these stones were indeed intended to fix lines of sight with events on the horizon their position is so inexact as to invalidate the purpose; any surveyor knows how difficult it is to establish a line of sight between two points even with the aid of a theodalite, much more if not impossible with gross structures.

Hawkins also sets up a complex 56-year lunar eclipse cycle in which the Aubrey holes are postulated as holding posts for movable counters to mark the passage of the moon toward that event. Although affirmed by a different method of counting by so eminent an astronomer as Fred Hoyle, this theory is widely doubted by prehistorians.[61] The Aubrey holes long predate Stonehenge III and may not have been visible, filled in and turf grown over, by the time this last phase was constructed; indeed, the earthen mounds in which the four Station Stones are embedded completely cover some of the Aubrey holes. Besides, they are cinerary pits. Nor are the proposed alignments in order. In Atkinson's words: "The observed irregularity of the alignments and sectors is thus at variance with the known capabilities of the builders, and with the precision and order

Plate 18.   Another view of stone circle in Northern Britain. (Hans Schaal)

which is implied by their apparent interest in geometry and mensuration. It is as if, having a need for graph paper and the means and ability to rule it accurately, one were to settle for drawing it freehand on blotting paper with a Post Office pen."[62]

On the other hand, C. A. Newham notes that the number of bluestones arranged within the trilithons is nineteen and that the number of uprights in the sarsen ring comes to 29½ stones, the half-length of stone no. 11 being intentionally short. Nineteen comes close to representing the 18.61 year Metonic cycle and 29.5 days of the lunar month, counting stone no. 11 as half a day. Knowledge of these numbers was gained, Newham suggests, from a series of posts fixed and refixed experimentally in the entrance of the causeway (judging from the numerous post holes there) as a method of observing moon positions and thus the Metonic and eclipse cycles were discovered. In the completed structure, an observer standing at the center would see the full moon nearest the winter solstice rise over the Heel Stone and alert him to a subsequent lunar or solar eclipse.[63] Newham needed no computer to make his observations and notes that the same were possible to the ancients with a simple rope and peg together with a knowledge of triangulation, an aspect of Pythagorean geometry (more than a millennium and a half before the man himself).

Plate 19.   The man is leaning against stone no. 11, the short stone in the sarsen ring. (Hans Schaal)

Plate 20.   Another view of stone no. 11. See Barclay's reconstruction, *p. xiii.* (Hans Schaal)

The foregoing, a very simplified version of some intricate theory, indicates a relatively sophisticated series of calculations by the peoples in this part of Neolithic and early Bronze Age Europe. To this end Hoyle has gone so far as to suggest a group of prehistoric geniuses who did the mathematical work. Thom would place the experimental center of this activity in Brittany. At Er Grah near Carnac he has proposed a universal observatory based on a tremendous menhir weighing 340 tons. Of eight linear sight lines predicted, most running along avenues of standing stones, he claims to have discovered five at the least.[64] All of this may be so, but it is really farfetched to require a band of Einsteins to build Stonehenge or even to observe fairly simple astronomical events. This, like Hawkin's Neolithic computer, is to take modern ideas out of context and put them in a wholly inappropriate place and time.

To work backward from modern presuppositions is to show only how the structure *might* have functioned if its architects shared the same outlook. In some cases our minds meet theirs, but we cannot be sure of that. One example will suffice. Stonehenge now and again is compared to the Mayan cult centers of Mexico and Guatemala, whose monumental architecture is inscribed in hieroglyphic writing with calendrical records of extreme sophistication and great accuracy. While Mayan farmers practiced a primitive, slash-and-burn type of agriculture, their priestly rulers were able to build magnificent temples of refined construction that seem to have been oriented toward solar and lunar equinoctial positions.[65] Yet, in the words of the eminent Maya specialist, J. E. S. Thompson,

> we must not try to look at Maya astronomy through European eyes. Maya emphasis was almost wholly on helical risings after inferior conjunction because of the astrological importance of that position. . . .
>
> The Maya astronomer—astrologer if you will—completely ignored phenomena that seem important to us . . . presumably because those phenomena had no effect on mundane affairs.[66]

Can we even guess at the details of cult affairs on Salisbury Plain four thousand years ago, much less an astronomical system, lacking any records?

With the above poser in mind, we are all the more aware that what theoretical matter follows is in hot dispute. If we dare enter the controversy it is only because we have taken pains to set out those relevant factors without which nobody can be prepared to unriddle the astronomical plan, if any, of Stonehenge and, more important, the mentality of the peoples who built it.

For one thing, we find it helpful to divide all large stone monuments, not just circles, into those which are directionally oriented and those aligned. The former class yields easily to our own theory of tribal cosmology while the latter, perhaps, has more to do with "pure" astronomy. Beginning with alignments, the massive researches of the Thoms[67] have convinced many archaeologists that their builders were keenly interested in, and possessed a deep knowledge of, mathematics and that all this had an astronomical focus of interest. Lacking blackboards, the ancients laid out in stone their preoccupation with "integral lengths and perimeters, and with Pythagorean and near Pythagorean triangles,"[68] going well beyond the needs of practical surveying. By implication, numbers and an understanding of their values preceded writing in northern Europe, not to say in the earliest civilizations of the Near East.

How might such a body of knowledge, if it existed, have come into being? Two main streams of thought come to mind, one Neolithic and the other Bronze Age. Already we have seen that Neolithic long barrows were oriented toward the rising sun, without doubt the result of cosmological thinking. These were set on high ground, on ridges above the tree line, so as to catch the early rays of the rising sun and at the same time focus the attention of the group that built it, the "we" symbol of a communal society. But to which sunrise were these barrows oriented? The sun rises over different portions of the horizon almost every day, except on the solstices when its risings seem to stand in place for a day or two. Most opinion holds that barrow entrances face the rising sun on the contemporary midsummer's day, but this proposition is not yet clear if it assumes reference to a common horizon. More likely orientation was irregular, and each community may have used its own local calendar based on the immediate horizon. Otherwise we must assume the existence of a megalithic church with the ritual power to establish a translocal calendar, as does the Catholic church in setting the saint's day of St. John the Baptist on 24 June.

How Neolithic calendars were reckoned on the basis of local topography has lately been evidenced by interviews with old timers from North Ossetia in the Caucasus Mountains. They report that into the early part of this century, village presbyters chose as their meeting place a house with its door facing north, next to which an old man was employed to sit on a bench and tell the seasonal time by observing the sun setting behind the mountain range before him.

> In each village there was a man who would observe the sun set each day. In the summer the sun set farther and farther to the right every day. It then reached the farthest point to the right and started to set at points farther and farther to the left. The silhouette of the mountain range is so individual from every view angle that it is not difficult to memorize the place of sunset at the farthest point to the right. When the sun returns to this point the year has passed. The sun sets at this point on the longest day (summer solstice). . . .
>
> Days of equinox were established by fixing the position of the setting sun on the day half way through the period between the solstices. If the sunset took place at a certain spot before the next movement of the point of the sunset from right to left, this occurred on the day of the autumn equinox. In some villages the space between mountain peaks where solstice occurred, was halved and at this point was fixed on the mountain profile. The day on which the sun passed that point, while setting, was the day of the equinox. . . .
>
> In this calendar the mountain profile is essentially outlined against the firmament; the position of the center of the sun is then fixed in relation to this profile against the firmament.[69]

Here is a good example, in how Ossetian villagers set their festivals, of what we have been calling a "farmer's calendar." Significantly, its use was predicated on seeing a distant horizon.

The same must have been true at Stonehenge. The forest growth on Salisbury Plain had not yet been reduced until the early or middle Bronze Age, therefore heliacal risings may have been observed with reference to large trees. Each community in the surrounding area probably had a different perspective. As the Neolithic population on that great plain began to grow and evolve a dominant chiefdom of ever greater scope, some uniformity in calculating events in the sky would have been required to regulate the ceremonial year on earth. Elsewhere in Britain, and especially in Brittany, multiple rows of standing stones or menhirs were set up presumably for sighting purposes. The most notable monument of this alignment type is at Carnac in Brittany, where nearly three thousand menhirs still remain, an area also noted for its great number of chambered tombs, monuments of the orientational type. The work of the Thoms on alignments tends to show that they often served as backsights to distant hills or notches between hills. Thus menhirs replace trees. One possible origin for the astronomical observations that led to the construction of stone alignments, we conclude, may be traced to the Neolithic practice of orienting funerary monuments, coupled with the practical requirement to predict seasonal festivals.

Boats and dancing figures, together with sun symbols, from the rock carvings of Bohuslän in southern Sweden. Observe, too, the sacred tree which appears commonly in this series of carvings. It seems clear that the ideas inherent in these go back well into the early part of the Bronze Age and are likely to have been related to Beaker folk. The boat and sun symbols are prime examples. (after Gelling and Davidson, 1969).

Megalithic alignments at Carnac.

Boats and ceremonies connected with them from Bohuslan. While none of the carvings are clearly datable, these seem to be later Bronze or Iron Age. The helmets on the tall figure in the middle picture closely resembles horned helmets of the Celtic era. Lurs or musical horns, common in Celtic contexts also appear in the bottom illustration. At least one of the ceremonies is echoed in heroic literature. The top picture shows figures leaping in graceful arcs over a boat and this seems connected to a "salmon leap" executed by the Irish hero, Cuchullain, before battle (after Gelling and Davidson, 1969).

Stonehenge at the very least is a monument of the orientational type, which we know from the simple fact that its causeway (phase I) faces east, as do the entranceways of almost all megalithic tombs built during the same Neolithic period; the connection with tomb building remained unbroken, as we have seen in the previous section, insofar as the architecture of Stonehenge III is designed after a sepulchral model. If the final phase has alignments built into its stones as well, we may now begin to see how an astronomical purpose could have been realized out of burial customs dating back to the Neolithic in Britain. In fact, if astronomy has one of its origins in a cult of the dead, and given the general principle that cultural continuity is just as much a fact of human life as culture change, then we should expect to find a trace of those origins in the pure astronomy of the scientific age. The first celestial body whose features were discernible by telescope, the moon, has come to be the graveyard of astronomy itself, owing to the custom of naming lunar craters and other formations after noted astronomers of the past; a custom that began in 1645 when Langrenus of Brussels published a first map of the moon.[70]

The other line of thought we promised to pursue derives from the early Bronze Age and is associated with the Beaker folk. As we have seen from their voyages to the Irish Sea, not alone across the English Channel, they possessed the navigational skills to travel far by boat. In fact, the Beaker folk are but one branch of the Bronze Age peoples of Europe whose rock-engravings of boat, sun, and axe remain on display throughout Scandinavia and in other Continental parts. As such, they represent one of the strands of culture history that finally went into the composition of the Vikings, although the Beakers were archers, not battle-axe warriors. Some of the boat images, particularly those from southern Sweden, show elaborate vessels with great curved prows and sterns that carried up to thirty passengers.[71] Evidently they were plank-built, hence capable of long sea voyages, and look very much like the long canoes of Oceania. The comparison is of more than passing interest.

A recent study of navigational techniques in Micronesia and Polynesia reveals that the natives are capable of steering by the stars, indeed that they command a precise not to say empirical knowledge of the entire heavens within their view. They pay careful attention not only to the stars and constellations, but to solstices and equinoxes by which they reckon their year. All of this is secret knowledge held by a caste of priest/navigators who by means of it have established themselves as chieftains of one rank or another. What they know is passed on from father to son and based on practical experience. This basis for chieftainship is not a new one, to judge from archaeological relics. Young sailors may once have been instructed to take their bearings from the rows of standing stones that have been found on some islands; a possibility made all the more likely by the discovery on Tonga of a stone canoe oriented east-west and with a sighting stone in front of it, surely a training device. Yet these peoples are nonliterate and innumerate, for all their astronomical knowledge. And so it cannot be organized in the same way ours is. For example, Oceanic navigators take this or that star to mark the place of certain islands and they steer their vessels accordingly, making adjustments for ocean currents which are said to be guided by certain other stars. That gets them where they want to go, but does not accord with reality as we know it.[72]

All of this is to say that literacy is not required to study the heavens, make practical use of that knowledge, and pass it on from one generation to another. Nonliterate peoples are thus able to arrive at solutions to problems that we would formulate differently, in the light of modern astronomy, but to the same practical effect. An exotic belief system, however untrue from the viewpoint of western science, will get the job done if it meets the test of experience. The same must apply to the megalithic engineers of Europe, whatever their purpose.

Indeed, their purpose may not have been very different. If the megalithic alignments we have been discussing bear out any astronomical significance, it may very well turn out to be navigational astronomy. The Beaker folk, who most certainly traveled long distances over open seas, and their Neolithic predecessors who plied rivers and coasts probably had developed navigational techniques the equal of modern Polynesians. If the Polynesians gained their experience in navigating open waters from island to island we must remember that the Beaker folk are related to the Kurgan folk, a pastoral people who were accustomed to moving from point to point over the open steppeland, and who probably made the same use of the heavens for guidance. Likely any peoples who spend much time in the open, sailors or shepherds, would develop some accurate knowledge of stellar positions and invent constellations to go with them. In the absence of written records, the knowledge will be cast perforce in the form of folktales and mythology.

We may imagine that in stone alignments the two traditions of astronomical thought mentioned above came together and at a propitious moment in time. Throughout much of the Neolithic period, northern Europe passed through a climatic phase similar to the present, cool and wet with much cloud cover. Modern Britain is hardly the place for prolonged astronomical observation. By about 3000 B.C. and certainly by the middle of the third millennium, however, the climate grew warmer and drier with a greater frequency of cloudless skies.[73] Longer observation of the heavens was now possible in the clearer air. The drier climate also aided in the destruction the forest cover, as on Salisbury Plain. Another major effect of the change in climate was to make for relatively calm seas, especially around 2000 B.C. This latter factor would have helped small bands of Beaker and allied peoples to migrate over wider stretches of open water, all the way to the west coast of Ireland, for example. At the same time, the climate was ideal for navigation by the stars.

But the question remains, why build gross alignments for the purpose of making refined astronomical sightings? Why construct them of rough stone (particularly given the exactitude of measurement supposed by the Thoms, down to tenths of inches) when they more accurately could be made of wood? The answer must lie in the method by which knowledge of the heavens was collected and transmitted. If the knowledge were scientific, as we understand it, then it would have to be cumulative, built up and added to by generations of observers, and it would have to be accessible. No evidence at all exists for anything resembling an information storage and retrieval system in Neolithic and early Bronze Age Britain. No record of numerical notation has ever been found by archaeologists, to say nothing of writing. Perhaps it was all done on perishable material, but perhaps not. At any rate, as Atkinson has remarked, the life span of individuals living at the time was markedly shorter than today so that even the Metonic cycle may not have been observed even once in the lifetime of a trained observer.[74] Even if a few persons lived into what we now consider middle age and did observe the Metonic cycle, there still is no evidence that knowledge of it was storable for future use. The logical reply to this objection is that astronomical data were not filed in almanacs but kept alive in the minds and mouths of learned men. That is not out of keeping with what we know of later Druids, they who are "thrice wise"[75] and who spent twenty years or more in memorizing a vast amount of poetry. But the content of this, on the whole, seems to have been more religious than scientific. That the detailed information of a celestial ephemeris could have been reduced to verse and passed on orally, generation to generation, is a mind-stunning notion. Not only is that unprecedented in all oral literature known to us, past and present, but it is likely impossible.

Hundreds of years of recorded observation went into compiling the first astronomical/astrological handbooks of Mesopotamia. The Maya in carving their calendrical notations in stone likewise made use of a writing and numerical system, a resource not available to nonliterate societies by definition. They may employ mnemonic devices that work on the principle of the Catholic or the Buddhist rosary, but for the most part we may say that specialized knowledge will be passed on by means of practical demonstration or versified lore. To say this is to suggest a specialist in the role. As a model for prehistoric Europe we perhaps may look to the North Ossetian elder who watched the sun over the mountains or to the Oceanic priest/navigator. We may be fairly certain, however, that ancient specialists of this sort held religious authority, that they were in fact one and the same as the shaman/priests who directed the construction of megalithic monuments. Evidence of seasonal construction attests to that.

Religion was the only means the ancients had of holding on to retrievable information, and that would have been set in verse and mythology. In fact, actual data may not have been recoverable by this method at all, only symbolic ideas. By analogy, then, stone menhirs represent only a general idea of accurate alignments which may once have had the force of actual navigational practice or farmer astronomy behind it. In either case, they stood as monuments to a dead idea even in their own time.

We may go so far as to suggest that the alignments at Carnac and other portions of Brittany were placed there for a social purpose that replicated a cosmological idea. The tremendous monolith at Er Grah may have provided a universal foresight for a number of backsights directed at it in making solar and lunar observations from the surrounding country-side, as Thom suggests, but if that was the purpose it was not the only one. We may well imagine that each menhir, referring to the solitary "back-sights" as well as to the ones standing in rows, was set up as the representative of a family or a noted individual during some annual festival. That is, at the ceremonies of any given year, some tribe, family, or Big Man might have been responsible for erecting a menhir as the symbol of social and cosmic solidarity. The gigantic one at Er Grah might have been put up by some ambitious chief for the same reason, looking to bring a number of local communities into alliance with him by way of a cooperative task of megalithic engineering. That must have been the way henge monuments were built, for unlike rows of standing stones, there is no question but they were oriented and not specifically aligned. Henges thus conform to a general religious idea: the sun rises in the east and sets in the west with special positions at various times of the year. The moon does the same thing. Above all, henges carry out a social theme not unconnected with the politics of chieftainship and the rota of a ceremonial year, itself calculated by shaman/priests from a devotional, not a scientific, study of the heavens.

Stonehenge cast in this light is by no means an astronomical observatory, a prehistoric version of Mount Palomar. The purpose its builders had in mind was far more immediate and that was political enhanced with cosmological pieties. How else could a group of religious specialists have organized the manpower to build it, or to erect the lithic monster at Er Grah, if not in the service of some powerful chief extending his authority in the very course of undertaking such projects? And why should anybody volunteer his labor if not to rejoice in the seasonal festivals that took place at the same time? And again, how could any large gathering of people be brought together, year after year, except at a place hallowed for the purpose in a tradition kept memorable by shaman/priests? The cosmological meaning of the megalithic structures erected bit by bit on these occasions is to be found in the building activity itself in all its social, religious, and political aspects, and cannot be divorced from them. Therefore it is quite misleading to compare ancient cosmology with modern astronomy, although both have features in common. To do so is to suppose that a group of professional astronomers could take upon themselves the power to rally a preliterate society behind their isolated purpose of conducting experimental science. It never happened and couldn't have. Stonehenge is of a piece with the other henge monuments.

Cosmology and Politics

Henge monuments grew out of a confluence in Britain of Neolithic and Mesolithic peoples (see Map 8). They are, as noted, closely related to sepulchral traditions among these peoples and later immigrants of the early Bronze Age. It also bears repeating that henges are symptomatic of rising chiefdoms and all that implies. The earliest henges are related to a cult of the sun particularly as it marks the different seasons of the year.

Autumn gatherings are known from the Neolithic at Windmill Hill and other causewayed camps. The continuity between causewayed camps on hilltops and circular monuments on the plain we previously have stressed. That is, both serve the same purpose—a gathering at important seasons of the year. The astronomy involved is agricultural astronomy; it is concerned with the calendar of farmers and herders. There is a noticeable association of jadeite axes with a large number of henge monuments from Avebury to the Orkneys, goods that probably were traded ceremonially during seasonal gatherings. That trade in turn has both religious and political implications. Control over the distribution of precious axes, the symbols and probably spirit of the god of rain and sun, was the means by which chiefs rising to aristocratic status could accumulate prestige and win followers. All of this centers on the henge monument, at once a temple of the sun, a symbol of tribal association and communal chieftainship, and even a place where the *axis mundi* turns under the pole star. As we have seen already, this same polar theme was imported to Britain once again by the Beakers, whose burial traditions may be traced back to those of the Kurgan pastoralists; therefore the earlier presence here of a stone circle with a pillar or perhaps a cultic meeting house at the center (as at Durrington Walls) must indicate a Neolithic belief system widespread enough to have reached all the way across the northern European plain. Certainly the axe symbol lends credence to solar associations which run straight through European prehistory. There is a whole nexus of symbolism—sun, axes, and circles—to which may be added the moon from a later developed tradition, but quite possibly it may belong to the Old Europeans. Lest the cultic implications of henges be forgotten, near the center of Woodhenge is the grave of a small child. It faces the midsummer sunrise and its skull has been cleaved in two.[76] No doubt a stone axe, sacred to the thunder god, was used for this.

This describes henges as they must first have been. In the course of time religious ideas changed as tribal organization began to stratify. One thing to come out of all the astronomical speculation about henges is to highlight their lunar aspects in accord with classical tradition. For example, a Greek writer of the first century, B.C., Diodorus Siculus, quoting a certain traveler of about 500 B.C. named Hecataeus, says that the priests of Alba worship in a circular temple dedicated to Apollo. This much we have adverted to already; but Hecataeus goes on to say that the priests meet every nineteen years (the Metonic cycle) and sing accompanied by harps to the rising Pleiades at the vernal equinox. The Pleiades is a cluster of stars in the constellation Taurus (the Bull). In Mesopotamian astrology that same cluster is described as fire burning between the Bull's horns and is said to herald the coming of spring.[77] Again, it is tempting to place the report of Hecataeus in Stonehenge, though the date is quite late.

The idea of the Pleiades as a heavenly fire directs our attention to the pan-European sun cult. Monuments all over Europe face to the east, from the passage graves of the north to anthropomorphic stelae on Sardinia and Corsica, with which evidence of cremation is associated. Celtic folklore about bygone peasant rites almost invariably recalls the lighting of

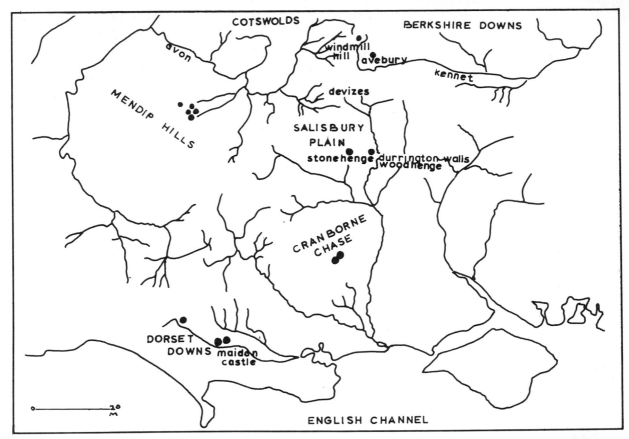

Map 8.   Distribution of henge monuments in the Wessex region. Note that all the groups are located on high chalk land and are close to rivers. They are prominent and accessible to water transport.

bonfires at the summer solstice and the practice must be very old. In this regard it is possible that Silbury Hill, built originally as a stepped structure with a flat top, was a high platform on which to light midsummer fires. They may have been ignited at the first glint of the rising sun, so that the mound was both a lookout and signal station for the coming festivities.[78] Throughout later European history from the Bronze Age onward, as we know from plentiful rock carvings in the northern countries, the advent of the summer sun meant ritual mating and human sacrifice.[79] Perhaps the related symbolism assigned female sex to the moon, male to the sun. The cosmology would have focused on the circumpolar constellations, since these are seasonal indicators. The Old Europeans appear to have symbolized certain constellations in their pictorial art, especially the bull (for Taurus) and the stag (for Leo). There is no reason to suppose that astrological thought about constellations was not widespread in Europe at an early date.

What then is Stonehenge III? It is the symbolic center for a Wessex chiefdom, and as such it has religious significance, a marker of important seasonal gatherings. It is the meeting place of a tribal chief, his men, allies, and clients. That it embodies a very ancient tradition of calendrical observation is really incidental to its political function. The work of priests is part of their special function in the social order and that would have been understood. Thus, when Stonehenge was built, the priests gave it the benefit of supernatural sanction. For what is in the heavens will be found on earth. But the priests gave it only that, they did not build themselves a giant computer; the chiefs who wanted it were not a modern government subsidizing astronomical research.

If we are to look for analogies, why not choose something closer to the Wessex folk in both time and outlook, not twentieth century industrial society. Take ancient Athens, for example. Were the wonderful temples on the Acropolis erected merely to indulge the religiosity of their priests? Or take the great cathedrals of later Medieval Europe. Were they built solely to the glory of God? The answer is, of course not. Building projects in both examples were undertaken to memorialize the glory and power of a city and its government. They were civic projects dedicated to public pride in the ideals around which the community had been traditionally organized before it grew to urban greatness. Yet a monument to these ideals was erected just as the society in each case was leaving them behind, when the old order was in fact passing away. This is much closer to the reality of Stonehenge.

Parkinson's Law and Megalithic Decadence

Stone is the oldest of man's industrial raw materials known to archaeology. Perhaps wood came first, although the artifacts have vanished, and early man viewed stone as another kind of wood to be chipped and split and rubbed into shape. This is likely from the equivalent use of wood and stone in what we have been calling megalithic structures. Nonetheless it is from stone that the first edge tools were made: the Paleolithic core tools, the Mesolithic knife blades, and the Neolithic axes and adzes. The first plastic material, contrasting with stone, was clay shaped by hand in its natural state and then hardened by the heat of an oven used also to bake bread, a Neolithic invention. The same invention led to the Bronze Age discovery that metal, originally treated as another form of stone, was a plastic substance if heated to a liquid state, then poured into a mold and allowed to cool.

We moderns who are dependent on the molten metals of the blast furnace for our tools find stone for the purpose so obsolete as to deserve conscious attention only in museums. But the technology of stone knapping and stone polishing was not replaced overnight with the beginnings of metallurgy nor did stone itself then suddenly lose its ancient prestige. During the transition stone would have attracted a heightened awareness by contrast with the very novelty and preciousness of metal. The Wessex warriors, for example, must have valued their bronze daggers and axes more as finery than as weapons, for which they still relied on their stone battle axes.

Yet it is the Wessex warriors, the first big-time users of bronze in Britain, who built the final phase of Stonehenge, the island's biggest pile of pure stone. In this it brings the old megalithic tradition of all northern Europe to a stupendous climax, or rather, to a dead end. In fact, that dead end was reached at Stonehenge even before the monument was completed. But in this climax, it celebrates the raw material of the stone age following the advent of metal. The medium is the message, as Marshall McLuhan would say. Direct attention is given to stone, an older material freshly perceived in contrast with the new, precisely because it is now obsolete as a medium for edge tools or weapons and thus acquires a symbolic meaning of added potency it lacked when the utility of stone was taken for granted. The extravagantly large stones used at Stonehenge, and in other megalithic monuments at the turn of the Bronze Age, suggest a decadent phase in stone-age technology, a dramatic increase in size and numbers at the moment of obsolescence. Parkinson's Law, which states that extravagant monuments are tombstones to the idea commemorated, seems to reach far back into prehistory. In Stonehenge can be seen a precedent for the American battleships of World War II, those dinosaurs of the sea built on the eve of a newly developed air power that could span oceans and continents alike; or New Delhi House, a palatial monument to colonial government occupied by the British resident in 1929, the very year in which the India Congress demanded independence.[80]

Having made that comparison, let us admit that it is facile. But we are not facetious. If we are overly clever in our application of Parkinson's Law to the stones of Stonehenge, it is only to draw attention to a more subtle version of it. There *is* an element of decadence in megalithic monuments, but it lies not so much in their substance as in the dead-end policy behind their construction. As time goes on, their symbolic meaning drops further behind social reality and that seems inherent in the political economy of the chiefdoms that built such monuments. Stonehenge was built under the authority of an aristocratic chiefdom, or one that made itself aristocratic during the course of construction. Yet the sepulchral continuities of that structure give it a symbolism harking back to the days of communal chiefdoms, when equality was a social fact and megalithic tombs its real memorial. Or at least the shaman/priests, acting as communal chieftains, who directed the work were self-effacing about it and did not dramatize the individuality of their leadership. Somehow the big chief at Stonehenge, or a succession of chiefs, was able to exert heroic authority to the same ends as did the communal chiefs of old in building family tombs. We doubt, however, that he needed to call upon the modern tricks of Orwellian double-talk in order to achieve this. He and others like him had only to exert himself as a Big Man in the economics of redistribution, and the evolution from a communal to an aristocratic chiefdom would take care of itself, with ever bigger megalithic monuments following in due course until the imperatives of growth under this system reached their limit and collapsed. Expand outward or die.

An aristocratic chiefdom is a pyramidal society; it is stratified in layers and does not articulate a division of labor into an organic whole as does a civic society. The lower layers merely reproduce the whole to a smaller degree: smaller clan heads and chiefs defer to higher chiefs and they to the highest chief. They collect goods at the local level (given a territorial division of labor but not a social one) and pass them on to their ultimate lord while keeping a suitable amount for themselves.[81] The big chief at the top (given the rapid evolution of dynastic lines out of a non-heroic order) will derive from a clan of the egalitarian type, except that his branch will hold a higher status relative to the others and will claim a more immediate descent from the family of the clan's tutelary god. The politics of inequality is thus validated by a belief system no less than is the apolitical society out of which it emerged. The resulting hierarchy accords with the will of the gods and is ranked at their behest. Envy from below is checked by sacrificing to these gods, so that the treasure hoard of the big chief is really an offering to them, who in turn distributes favors to humans. Naturally the god-system is organized in exactly the same way as the temporal one with a chief god, a male warrior or thunderer among the Indo-European peoples, who rules wisely, defends the cosmic order, and accumulates wealth. While this describes later aristocratic chiefdoms, it would not be amiss to give the gods credit for organizing as well the re-distributional economies of the earlier communal chiefdoms. These were led or advised by the same shaman/priests who in time formed a subordinate class, with craftsmen, in the service of heroic chiefs.

It is a feature of the early chiefdoms, when led by religious specialists, that the process of redistribution is often objectified in the construction of megalithic monuments. Why these are so expressive of the social order may be explained in part on the grounds that an economic surplus was thought to have included labor, a self-evident observation in a non-mechanized society. As the religious specialists developed a theology and as chiefly centers became more aristocratic, perhaps the gods needed more tangible proof of devotion. At least there would have to be some well-defined location where redistribution could take place. That is clearly the significance of the first cities in Mesopotamia where temples served as the storehouses and market places for the community as a whole. Therefore, a stage-set where the community interacts must need be built by that community on a cooperative basis. The earliest markers are small—in northern Europe megalithic tombs—but eventually they increase in scale probably in direct correlation to the degree of social organization, that is, the bigger the buildings the more people embraced by the system of redistribution. Competition between chiefdoms at potlatch festivals will have made for bigger and more elaborate monuments at the potlatch site, if not for the prestige of any individual chief then for the community and its god. We already have associated these motives with megalithic tomb construction. Renfrew has described the extraordinary temples on Malta, albeit a resource-poor island, in just these terms.[82] How much more favor would the gods bestow on that group with better offerings. Viewed in this way, monumental architecture must play a part in the evolution of chiefdoms and it must also take place in areas where there is a stable and growing population, utilizing local resources intensively, and under some competitive pressure from neighbors. Under these circumstances it is preferable to utilize labor for building projects rather than for warfare. This was as true for early state societies as it was for all heroic societies.

Let us imagine a society which produces considerable agricultural surplus and has plenty of manpower available, one with a literate priesthood and full-time craft specialists; in short, a civilization—a civilization covering a large territory divided into townships of Neolithic villages and no true cities, at least not cities as foci of craftsmen, traders, and merchants. This society, or state, is held together by a divine king, literally a god on earth, who will ascend to the heavens after the death of his mortal body to become president of the gods. That king is called pharaoh, that state is Egypt of the Old Kingdom. The reason we turn to Egypt, briefly, is to illustrate a parallel feature of monument building. In Egyptian theology the soul and body always comprised a unity and so after death the latter had to be preserved. In the king's case it had to be housed in a style befitting a god. In a cosmic reenactment of wealth accumulated by a potlatching chief, each pharaoh's preparation for the afterlife would have to be more elaborate than that of his rivals, that is, his predecessors. While tombs of the early dynasties were not very large, as time passed they grew in size as did the amount of furniture until a new departure was taken by Imhotep, the chief court official of the Third Dynasty king, Djoser, sometime in the middle of the twenty-seventh century B.C. It was Imhotep who designed and executed the first great pyramid, the Step Pyramid at Saqqara. Now, pharaohs were divine beings from the foundation of the kingdom some six hundred years previous; but by the time of Imhotep there is good reason to think that pharaoh had descended to at least a quasi-human level. Of course, he still became divine after death (though no longer the chief god) and so members of his court went with him. On a more mundane level the pharaoh was a redistributing chief, though on a very grand scale. He took in great wealth and in return gave out less costly but impressive favors. His chief services, arranged through a court bureaucracy, were to protect the kingdom, see to its prosperity through the flooding of the Nile (and this magical property of kingship is one explanation for its rise over the whole Nile Valley), to render justice and to see that the rest of the gods were happy. Egyptian cities from the start of the kingdom were centers for the administration of this exchange, which always favored the royal house.[83]

What made the first pyramids possible was the efficient collection of taxes in the form of goods and labor services almost from the start. Local labor had always been employed for building temples; shifting it wholesale to pyramid building was a matter of organization and at that Imhotep was a genius. The pyramids employed tremendous quantities of manpower sustained by the availability of enormous agricultural surpluses. The focus of a redistributional economy was now construction of pyramids. Whole towns were built to house the labor force (mostly voluntary, not the slaves whipped into submission by historical novelists and movie directors), grain collected and bread baked in a massive array of ovens to feed the thousands of festive workers that gathered to do their turn. By the time of the great pyramids of the Fourth Dynasty the whole state system was organized around the construction of these monuments. Not only were there religious reasons for building pyramids, though these were less pressing as time wore on, but reasons of state. Once begun, the building program had to continue; it could not stop, because it was the only effective means of redistribution, the only thing that held the state together. At least this must have been the perception of the bureaucrats, priests, who ran it. Not only were surpluses used during construction, but thereafter in tremendous ceremonies held at the pyramid sites monthly. Here indeed is a monument to a dead idea. Pyramids were built even after other gods took precedence over the divinity of the pharaoh. But the system had to continue and as long as the factors of manpower, resources, and political control remained in balance, pyramid building would continue.[84] Whether the building program outstripped resources or whether political control fell behind (and this would have been tied to changes in theological ideas), the whole system eventually collapsed leading to loss of a centralized monarchy in the First Intermediate Period.

What has this to do with prehistoric Britain? It is likely that the large monuments of southern Britain were built under roughly analogous circumstances. Megalithic tombs were built by extended family groups and their neighbors, but the huge ring works surrounding the largest henge monuments required considerably more labor. The embankment at Stonehenge is estimated by one authority to have taken close to 30,000 man hours to construct, perhaps over a period of decades.[85] This is no work of a mere family gathering but evidence for evolving centralization in late Neolithic society before the arrival of Beaker folk. Durrington Walls nearby, which may have incorporated a large roofed wooden structure—perhaps a *kiva* of sorts—must have taken 900,000 man hours to construct.[86] The greatest monument in point of size and labor is Silbury Hill. This tremendous barrow on the Roman highway from London to Bath (the Romans, in fact, detoured their road around it) some 120 feet high, is estimated to have taken 18 million man hours, or 500 men working for 15 years, to construct. As Atkinson says: "In view of the small size of the Neolithic population, this represents a fraction of the 'gross national product' at least as great as that currently devoted by the United States of America to the whole of its space program."[87] Despite great hopes by archaeologists, excavation of Silbury Hill has revealed no grave inside it. As interesting, perhaps, is the date and construction phases. Built in several stages, the central core is dated to about 2750 B.C. by recalibrated carbon-14 dating. It is therefore contemporary with the building of the middle date henges. All of these can only have been built under some sort of central direction and that must have been religious. The cosmic implications of henges we have discussed at length elsewhere, but it is well to recall that the monuments cited were of paramount interest to all the people who took part in building them, not just the specialists who directed the work. As the Egyptian model suggests, these monuments would have focused the organizational powers of emergent chiefdoms. The later phases of Stonehenge must express the same forces, while only the third one will have been a tribute to fully evolved chiefs. That it was never finished is indication only of the fluid nature of warrior society at the rim of the barbarian world. Massive political collapse, as in Egypt, is a function of size; the abandonment of Stonehenge is evidence of shifting tribal hegemony and alliances in a precivilized, heroic society.

5. Indo-European Warriors & the Heroic Tradition

Metallurgy and megalithic architecture are among the inventions of barbarian Europe that we now know found their way into the original civilizations of the Mediterranean, not the reverse. This is the ultimate meaning of the radiocarbon revolution and the new dating system. Civilization started as a home for corporate civic life rather than of technological invention. Europe built rude megalithic tombs before the Egyptians built bigger ones of dressed stone in the form of great pyramids. The alloy of copper and tin that is the signature of Bronze Age civilization was invented beyond its borders, for no metal ore is located within Sumer, and Egyptians did not make bronze until a millennium and a half after the founding of their kingdom. It is social organization that creates economic surplus for the building of cities and states, not surplus that creates the organization, such as chiefdoms.

Barbarians on the Edge of Civilization

But once the urban order carried forward inventions of the hinterland, it then radiated its own cultural glamor, inspiring imitation. This is an old story, going back to the very beginnings of the transition from the Neolithic to the first Bronze Age civilization in Mesopotamia. The basic technologies of the Neolithic—plant and animal domestication, weaving, house building, settled village life—originated outside Mesopotamia. The Sumerian civilization that evolved there along the Tigris-Euphrates gathered in these basic technologies from the hilly flanks of that river system in Palestine, Syria, Turkey, and Iran. Neolithic settlements in these semi-arid highland places then found themselves marginal to the well-watered lowland civilization their inventions made possible.

Even those technologies most distinctive of the Bronze Age itself—metallurgy and writing—were not developed in its urban centers, which served rather to concentrate the inventions of "barbarians" as before in the case of Neolithic technologies. The political and economic context for this concentration of scattered innovations is the kingdom, whose ruler is the patron of craftsmen attached to the palace within city walls—a ruler who pays for his specialists by arbitrating a complex system of redistribution involving trade and the taxation of Neolithic farmers in the surrounding countryside. The original centers of civilization in Mesopotamia and Egypt thus evolved out of the peaceful occupations of trade, commerce, and agriculture. Imitation civilizations, always partial and militarized versions of the archetype, grew by way of war and piracy.

The most spectacular of the derivative civilizations is the Mycenaean, an aggregation of kingdoms in the Argolid reported by Homer to have stopped raiding each other only when organized under the mythological Agamemnon in a joint effort to sack Troy. We should recall, however, that the achievement of kingship in the Argolid was conditioned by the indigenous rise of aristocratic chieftains, as elsewhere in Europe, and thus had the Mycenaeans already developed the potential to imitate the real thing as known to them from truly civilized kings close to home. Like these exemplars, Mycenaean kings were patrons of craftsmen, artisans, and court poets but whose products, used either to conduct or celebrate internecine war, made their occupations insecure. Herein lies the essential difference between heroic societies and civic societies. Even Mycenae itself, chief of the Mycenaean states, is not a city proper as we explained before. Its walls of cyclopean masonry enclose only the palace quarters, graves, and homes of the warrior nobility, not the full round and roster of civic life contained within the urban precincts of the great Near Eastern cities. While chiefdoms expand outward over wide spaces and thus reach their limit, civic societies expand inward and make inner space dense.

Mycenae, in turn, may have done its share in eliciting a distant barbarian response to its own heroic version of Mediterranean civilization. This was the by-product of its long-range trade—not always distinguished from gift exchange or piracy—in pursuit of copper and tin essential to bronze making. Bronze was essential for the king's craftsmen to make weapons by which his warriors could win booty and by which his diplomats, making gifts of weapons and other luxury products, could win allies.

One step further removed from Mycenae in development are the native chiefdoms of Europe north of the Alps, more distant from the

Lion Gate and cyclopean masonry at Myccenae.

Mediterranean and less civilized but no less militarized. In the heroic burials of the Wessex warriors are all the trappings of a barbarian aristocracy: the weapons of war (stone battle axes and bronze daggers), the drinking vessels (clay beakers for barley beer, if not gold and silver service for wine), and the objects of personal adornment, emblems of a treasure-seeking greed and treasure-giving generosity that is the very essence of warrior chieftainship. The same may be said for the heroic burials of Únětice.

These warrior societies in Britain and central Europe of the third and second millennia B.C. did not attain the level of political organization—the kingdom—evolved by their civic counterparts in the Mediterranean; but if they remained precivilized, they at least reached a degree of social stratification that marks all the evolved chiefdoms of Indo-European origin. That is, a tripartite organization with kings or aristocratic chiefs at the top, together with a warrior nobility, followed by a class of priests or praise-poets, then a foundation of commoners which include craftsmen, farmers, herdsmen and horse trainers. This is the kind of barbarian society, found outside the walls of corporate city life, that is clearly visible in the epics of Homer, in the classical accounts of the Iron Age Celts, and may be inferred from the burials at Stonehenge and Únětice. Indeed, it would not be amiss to classify the Wessex and Únětician warriors as formative Celts. If so, then the eyewitness accounts of Posidonius and Caesar[1] can be used as sources for breathing life into the bones of Wessex warriors, buried in the tombs near Stonehenge a millennium and a half before the Celts of Gaul fought Roman armies. The difficulty is that the proto-Celtic Britain of Stonehenge III and the Celtic Gaul of Caesar's conquests are separated by almost two thousand years, the English channel, and the difference between archaeology and history. These are not unbridgeable gaps if the term Celtic be taken as a term identifying a distinctive branch of the Indo-European peoples whose marginality to Mediterranean civilization, be it to Bronze Age or Iron Age developments there, is invariably militarized and provincial. Of the Gauls, Caesar said in 51 B.C., before his arrival "it used to happen every year that they either attacked another tribe or warded off attacks of another tribe."[2] Strabo before him had already written that "The whole race . . . is madly fond of war, high-spirited and quick to battle."[3] The same might have been said of the Wessex warriors, as Homer did of the Mycenaean warriors.

"Beyond Our World"

To linguists, Celtic means a family of languages, whose living representatives are the Brythonic ones of Breton and Welsh, and the Goidelic ones of Irish, Manx, and Scots Gaelic. In the time of Caesar, however, the languages of Gaul, Britain, and Ireland may have been much closer to each other than they are now.[4] The linguists then allow that "Celtic" may apply as the name of a cultural heritage in any areas in which Celtic is spoken, in Ireland, the Scottish Hebrides and Highlands, the Isle of Man, Wales, Cornwall, and Brittany. Or on the Continent, where Gaulish, allied

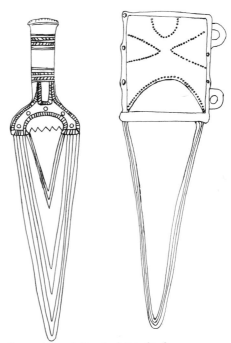

Bronze dagger (left) and a dagger sheath, Únětice culture, Czechoslovakia (after Piggott, 1965).

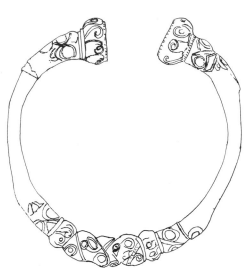

Hollow gold bracelet, 6th Century, from Waldalsheim, Germany.

Handmirror from Desborough, Northants, England.

with dead British forms such as Cornish, once flourished. But as a matter of historical fact, the cultural definition came first.[5] Herodotus, writing in the mid-fifth century B.C., took for granted the existence of a major barbarian people, the *Keltoi*, living beyond the Alps to the north and west of him. He distinguished the *Keltoi* from neighboring peoples by their tall fair appearance, quarrelsome behavior, ostentatious dress, and fierce warmaking. They are portrayed by themselves with wavy, swept-back hair, great moustaches, and wearing the torc or neck-ring. The Romans, in the words of Vergil, called them a people "beyond our world" who lived "on the edge of the habitable globe."[6] Archaeologists have identified them with a phase of the European Iron Age, early La Tène, dating from the sixth to the late fifth centuries B.C., and distributed from the middle Rhine east to the Danube, south into Switzerland, and west and north into France, the Netherlands, Denmark, and the British Isles. The type site is on Lake Neuchâtel in Switzerland. The most thoroughly excavated site is the British one of the Glastonbury lake dwellers in Somerset. To the art historian, La Tène crafts are known by a distinctive curvilinear style with linked spirals and expanding tendrils drawn from Etruscan and Scythian motifs. It appears most commonly in bronzework associated with war (buckles, scabbards, helmets, shields, chariot fittings, and horse gear) and with eating and drinking (cauldrons and wine flagons), just those fields of activity emphasized by the Celts.

All of this shows a mixture of cultural connections: a new one to the urbanized Mediterranean on the one hand, and on the other an older one to the nomadic Indo-European homeland, now occupied by Scythians and Cimmerians. The resulting mixture that is the culture of the La Tène Celts flourished until assimilated by the Roman Empire, with the exception of Ireland. By this time the Celts were somewhat fitted for assimilation by a civilized power, for they had already borrowed the chariot (from either Etruscan and Greek ceremonial or Assyrian and Persian war models), the Greek rotary millstone, and the all-pervasive iron axe for the clearing of land worked by means of Iron Age plow agriculture. And they lately imitated the currency and urban centers of civilized lands, with which they exchanged cattle and slaves for wine, by minting a crude native coinage and by adding commercial centers to their fortified townships, the *oppida* finally assaulted and conquered by Caesar.

Caesar, with the help of some passages drawn from Posidonius, described what he came to destroy. The accounts by classical authors thus date from the termination of Celtic life. But we are interested in its antiquity. All authorities agree that as a cultural if not a linguistic term, Celtic refers to a tradition maintained through a number of centuries of common history in the same general area of temperate Europe. The question is, How many centuries? Conservative opinion allows the tradition to date back no further than the Iron Age, beginning with the Hallstatt culture.[7] Another opinion, the one we favor, holds that Celtic is applicable to the Bronze Age forebears of Hallstatt and La Tène, to a population occupying southwest Germany and eastern France from well before 2000 B.C.[8] Conservative opinion draws a line between Bronze Age and Iron Age peoples in the same region. But as we shall see, their origins are to be found in the rise earlier of a heroic society. The discontinuity, then, is not as great as it might appear. Iron Age Celts and Bronze Age Celts were only partially influenced by the progress of Mediterranean civilization at whatever stage of development; they never duplicated the whole of its technology and social structure, but always remained in a marginal position on its nonurbanized, tribal frontier.

The Iron Age, in its fundamental pattern of development, includes not only cheap iron for swords and axes, but also horseback riding, the alphabet, coinage, free craftsmen organized in guilds, and large scale political organization tied together with a system of posts, as in the Persian, Assyrian, and Roman empires.[9] Armed with iron swords but riding Bronze Age chariots, La Tène Celts rapidly spread throughout Europe, south into France, Italy, and Spain; they penetrated Asia Minor and raided Hellenistic settlements there, and preceded the Romans into England, noted by Caesar as the invasions of the Belgae. But for all that, they remained a peripheral Bronze Age people, touched by the Iron Age only in sword making and in the use of ox-drawn plows and wagons. Iron Age Celts were politically organized into no empires; their craftsmen worked not for a free market but for the war chiefs they were attached to; and coinage and alphabetic writing were products of so late a culture contact as to verge on collision with Caesar.

Celtic chariot with warrior from Roman coin. Compare this with scene from Mycenean ring showing two riders, which is closer to description in epic poems.

Likewise were the proto-Celts of Bronze Age times incompletely touched by the kingdoms of Mediterranean civilization, based on the technologies of bronze metallurgy, wheel making, and prealphabetic writing. While Homer's Mycenaean aristocrats fought with bronze swords and rode in chariots, the Únĕtician and Wessex warriors were organized into no kingdoms and they lacked writing, and, in Britain, bronze weapons other than daggers and axes too rare to have replaced stone altogether.

The Celts emerged as a dominant people in Europe by the beginning of the third millennium B.C. with their own internal traditions developed outside the bounds of Mediterranean influence. Their cultural coherence over the centuries need not be stated as a militarized response to civilized developments. If that view has any validity at all, it applies to the latest phase of Celtic culture, not to the long centuries during which it developed. Yet these peoples, Celts and before them proto-Celts, were in contact with their neighbors, both lending and borrowing. And they migrated. The first proto-Celtic settlement of Britain may be dated to the early Bronze Age, by about mid-third millennium at the earliest, and might be identified with the infiltration of the Beaker folk who, in turn, would then be ancestors of Goidelic speaking peoples. If not Beakers, then their descendants, the Únĕtice peoples (who more clearly belong to the Battle Axe/Corded Ware tradition) must be regarded as proto-Celts. Continental Gaulish, with Brythonic, would then be a later form of Celtic speech, specifically associated with a central European culture called Urnfield. The

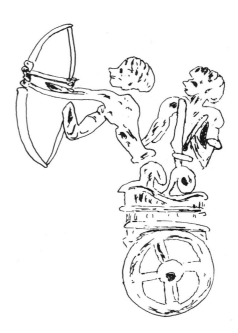

many centuries between the first Beaker migrations to Britain and the Belgic ones that Caesar mentions, is long enough to explain the absence of Goidelic in Britain outside the areas of later Irish settlement.[10]

The last surviving stronghold of Celtic culture was that found by St. Patrick in fifth century Ireland, a belated Indo-European culture of Bronze Age heroism, complete with chariot riding, cattle raiding, loud-boasting warriors whose chief virtues were courage and violence, and with an oral literature that praised such doings. Christian monks recorded this literature, including the *Táin Bó Cúalnge*, the finest of all the Irish sagas whose Homeric qualities recur only in the *Rig Veda*. Ireland and Aryan India are the western and eastern extremes of the Celtic conquest whose heartland was swallowed by Iron Age civilization, leaving only these two wings beyond the reach of Roman conquest.

The heroic tradition can be pushed back in epic literary remains to the second millennium; archeologically it is much older than that. If we are to identify and place in time and space the warriors to whom heroic society belongs, we must begin by looking at the first appearance of their literature, then examine the origins of the Indo-European speaking peoples that literature typifies.

The *Rig Veda* and Indo-European Society

The oldest epic in the history of Indo-European literature is the *Rig Veda*, which dates back to the middle second millennium and supposedly celebrates the Aryan conquest of a Bronze Age civilization in India, the Harappān of the Indus river valley. These migrants flow from the same source as the Battle Axe folk who moved into the region of the Rhine and Lowlands in Europe, who blended with the Beaker folk there and emerged as the proto-Celts who entered Britain and built Stonehenge III.

That source is the Ukrainian grasslands above the Caucasus, where a Neolithic people began domesticating the horse by 4000 B.C. It was the domesticated horse which gave this nucleus of the Indo-European peoples the mobility to move in waves into Europe, first with the horse as a pack animal then later as a draft animal for pulling wagons; with a team of animals hitched to war chariots they rode into Anatolia and Greece as ancestors of the Hittite and Mycenaean rulers, into Egypt as the Hyksos, into Mesopotamia as the Kassites who conquered Babylonia, and into India as the wreckers of Harappā. The Indo-European chariot appears to have been modeled after the Sumerian battle-car, drawn by onagers and rolling on solid wheels. The imitation was drawn by horses and rolled on spoked wheels, a combination that gave the chariot a speed and lightness that carried the Indo-Europeans rapidly through the east-west corridors of steppeland from Hungary to Mongolia. The Battle Axe folk who entered Europe were an advance wave who brought with them hole-shafted axes of stone modeled after Kurgan bronze axes but not yet horses, wagons, or war chariots. These were passed on to the Celts of Hallstatt times and were brought to Britain by La Tène Celts from the Marne region of France in about 250 B.C. and from thence to Ireland in about 1 B.C.

At all events, the Aryan chariot is named in the *Rig Veda* with a Sanskrit word *(ratha)* which is cognate with words in Latin *(rota)*, Celtic *(roth)*, Old High German *(rad)*, and Lithuanian *(ratas)*. Sanskrit words in the *Rig Veda* for wheel, axle, nave, and yoke also appear in related forms throughout the whole Indo-European group of Celtic, Germanic, Italic, and Balto-Slavic languages. Furthermore, the chariot itself, as shown by correlations between descriptions in the *Rig Veda* and archaeological evidence, is essentially the same vehicle—from wheel base to length of yoke—as known throughout the whole area of Indo-European colonization, from Mycenaean Greece to Celtic Britain—even to China, where chariot burials appear concomitant with the first historical dynasty (Shang) and cities.

The subject of the *Rig Veda* is the glorious deeds of city-wrecking, cattle-reiving heroes of the Punjab, personalized in a number of Aryan deities whose greatest is Indra.

> With all-outstripping chariot-wheel,
>> O Indra, though far-famed, hast overthrown
>> the twice ten kings of men
> With sixty thousand nine and ninety followers.
> Thou goest on from fight to fight intrepidly,
>> destroying citadel after citadel with strength.

Strong-armed, drunken, beer drinking, beef eating battle leader, Indra hurls thunderbolts in his divine moments, otherwise fights with bow and arrow from a chariot. "He sweeps away, like birds, the foe's possessions." Warriors appeal to him in their "resolve to win a cow, to win a steed." Indra is the apotheosis of the Indo-European warrior chieftain; it is "He under whose supreme control are horses, all chariots, and the villages, and cattle." Above all, he is a "city destroyer."[11]

The phrase "city destroyer" reverberates throughout Indo-European literature. Professor F. J. Tritsch recently has commented on its factual basis among the ancient Greeks:

> Small groups of people consisting mainly of chieftains with their bands of followers appear at various places. . . . Almost in every case we find small bands of chiefs and adventurers going forth in the Aegean region to carve out for themselves a new home, or little principalities, or lives of romance. . . . They had among them a special title of honour; *ptoliporthos*, "Sacker of Cities". . . . The greatest thing was to be a sacker of cities. . . . In the Homeric epics not only the great heroes like Achilles bear this title. . . . One does not sack a city in order to increase one's power or political influence, or to capture its trade and commerce. The real purpose is to capture booty, silver, gold and bronze, horses and cattle or sheep, but especially: women! Again and again the phrase occurs in the epics of the fight for "the city and the women."[12]

The warriors who did these things, or boasted of doing them, are the main subject of epic poetry.

The Vedic hymns, like the poetry of the Homeric minstrels and Celtic bards, were composed by a class of artists for the praise of their heroic patrons, who stood at the head of a chiefdom stratified in three layers. The Sanskrit words for these are *Kshatriya, Brahmin,* and *Vaishva* in which the praise poets, shaman/priests in another role, occupy the middle stratum. All three layers correspond with the *equites, druides,* and *plebs* described by Caesar for the Celts of Gaul, and which have their exact parallel in the Gaelic society of old Ireland. They are the warriors, priests, and husbandmen which make up the social order of Indo-European chiefdoms everywhere.[13] To summarize:

	India	Gaul	Ireland
Warriors	*Kshatriya*	*equites*	*ri*
Priests	*Brahmin*	*druides*	*fili* (or *drui*)
Husbandmen	*Vaishva*	*plebs*	*aire*

Exceptional craftsmen rank with priests and poets; ordinary artisans are joined with husbandmen and other lower class freemen. Warriors constitute a self-equipped nobility from whose upper ranks a chief or king is elected by the sovereign assembly of the tribe, the totality of fighting men, the *teuta*.[14] Derived from this Indo-European root word is the tribal name of the Teutones and the Irish *tuath*. Rarely mentioned in heroic poetry are the bondsmen and drudges named *Sudra* in Sanskrit.

Ireland and India are the two extreme reaches of Indo-European colonization in which literacy was delayed the longest, hence the longest viability of oral literature in these parts. St. Patrick brought Roman writing with the conversion and by the eleventh century native monks patriotically recorded the Irish counterpart of the *Rig Veda* known as the Ulster cycle. Paper was introduced to India by the Moslems in the thirteenth century and the *Rig Veda* was recorded in the late eighteenth by British scholars from Brahminic sources for whom the exact reproduction of every syllable and accent was a sacred duty. This is nothing unusual if we accept, on Caesar's word, the twenty years taken by the British Druids to memorize a body of oral literature.

That the Druids were heir to the same tradition as the Brahmins is further exemplified by the heptasyllabic line in Irish verse, which is derived from the same metrical standards of the oldest known form of Indo-European verse in the *Rig Veda,* a heritage shared by the Greek meters of Homer as well.[15]

Indeed, the *Rig Veda,* the Ulster cycle, and Homer may all spring from a common literary work. Or so Robert Graves believes. (In the quotation below, he translates the title of the main epic in the Ulster cycle, the *Táin Bó Cúalnge,* as "The War of the Bulls.")

> Sometimes the similarity of Greek and Irish myths tempts us to reconstruct a lost Indo-European original. Thus the Irish *War of the Bulls* describes the hero Cuchulain's divine chariot team, named "The Grey of Macha" and "Black Sanglain," which correspond to Achilles' horses Xanthus and Balius and, like them, shed tears of grief. Cuchulain and Achilles both have a charmed spear, each mourns for the death of a blood-brother and fights desperately at a ford; but Cuchulain kills his blood-brother, who has been enrolled by fate among the enemy. *The War of the Bulls* being far earlier in sentiment and style than the *Iliad* (though consigned to writing a thou-

sand years later), their common Indo-European original may have been the *Mahabharata*, before it was heavily and clumsily rewritten, where Karna, son of the Sun-god, possessed a similar weapon and fought his own brother. I make this suggestion because, on the battle-field, Cuchulain and Achilles share the unusual characteristic of shining with a "hero light" compared to the Sun; and because Cuchu-lain is held to be a reincarnation of the Sun-god Lugh. When the River-god Xanthus attacks Achilles at the ford, Hephaestus, God of the Forge, rescues him by scorching the riverbanks and making the waters boil. Since the Greek Sun Titan Hyperion never intervened in human affairs, and since Hephaestus' use of coals from his furnace has an artificial ring, we may presume an earlier version of the leg-end in which the Sun-god comes to the hero's rescue.[16]

The *Rig Veda* was composed during the entrance phase of the Aryan invaders, whose verses about city sacking once were thought to accord with the time of actual destruction in the archaeological record.[17] In time, the Aryans were absorbed by the civilization under attack, to contribute their epic poetry to the evolving tradition of Indian high culture. Sanskrit poetry thus has something important to say about the Indo-European background of the Wessex warriors, who built Stonehenge III at about the same time the *Rig Veda* was composed. Both the Vedic and the Wessex warriors belong to the same heroic age of aristocratic chiefdoms.

Proto-Indo-Europeans and Celtic Origins

The basis for the heroic age, in turn, is Europe of the eighth millen-nium B.C., when the first Neolithic communities were established there. The Neolithic state of culture is peaceful, or at least that is the picture pre-historians like to paint. There is nothing inherently peaceful about the food producing economies that characterize the Neolithic, for when crowded by growth of population and expanding herds neighboring tribes can fight over land. Nevertheless, the mixed farming of Old Europe seems to have been relatively peaceful, where the lives of garden plants and barnyard animals dictated the round of human life. Impinging on this substratum are warrior herdsmen from the steppes of southern Rus-sia, who established themselves as the dominant element among all Neo-lithic communities in which they settled. They brought with them ev-erywhere the battle axe and the individual burial mound, with timber mortuary house within the tumulus, a custom which persisted in Europe down to the Viking age when the house became a ship and the stone bat-tle axe a weapon of forged iron. Were these people, previously called Kurgan folk, the speakers of Celtic, Greek, and Sanskrit languages among many others? Did the speakers of this great panoply of related languages originate in the steppe region and mixed forests north of the Black Sea? That is a question which has vexed scholars for almost two hundred years.

Ever since the first identification at the end of the eighteenth century of a generic relationship between Indo-European languages a search has gone on among philologists, later archaeologists and historians, to find the homeland of the people from whom these languages arose, that is, to

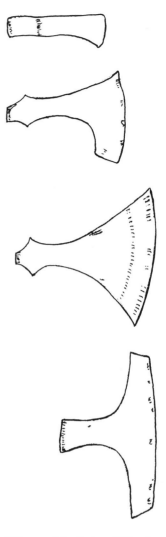

Viking axes (after Foote and Wilson).

Anatolian		Hittite*
Baltic		Latvian
		Lithuanian
		Old Prussian*
Celtic		
	Brythonic	Breton
		Cornish*
		Welsh
	Continental	Gaulish*
	Goidelic	Old Irish*
		modern Irish
		Manx*
		Scots Gaeolic
Germanic		
	East Germanic	Gothic*
	North Germanic	Old Norse*
		Icelandic
		Norwegian
		Swedish
		Danish
	West Germanic	High German
		Dutch
		Frisian
		Anglo-Saxon*
		English
Greek		Ionian (Homeric Greek)*
		modern Greek
Indo-Iranian		
	Iranian	Persian
	Indo-Aryan	Sanskrit*
		Kasmiri
		Punjabi
		Urdu
		Hindi
		and other modern
		languages of India
Italic		Latin*
		French
		Spanish
		Italian
		Portuguese
		Rumanian
Slavic		
	East Slavic	Russian
		Ukrainian
	South Slavic	Slovene
		Serbo-Croatian
		Bulgarian
	West Slavic	Czeck
		Polish
		Slovak

Major Indo-European Language Families (boldface), with some representatives. (An asterisk indicates a dead language.)

determine the origin of the Proto-Indo-Europeans (PIE).[18] By a process called glottochronology scholars have been able to trace back certain words in all the languages classified as Indo-European to specific roots. This is not the easiest process and many mistaken assumptions have been made, but the body of work shows that since many words are of the same origin they must be cultural indicators, and therefrom perhaps something of PIE social structure can be reconstructed. Words for domesticated animals (sheep, oxen, pigs, horses), barley, boats and related nautical objects and, as noted already, the horse and wheeled vehicles, all are of similar etymology. So are words for chiefs or kings, rulers of a stratified social order. The well-known correlations of the words for father—Sanskrit *pitar*, Greek *patēr*, Latin *pater*, Irish *athir*, German *fadar*, Armenian *hair*—together with words for brother (in ten different linguistic stocks) indicate a patriarchal kinship system. This kind of male dominated social structure is well known among pastoral peoples from many parts of the world. The extended family presided over by the eldest male, a clan chief, lay at the foundation of PIE society.[19]

The Indo-European tradition is that of mixed farming with a heavy pastoral element. The plants are passive, though not the animals because they are not stabled but transhumant. The background is a Neolithic economy which includes the growing of grain by a subordinate population (words relating to the soil are feminine) and the control over herds of cattle, sheep, and goats by a dominant warrior population. The heroic aristocracy we know so well in Homer owes its wealth in cattle to a tradition as old as the PIE root language itself, in which "pecunius" means holding property in cows, the word for war-band means a horde seeking cows, the root of the word "protection" means to guard cows, and the title of the chief is "cow chief," for whom the measure of hospitality is slaying cows for guests.[20]

Indo-European society is a society of warrior chiefdoms, who sought and forged metal, traveled by horse and wagon, and by the turn of the second millennium, at least, made use of war chariots. Their class system was tripartite consisting of king and his assembly of warriors, priests, and farmers or herdsmen (the word in Old Persian is the same for both). The king himself bore three titles as war chief, judge, and high priest. Even the cosmos was layered in three parts around a polar axis: male sky, female earth, and the underworld of spirits. Gods were those of the sun and thunder, their symbols fire and the axe; and they required sacrifice of horses and dogs (always sacred to female deities). Mithra was a sun god and later a radiant hero, son of the sun; the shining warrior Cuchullain of the Gaels is the descendant of that God.

Another characteristic of Indo-European society is the rapid mobility of its peoples in space and the speed in time with which they melded with other peoples they encountered, making for new cultural blends. In the east, among the Aryans, class quickly froze into caste while in the west it remained uncrystallized. The determinant factor must have been population density.

Was the society of proto-Indo-European speakers very different? We think not. For it must be apparent by now that the peoples we identify linguistically as proto-Indo-Europeans are the same as those identified archaeologically as Kurgan folk and that being the case, their homeland is a belt of country running from the North Pontic steppe country on the Dnieper River across the Volga into the Ural steppe region. That is, it lay alongside the eastern reaches of Old European culture and likely rose from it. This identification of Kurgan peoples with PIE origins has always been a point of contention. One of the sticking points is the geographical distribution of certain diagnostic words among all later Indo-European languages. Many of these seem to indicate a temperate forest environment, hence a number of authorities give a north European center of origin. Such a word is *lachs*, PIE for salmon. If salmon is a northern fish, then the Indo-Europeans must have originated somewhere near the Baltic Sea. Such is the argument that has engaged many philologists for a long time. As it happens, there is a salmon-like fish found in the lower Volga of southern Europe which fits this word just as well. And because Kurgan I and II sites always contain lots of fish bones, there is nothing here to contradict location of the PIE homeland in the combined steppe and forest environment of the same people who occupied these sites.[21]

Less conjectural is the distribution of European river names worked out by Hans Krahe; those which end in some form of -al relate them to the word "to flood" in Lithuanian, that language considered the most conservative, hence the most archaic Indo-European language. These river names seem to coincide with the area occupied by the necked beaker complex of northern Europe, hence old as Neolithic. Pushing the argument a little further, Ward Goodenough has speculated that PIE was a language widespread in Europe from the Neolithic at least, and that the Kurgan folk were only one speech community among others.[22] This is a very attractive theory, as it accords with our view that chiefdoms were self-developing all over Europe, not dependent on stratification by conquest from a single, sweeping invader. All of that notwithstanding, we are concerned with a culture complex and not necessarily the specifics of language. Indo-European languages span the European continent, they are all related, and the society that fits the linguistic evidence also fits that of the various Kurgan peoples. Those who took the Indo-European heritage to the west were the Battle Axe folk.

Yet it is obvious from all we have said previously that chiefdoms arose among the Neolithic peoples of western Europe long before the Battle Axe folk arrived. We have also seen that the invasion hypothesis, and the domination of locals by a superior culture, does not necessarily work in this setting. At the same time, it is clear that intrusive elements do penetrate older farm settlements at the onset of the Bronze Age. Both views may be reconciled, however, if our model for the spread of farming itself to western Europe is borne in mind. Kurgan culture emerged in response to certain conditions making for pastoralism and chiefdoms evolved on that basis. These chiefdoms, reflecting the same conditions,

Carved stone stela, one of earliest examples of Celtic art, Pfalzfeld, Germany. Note the cult of the head appears at a very early date.

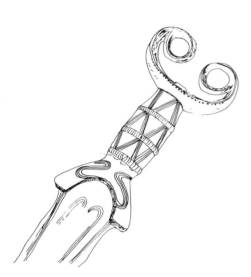

Antena sword, Urnfield culture,
Czechoslovakia.

ranged over both steppe and forest lands. Perhaps their language was exactly the same in all parts, more likely it was already divided into regional dialects. The Kurgan complex, and that is the way to look at it, not as a single culture, was formed as a result of the melding by steppe farmers with forest-dwelling hunters. When fully developed Kurgan peoples went on the move, now heavily pastoral, they ran into settled societies. But Neolithic peoples of the west had already developed chiefdoms of a communal sort and thus were the more easily dominated by warrior chieftains from the east. This should be obvious from historical evidence. Barbarians normally are not inclined to reorganize peoples with dissimilar lifestyles. The Kurgan invaders simply replaced native chiefs either by conquest, intermarriage, or general acclamation, just as the Mongols (for example) replaced monarchs in China or princes in Russia. That is exactly the way a numerically tiny group of French-speaking Normans dominated Anglo-Saxon England much later in time. It is also the means by which their minority language mixed with the native one to produce modern English. That too is how the various Indo-European languages developed from PIE, spoken by Kurgan warriors.[23]

If Celtic origins may be ascribed to the same process, the question comes down to this: What cultural tradition in the west may we identify as the product of native blending with PIE migrants from the east? In short, who are the proto-Celts taking shape under the impact of infiltrating Kurgan war bands? They can be none other than the Battle Axe/Corded Ware folk of central Europe and clearly including Beaker folk, one branch of which stems from this same region. Thus the first Celtic speakers in Britain will have been composed of those diverse groups who arrived there during the early Bronze Age: Battle Axe folk as well as Beakers of Rhenish derivation. Later Únětice connections would vitalize the mutual development of Goidelic speaking Celts on both sides of the Channel. Their descendants, after that, proceeded alike even in the absence of further migrations from the Continent during the middle and late Bronze Age.

In keeping with their continental relatives, the proto-Celts of Britain abandoned inhumation for cremation and buried the ashes in special urns. At the same time, a whole new culture associated with this burial practice came to flower in central Europe, the so-called Urnfield culture named after its distinctive cemeteries. It is the Urnfield people that V. Gordon Childe and others have identified with the first authentic Celts, whose heroic tradition dominated Europe into the Iron Age long enough to be available for Greek and Roman historians to record. Going back in time, aspects of its militant chieftainship and Druidic religion are continuous with the early Bronze Age and the proto-Celts who built Stonehenge III.

The most interesting religious feature of the historical Celts viewed in archaeological retrospect is the striking similarity between their ritual shafts, which occur in both Britain and on the Continent, and those cognate with the shaft graves of Mycenaean cemeteries. One at Wilsford in Wiltshire is close to Stonehenge, although it has no discernible relationship to that monument; among other items thrown into it was the skull of an ox. Another at Swanwick in Hampshire, dated to about 1200-1000 B.C., contains traces of animal flesh and blood in it.[24] Both of these compare with a famous shaft located within an embanked enclosure at Holzhausen, one of many found in Germany and France and which dates from La Tène times.[25] It, too, contains animal remains at the bottom. We know from classical writers that springs and wells were sacred to the Druids. Such places we can be certain were regarded as entrances to the nether world. In fact, holy wells are venerated in Ireland to this day for the same reason, which shows how conservative folk tradition can be. Significantly, Ireland remained isolated in a state of heroic barbarism longer than any other Celtic domain.[26]

Celtic culture in Britain first assumed its better known Iron Age signature by the eighth century B.C. with iron swords and new burial rites, again inhumation but this time with wagons and horses. These were introduced by fellow Celts from the Continent bearing the Hallstatt culture with its even more highly organized chiefdoms. They came speaking the Brythonic version of the Celtic language family, displacing the Goidels who retired to the north and west and across the Irish sea, where they preserved their older customs and speech in isolation. Later Celts would adopt features of La Tène, the next culture to enter Britain. La Tène, however, is rather more a new cultural style than a wholly new culture; it is Hallstatt enriched by steppe influences, which begins at a very specific place in the middle Rhine valley. T. G. E. Powell has theorized that the earliest burials exemplifying it are those of one dynastic family in wide contact with the Mediterranean and with Scythians of the steppes.[27] He concludes that the word *Keltoi* meant to Greeks the Hallstatt people, while the La Tène folk were named *Galatae*. Together they are the classic Celts of historical record, the outcome of a warrior tradition with deep roots. Because these may be traced back through the archaeological record to the proto-Celts, we find eyewitness accounts of barbarian Europe relevant to the builders of Stonehenge III, as we do the epic poetry of Ireland, which long sustained Celtic culture in some of its preclassical aspects. Homer's *Iliad* is relevant, too, because its remarkable cognates with the Irish *Táin* help widen our view of Indo-European society and enable us to catch something of its heroic spirit even in its prototypical form.

The Celts in History and in Epic Literature

Caesar is the only one of the Greek and Roman authors to describe Celtic culture in both Britain and Gaul. His account of cavalry and chariot attacks when his men tried to land in Britain in 55 B.C. is well known. He speaks of British skill in handling the horses, in throwing spears, and how the warriors even danced out on the chariot pole and yoke. The two-wheeled war chariot of the La Tène Celts is verified by archaeology in Britain and the Continent, dating back to the fifth century B.C.

Perhaps the most spectacular episode in Caesar's commentaries is his account of human sacrifice in Gaul.

Ritual shaft from Vendée, France. About 36 feet deep (after Piggott, 1968). See Glossary.

> Some tribes built enormous images with limbs of interwoven branches which they then fill with live men; the images are set alight and the men die in a sea of flame.[28]

Strabo describes both stabbing and cremation as forms of human sacrifice.

> They used to stab a human being whom they had devoted to death, in the back with a dagger, and foretell the future from his convulsions. They offered their sacrifices not without a Druid. There are also other accounts of their human sacrifices; for they used to shoot men down with arrows, and impale them in their temples, or making a large statue of straw and wood, throw into it cattle and all sorts of wild animals and human beings, and thus make a burnt offering.[29]

This holocaust, whose victims are war captives, recalls various Irish stories in which houses are burnt down around the victims of a blood feud. In one case the sacrifice is interrupted by the appearance of a supernatural woman leading a cow which she directs to be offered in substitution. The story has a parallel in the Aryan traditions of India, where in time human sacrifice had been abandoned for animal surrogates, but not among the Irish Celts except perhaps in special ritual situations. Caesar himself found nothing extraordinary in the real thing among the Celts of Gaul; for him Gaul merely had retained the archaic practice of human sacrifice once at home in his native Italy until the first century B.C., although he could not know that Indo-European charioteers had probably introduced it at the time of their much earlier invasion.

A good many of Caesar's observations about Celtic life repeat those in the lost *Histories* of Posidonius of about 80 B.C., as do the works of Athenaeus, Strabo, and Diodorus Siculus. Posidonius is known only by quotation and paraphrase in these other writers.

Here is an account by Diodorus of the Gauls in battle:

> For their journeys and in battle they use two-horse chariots, the chariot carrying both charioteer and chieftain. When they meet with cavalry in the battle they cast their javelins at the enemy and then descending from the chariot join battle with their swords. Some of them so far despise death that they descend to do battle, unclothed except for a girdle. They bring into battle as their attendants freemen chosen from among the poorer classes, whom they use as charioteers and shield-bearers in battle. When the armies are drawn up in battle array they are wont to advance before the battle line and to challenge the bravest of their opponents to single combat, at the same time brandishing before them their arms to terrify their foe. And when someone accepts their challenge to battle, they loudly recite the deeds of valour of their ancestors and proclaim their own valorous quality, at the same time abusing and making little of their opponent and generally attempting to rob him beforehand of fighting spirit. They cut off the heads of their enemies slain in battle and attach them to the necks of their horses. The blood-stained spoils they hand over to attendants and carry off as booty, while striking up a paean and singing a song of victory, and they nail up these first fruits upon their houses just as they do those who lay low wild animals in certain kinds of hunting.[30]

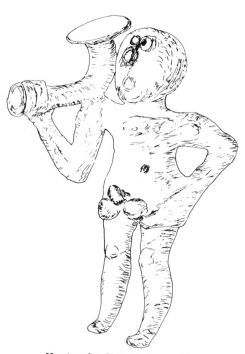

Heroic nudity. Statuette of man with weapon, Czechoslovakia.

The match between this and episodes in the Irish sagas is perfect. The warriors of the *Táin Bó Cúalnge* go into battle in chariots, and the chal-

lenge to single combat is as central there as it is in the *Iliad*. The hero
Cuchullain in his two-horse chariot, with his charioteer Láeg and armed
with shield, spear, and sword, is a Celtic warrior right out of Posidonius.

The custom of headhunting appears again in Strabo, who sees it as

> a trait of barbarous savagery which is especially peculiar to the north-
> ern peoples, for when they are leaving the battle-field they fasten to
> the necks of their horses the heads of their enemies, and on arriving
> home they nail up this spectacle at the entrances to their houses.[31]

Celtic society is a heroic society of aristocratic chiefdoms, warfare is its
business and severed heads, a dominant theme in Celtic art, are trophies
won in that business. So too in the Irish tales.

Headhunting betrays yet another connection with the steppes because portrayed in art work from that source among Cimmerians and
Scythians are trophy heads attached to saddles. The cult of the head itself
is well known and widespread in Celtic iconography. It seems to have
been associated with prophecy in Irish literature, as in the *Táin Bó Cúalnge*
when Sualdam's decapitated head is put on a pillar so that he can speak
and foretell many things. Both pillars of stone or wood and wells are the
repositories of heads; they are surmounted on the former or thrown into
the latter. One of the more grisly deposits in wells is known from Wookey
Hole in Somerset, where some fourteen skulls of persons aged twenty-five
to thirty years lay at the bottom.[32] This cult of the skull cannot be entirely
new with the classical Celts because we know that Beaker folk regularly
practiced trephining, probably to get at the brain. Something similar, perhaps, is found in an Irish tale concerning the hero Conall Cernach; he
took the brains from the head of one of his slain foes, mixed it with lime
so as to make a hardened ball of it, which he kept on a shelf in his house,
lined up with the brain balls of other heroes.[33] Whether Beaker folk did
this has yet to be determined.

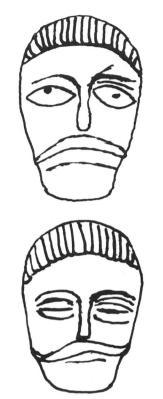

Stone heads from a Belgic burial, Hertfordshire,
England. These are simple examples of the
widespread Celtic cult of the head.

The warrior aristocracy and its deeds of raiding and fighting are the
only fit subjects of literature in the *Táin*, as in Homer. Diodorus, describing
the habits of the Gauls at a feast, makes an explicit Homeric reference.

> Beside them are hearths blazing with fire, with cauldrons and
> spits containing large pieces of meat. Brave warriors they honor with
> the finest portions of meat, just as Homer introduces Ajax, honored
> by the chieftains, when he conquered Hector in single combat: "He
> honored Ajax with the full-length chine."[34]

Posidonius describes such scenes; the Irish tales dramatize them. Here is
Athenaeus quoting directly from Posidonius:

> "The Celts sometimes engage in single combat at dinner. As-
> sembling in arms they engage in a mock battle-drill, and mutual
> thrust-and-parry, but sometimes wounds are inflicted, and the irrita-
> tion caused by this may lead even to the slaying of the opponent un-
> less the bystanders hold them back." "And in former times," he says,
> "when the hindquarters were served up the bravest hero took the
> thigh piece, and if another man claimed it they stood up and fought
> in single combat to the death."[35]

Head from Stupna, Czechoslovakia.

3-faced head from Jutland.

Head from Djeberg ceremonial wagon, Denmark.

Head from Lougrea, Ireland.

In the Irish hero tales, the champion's portion is the *curadmír*, the best cut of meat. It is literally a bone of contention. For who *is* the bravest hero present? In *Mac da Tho's Pig*, one warrior after another claims the right to carve the pig at a feast; each man in turn yields to a rival after a dialogue of boasting and abuse. Finally the Connacht champion, Cet mac Mágach is about to carve the roast after having put several Ulstermen to shame. Then Conall Cernach enters the hall, and there follows the very scene that Posidonius witnessed a thousand years before in Gaul. What better testimony for the archaism of Irish tradition!

> The Ulstermen gave Conall a great welcome. Conchobar took off his hood and waved it about. "We would like to get our supper," said Conall. "Who is carving for you?" "It has been conceded to the man who is carving," said Conchobar, "Cet mac Mágach." "Is it true, Cet," said Conall, "that you are carving the pig?" Then Cet said:
> > Welcome to Conall
> > heart of stone
> > fierce energy of the lynx
> > glitter of ice
> > red strength of anger
> > in a warrior's breast
> > a wounder, a conqueror!
> > Son of Findchoem, you are a match for me!
>
> And Conall said:
> > Welcome to Cet
> > Cet son of Mágu
> > Warrior's dwelling
> > heart of ice
> > plumage of a swan
> > chariot-fighter strong in combat
> > angry sea
> > handsome fierce bull
> > Cet son of Mágu!
>
> "Go away from the pig!" said Conall. "What should bring you to it?" said Cet. "Truly," said Conall, "that is to challenge me to a contest! I swear the oath of my tribe, since first I took a spear in hand I have not passed a single day without killing a Connachtman, nor a single night without setting fire, and I have never slept without a Connachtman's head under my knee." "It is true," said Cet, "you are a better warrior than I. If it were Ánluan who were in this house, he would contest with you. It is bad for us that he is not in the house." "But he is!" said Conall, taking Ánluan's head from his belt. And he hurled it at Cet's chest so that blood flowed from his mouth. He went away from the pig, and Conall sat down by it.[36]

Mac da Tho's Pig is one story from a body of heroic narratives, including the *Táin*, known collectively as the Ulster cycle. The point of reference in all of them is the king of Ulster, Conchobar, equivalent to the Mycenaean king Agamemnon in Homer. His champion is Cuchullain, the Homeric Achilles. The Irish Trojans are the men of king Connacht, one of whom is Cet mac Mágach. The *Iliad* is in fact a good guide to the life of the Celts of Gaul and Ireland. Homer's Mycenae is essentially an Indo-European culture transplanted into a Mediterranean setting, but not an urban one. Cattle are a staple form of wealth, the aim of much fighting and raiding in the Ulster cycle; the measure of wealth in Homer, a captured set of armor, is worth from nine to a hundred head of cattle, a prize well worth the risk of battle.

Perhaps the chief difference is that while the Ulster cycle delights just as much in court ceremonial as does Homer, Homer likes to depict ceremonies in progress, while the Irish bards prefer ceremonies in collapse. The most noble Irish heroes abandon their dignity to a youthful, rough-and-tumble melee despite the abundance of ritual niceties, especially in the feasting hall, the center of court life. Celtic feasts in Posidonius and the ancient Irish tales are peopled with swaggering, belching chieftains endowed with a strong arm and a big mouth, adored by an equally impossible following of adolescent gangsters, all hands twitching to the sword-hilt at the imagined insult, all greasy, mustachioed lips curling with snarled threats, boasts, and bombastic self-dramatization. Such may have been the rude barbarian builders of Stonehenge. Certainly the Irish tales are closer to them than Homer but we must also remember that Homer, no partisan of civic society, is just as much the celebrant of heroic society.

Freedom vs. Self-Awareness

We have not allowed ourselves to be blinded by the manifest poetic genius of Homer to think that the civilization he sings about is anything but an imitation civilization, not the real thing. For all the material splendors unearthed in the shaft graves at Mycenae, Homer cannot sentimentalize for us the barbarism of mind and action that sets off heroic from civic society. For all the perfection of his art and the parity with high civilization of Mycenaean technology, his world is strangely uncivilized, profoundly different and instructive. In Homer we may recognize some of our own particulars of honor, such as affection for wife and children and courage in their defense. But animating this is another working faith, another species of culture that also belongs to the Celtic world and to all other barbaric worlds created by the same process. Arising as aristocratic chiefdoms governed by warriors out of communal chiefdoms governed by priests or shamans, heroic societies were stimulated to even greater militarization everywhere they came into contact with their opposite.

Civilization not only creates corporate civic life within its boundaries; on its frontiers it antagonizes barbarians, making them even more so what they are, even as they envy civilization and borrow from it anything that fits their pattern of life. Heroic societies everywhere reached their greatest glory in the process of this culture contact, and everywhere they came to the same end. Striking at their civilizers they in time were absorbed by them. The waning of barbarism in Europe was prolonged into the Middle Ages, when the Holy Roman Empire stood for the moral authority of permanent and settled government against threats to public peace from a still viable heroic world of eternal war for booty and vengeance. To be sure, the citizen gained a deeper sense of a corporate "we" as against a despicable "they," while "they" had all the fun of ruthless individualism. But who would not side with Christendom in judging the nomad chieftain who in 1246 answered a papal reprimand in these words:

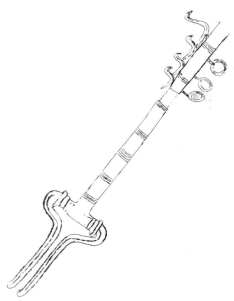

Fleshfork of the sort used by warriors for lifting meat at banquets. From Dunaverney, Ireland.

"It is said in your letter that the slaughter of men . . . puzzled and embarrassed you. We can simply reply that we are not able to understand this." Another barbarian reply, in the fourth century, to the Christian persuasion was: "If we do not plunder and rob the goods of others any more, on what shall innumerable masses as we are, live?"[37]

There is little in these replies to distinguish them from boasting about the same habits of feud and foray, raid and counter-raid, in the Greek and Irish epics. Nestor recalls his younger days of reprisal-making and cattle-lifting:

> We collected a world of spoil from that countryside—fifty herds of cattle, as many flocks of sheep, as many droves of swine, as many solid flocks of goats, bayards one hundred and fifty, all mares, many with foals at foot. All these we drove through the night to Pylos; and Neleus was a glad man that I had taken a great prize, when I went as a green hand into battle. Criers went out in the morning to noise abroad, that all those who had a claim on Elis should come in. The leading men of our people assembled and did the dividing; for we Pylians were few in number and much aggrieved, and many of us had claims on the Epeians. You see Heracles had come in former years and done a great deal of damage, when our best men were killed; for Neleus had twelve sons, and all perished but me alone. So the Epeians got above themselves in their impudence.[38]

In the *Táin* an Ulsterman tells one of the men of Ireland all the wrongs and injustice and treachery and evil deeds ever done to Ulster, and adds: "All your cattle will be driven before the Ulstermen. . . . There will be deeds of violence—mighty tales—and queens will be tearful."

Never in the *Táin* is there any hint of a different, civilized world for comparison. So too, must have the same moral gap divided the Celts from the Roman Empire. Looting and raiding the treasure and herds of one another, Celtic war bands supplied their economic needs in part by holding their neighbors to be eternal enemies with which to perpetuate quarrels, slaughter, and vendettas. Unthinkable to them the organized social context of labor among the Romans. With no superior technology, the Romans managed a higher productivity in their use of slaves (war captives exported for wine by the Celts) and in their reliance on a stable marketing system of trade and distribution sheltered by the state, with its published business laws and official standards of accounting. Such is the way of a civic society, totally alien to chiefdoms and unmentionable in their heroic literature. (Homer, however, from time to time does make civilized judgments of his characters both explicit and implicit. For example, he does say that Achilles has done an evil thing when he sacrifices twelve hostages at the funeral of Patroclus. No Irish hero would ever have such a thing said of him. This is one of the problems with Homer. How much is original and how much interpolation by later singers or scholars in Alexandria whose copies it is we have? Even if this sentiment is part of the original composition it must be understood that it dates to the late eighth century and thus on the borderlands of polis society. There are elements of the civic tradition, much of it Near Eastern, in Homer.)

Never in Homer among the Achaeans is there any intellectual reflection on the heroic ethic itself. Individualism is combined with a total lack of self-awareness. By contrast, in literate civilized societies, the loss of individual freedom necessary for corporate loyalties beyond family and tribe is compensated for by an intellectualized awareness of self, society, and other cultures. In Homer the Achaeans are the barbarians, while the Trojans are the civilized folk. Hector says that he fights for his fatherland. How unlike the heroic ideals of Achilles who fights (or does not) only as the cause is an extension of himself. Hector is the defender of the civilized world, a truly noble man; that he falls in its name is tragic, the way of an unstable world. Never can we think of Achilles in these terms; he is truly a hero of the old style, of a piece with Cuchullain.

One hundred and fifty centuries before Homer, an unnamed Mesopotamian story teller in the seventh century B.C. recorded the legendary adventures of Gilgamesh, King of Uruk, in 3000 lines of Assyrian cuneiform on 12 tablets of baked clay recovered from the ruins of Nineveh by Austen Henry Layard in 1853. Gilgamesh, who lived about 2800 B.C. in the epic named after him, is a builder of enduring walled cities.

> In Uruk he built walls, a great rampart, and the temple of blessed Eanna for the god of the firmament Anu, and for Ishtar the goddess of love. Look at it still today: the outer wall where the cornice runs, it shines with the brilliance of copper; and the inner wall, it has no equal. Touch the threshold, it is ancient. . . . Climb upon the wall of Uruk; walk along it, I say; regard the foundation terrace and examine the masonry: is it not burnt brick and good? The seven sages laid the foundations.[39]

Urbanism is precisely what barbarians lack by definition. The Akkadians to the north of Uruk described their frontier neighbors, the pastoral Amorites, as "a host whose onslaught was like a hurricane, a people who had never known a city."[40] Nor had they ever known the reflective intellect that distinguishes the citizen. The epic of *Gilgamesh* opens with these lines:

> O Gilgamesh, lord of Kullab, great is thy praise. This was the man to whom all things were known; this was the king who knew the countries of the world. He was wise, he saw mysteries and knew secret things, he brought us a tale of the days before the flood. He went on a long journey, was weary and worn-out with labor, and returning engraved on a stone the whole story.[41]

This is more than an artifact of literacy. Literacy itself is the product of civilized self-consciousness, purchased at the sacrifice of ruthless individualism. Here lies the moral difference that separates the citizen from the barbarian who is all freedom and no awareness.

This is one of the lessons of *Gilgamesh*, for the eponymous hero is a king who despoils his own city, who behaves like a barbarian (which, incidentally, he may have been!), but who learns through bitter experience to be wise and just. This comes about when he becomes aware of his mortality (he was mostly god). Cuchullain, on the other hand, has all the attributes of a god. Though he knows he will die it does not matter to him because immortal glory will attach to his exploits, thus he has neither wisdom nor reflection. Achilles also reflects on his problem, but only in the later *Odyssey* and after he is in the land of the dead. *Gilgamesh* has features of a parable on good rule and seems at the same time to be a model for the civilizing of barbarian peoples.

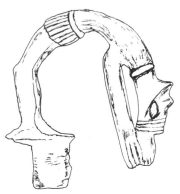

A feat of heroism in the *Táin* is Cuchullain's famous salmon leap, possibly illustrated in this figure from Denmark.

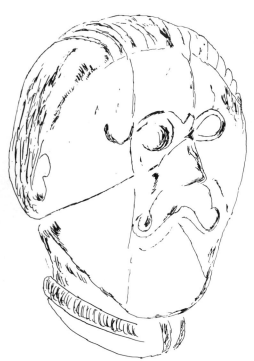

Stone head of a man wearing a neck ring or torc. Found together with bones of sacrificed animals in a sacred enclosure at Mšecké Žehrovice, Czechoslovakia. La Tène culture from about the second century B.C.

The feats of heroism in Homer, by contrast, are no occasion for intellectual reflection of any kind; they are merely described and praised, and with great art. Homer's art and poetic genius in the *Iliad* easily obscures the ideas and ideals of an unthinking brutality that we civilized men would find repulsive were we transported in time to his world, or to any locality of the heroic age for which as a whole he is its one prodigious spokesman.

Klea Andrôn—Glories of the Heroes

The first object which heroes set for themselves is to "win glory." Achilles stays at Troy to die for undying glory rather than desert his comrades. "Yet I pray that I may die not without a blow, not inglorious. First may I do some notable thing that shall be remembered in generations to come!"[42]

In *Beowulf* it is said:

> Let him who can do so win renown before death, for that is the finest thing left to a lifeless man.[43]

The *Hávamál*, or Sayings of Odin, speaks for the Viking warrior when it advises:

> Cattle die, kinsmen die, I myself die, but there is one thing which I know never dies: the reputation we leave behind at our death.[44]

Cathbad the Druid advises Cuchullain that if on this auspicious day he takes arms as an underaged boy, he would be "splendid and renowned but short-lived and transient." Cuchullain replies,

> It is a wonderful thing if I am but one day and one night in the world provided that my fame and my deeds live after me.[45]

What sort of deeds? Homer sings of *klea andrôn*, "glories of the heroes" who are savage in battle. When Hector falls, Achilles strips his body of armor and his comrades plunge their weapons into it; then, slitting the ankles and passing thongs through them, Achilles drags it in the dust behind his chariot intending then to chop it up limb by limb for the dogs. Women are the approved prize of war. After the men defending a city are slain in battle, the children are dashed to death and the women taken as slaves and concubines. Indeed, the subject of the *Iliad* is a quarrel over such victims. Theft is an honorable trade and perjury is admired, skills the god Hermes gave to Autolykos, Odysseus's noble grandfather on his mother's side, in unexcelled measure.[46] And should heroism fail, then the manliest warriors break into public tears. Agamemnon stands before his demoralized host, "weeping like a fountain."

The main themes of the heroic ethos are defilement, honor, and individual integrity.[47] The heroes in all the epics are touchy about their honor and, as indicated, if they have a chance to defile their enemies even after death they do so. The abduction of Helen is a defilement that must be revenged to the fullest note of savagery. Achilles sulks in his tent through much of the *Iliad* because of the merest insult to his integrity: he had lost face when Agamemnon took away his slave girl. That is why heroes boast about their deeds; modesty is a civilized virtue, safe only in an ordered, bureaucratized society where institutionalized roles replace individual reputation. In the world of heroes the greatest fear is loss of personal identity. This is not so much in battle; losing to a greater, god-endowed warrior is no dishonor, but to lose through mockery or deceit is. Thus Unferth is a coward who tries to impugn the integrity of Beowulf; he is wildly unsuccessful. Others had better luck. Throughout Indo-European poetry the figure of the *scop* appears, a man who can shame others in such a way that they must either go into exile or commit suicide.[48] This is the other side of the aristocratic coin, the half that emerges only rarely in the heroic epic. It is, after all, perhaps the only workable method of social control among such louts.

The Warrior's Mask of Barbarism

Heroes are likened to wild beasts. Cuchullain is "the hound of gore." Homer's warriors are "ravening lions" and "jackals." Indeed, the heroes themselves take for a self-image what they believe to be some outstanding attribute of ferocity in wild animals. The physical description of the Gauls by Diodorus is instructive. Diodorus, relying on his source, Posidonius, writes:

> The Gauls are tall in stature and their flesh is very moist and white, while their hair is not only naturally blond, but they also use artificial means to increase this natural quality of color. For they continually wash their hair with lime-wash and draw it back from the forehead to the crown and to the nape of the neck, with the result that their appearance resembles that of Satyrs or of Pans, for the hair is so thickened by this treatment that it differs in no way from a horse's mane. Some shave off the beard, while others cultivate a short beard; the nobles shave the cheeks but let the moustache grow freely so that it covers the mouth. And so when they are eating the moustache becomes entangled in the food, and when they are drinking the drink passes, as it were, through a sort of strainer.[49]

La Tène art commonly features the upturned Celtic moustache and backswept hair style, stiffened, no doubt, by lime as Diodorus reports. Cuchullain's hair is said to be three colored and standing up rigid, so that apples falling from trees are impaled on its spiky points. This description matches exactly the limed hair of the Celtic warrior. It is worth passing notice that the eyes of warriors in La Tène sculpture are portrayed large and bulging. Perhaps they are the eyes of a pastoralist, gazing upon far horizons, like those of "far-seeing Zeus" in Homer's words.

The Celtic moustache in La Tène art is modeled in shape after the tusks of the wild boar. This would not be the first culture to use the symbolism of the hunt as an index of valor in war. The lion, the bear, and the eagle still have their place in the heraldry of all western nations. Hunting, the sport of kings, is no fun against animals of no dangerous challenge. Odysseus was wounded on Mount Parnassus while hunting the wild

Life-size head from Glouchester, England. The bulging eyes suggest a far-seeing Indo-European pastoralist.

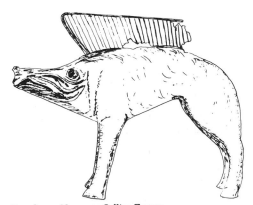

Boar figure, Neuvy-en-Sullias, France.

Boars' tusk helmets, Mycenaean period, Crete.

boar, gored in the thigh. Boars' tusk helmets are mentioned in the *Odyssey*, and fragments have been found buried in several Mycenaean sites. Beowulf and his followers wear boar-crested helmets. Roman legionaries wore helmets topped with a crest of bristles made of horsehair, but the only animal with a standing mane the helmets could have imitated is not the horse but the wild boar. The two distinctive features of that animal in Celtic sculpture are its high mane and its long, curved tusks. The long curved moustache for which the Celtic warrior is famous, not to mention his swept up head hair, is evidently intended as an ensign and battle emblem of the boar.

The difference between the Celtic moustache and the Roman helmet is that the former is a growth of the warrior's own body and the latter is an attachment taken from the body of the animal symbolized. The moustache is consistent with an oral culture, the helmet with a literate one. In a culture that lacks the written word, the only word is the spoken word, the only memory is unwritten memory, as recorded in body decoration. The human body, with its boar-toothed moustache and boar-bristled hair, is made to stand for something else, as a symbol; that is, as a reminder and emblem of the tribe's militant ferocity. The boar-maned helmet of the Roman soldier is government issued equipment, symbolizing the mission of an organized army of the state, to which the heroics of the individual warrior are deracinated for systematic butchery of the enemy by the numbers. When Roman helmet met warrior's mask, trophies of severed heads yielded to captured real estate; warfare as the personal achievement of prestige and wealth through killing and looting was swamped by the legions of Caesar, who fought in the name of territorial annexation. Feud and foray is for warriors, conquest for soldiers. The boar-crested helmets in *Beowulf*, a composition of the eighth century A.D., probably reflect the imitation by a changing heroic society of the civilized trappings of government-led armies.

At all events, only warriors in Celtic society were allowed to wear the moustache. The Druids were required to shave it off but grew beards, looking like Herman Melville or Alexandr Solzhenitsyn before he left Russia. Like Melville and Solzhenitsyn, the Druids were, as the Irish sagas say, "men of art."

Praise Poetry and the Druids

The men of art, Druids and the best artisans, belonged to a social sphere just below the warrior-aristocracy. The more distinguished ones were themselves of noble birth. According to the Posidonian authorities on Gaul, the Druids specialized in three fields; Druids proper in theology, *vates* or seers in sacrifices and omen reading, and *bardos* who, Athenaeus notes, "deliver eulogies in song." This corresponds exactly with the Irish *drui, feaith* and *bard*. The Christian monks who edited the Irish tales, however, removed most references to Druids on religious grounds, for they are particularized there almost solely as confidential advisors to petty kings on lucky and unlucky days. The classical authors, on the other hand, were themselves pagans and commented at length about the importance of a class of priests no longer highly respected back home, now that human sacrifice had lately been given up, in their own native Graeco-Roman civilization. The story about the functions of Gaulish bards told by Athenaeus, quoting from Posidonius, could have been told of Irish court poets right up to the time of Christian conversion. A certain wealthy chief, Lovernius, to win a following after the Romans dethroned his father, rode over the plains in a chariot, distributing gold and silver to those who followed on foot. Moreover,

> he made a square enclosure one and a half miles each way, within which he filled vats with expensive liquor and prepared so great a quantity of food that for many days all who wished could enter and enjoy the feast prepared, being served without break by the attendants. And when at length he fixed a day for ending the feast, a Celtic poet who arrived too late met Lovernius and composed a song magnifying his greatness and lamenting his own late arrival. Lovernius was very pleased and asked for a bag of gold and threw it to the poet who ran beside his chariot. The poet picked it up and sang another song saying that the very tracks made by his chariot on the earth gave gold and largesse to mankind.[50]

Small wonder that Irish monks censored the Ulster cycle. The purpose of a chieftain in gathering followers is usually to make war, and in Gaul and Ireland this meant taking heads and the sacrificial butchery and burning alive of war captives, all sanctioned by the praise poets. In the *klea andrôn* there is everywhere the smell of blood.

There is plenty of evidence in Homer for the court minstrel who composes for his lord's gratification by singing "glories of the heroes." Like Celtic and Germanic bards, Homeric poets occupy a high social position. Agamemnon left his queen in the care of one before he departed for Troy. Demodocus, a royal minstrel in the court of Alcinoös in Phaiacia, is represented in the *Odyssey* as singing of the adventures of the Achaeans on their return from Troy. The song is accompanied on a lyre in the same way the Teutonic minstrel uses a harp in *Beowulf* (archaeologically reconstructed as a lyre from the Sutton Hoo burial ship).[51]

The Wessex chieftains must also have kept men of art in their employ, Druids of some sort, shaman/priests who could direct the construction of monuments, endow them with cosmological significance, and preserve and sanctify genealogies, if not sing glories of the heroes.

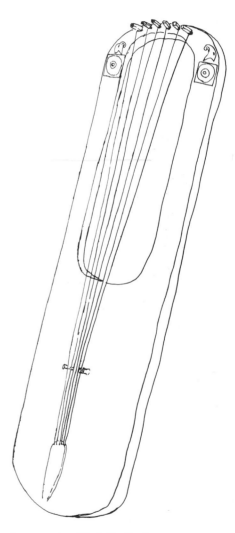

Reconstruction of the Sutton Hoo lyre.

6. Stonehenge: Parliament of Heroes

A Window on the Wessex Warriors

If in the light of archaeology, history, and comparative literature we interpret rightly the epics of La Tène Ireland, they will open for us a window onto the cultural landscape of early Bronze Age Britain in 2000 B.C. at the time the Wessex warriors built Stonehenge III. La Tène culture died out in Gaul at the beginning of the Christian era, in Britain at the end of the first century A.D. The Irish La Tène is of Gaulish origin, and would have died out in about 150 B.C. had the Roman conquest extended far enough. It didn't. Rome never came to Ireland. La Tène lived on there in isolation as the oldest surviving stronghold of Celtic culture, the one discovered by St. Patrick in the fifth century A.D.[1]

Later monks recorded a heroic literature whose bardic transmitters had drawn on an oral tradition going back at least as far as the Irish adoption of La Tène culture in the fourth century B.C. Iron Age Ireland at that time differed from Bronze Age Britain, ever since Goidelic-speaking ancestors of the Irish were displaced a thousand years earlier by Brythonic invaders. This cultural gap is not quite as wide as it might seem if we allow geographical isolation to compensate for temporal distance. Ireland is situated on the far periphery of the fundamental developments of Iron Age civilization, only a few of which penetrated. The full inventory of these developments include iron swords, horseback riding, the alphabet, money, craftsmen organized in guilds, and the politics of empire. In the Ulster cycle both Conall and Cuchullain use iron swords and one or two references to the ogham alphabet, invented under distant Roman influence, occur. But Irish heroes still ride war chariots, not horses, chariots that could have been Bronze Age weapons described by Homer for Mycenaean times. There is no empire in Ireland, only the Bronze Age politics of petty kingdoms, under whose patronage craftsmen still work. Take away iron swords and the Irish hero tales would describe the doings of Bronze Age kings. Take away more, chariots and kings, and what is left is a barbarian Europe as peripheral to the developments of Bronze Age civilization as it was to Iron Age ones, the very position of Celtic chiefdoms in the Wessex district of southern Britain at the time Stonehenge III was built.

If the tripartite grading of Indo-European society obtained in Wessex, well documented for the heroic chiefdoms of later times, then the pre-eminence of a warrior class is undoubted. The importance of a priestly class is also undoubted. Indeed, religious leaders had to precede or act with political ones in what we know to be the pattern, repeated over and over again, in the evolution from communal to aristocratic chiefdoms. The cosmological meaning built into the collective tombs of megalithic construction in Europe is sufficient evidence of this. When heroic chiefs built henge monuments to their aristocratic power (in the name of old communal ideals) and were buried in single grave mounds, priestly influence continued, if only in a subordinate role. The old politics had become the religion of the new politics. This is evident from the fact that British henges, circular places with their own cosmological significance where chieftains gathered their tribesmen for seasonal observances, were located in or near burial grounds. Or so we may deduce from the example of the classical Celts, whose tribal assemblies almost invariably met in cemeteries. Assemblies among the Irish, we know from hero-tales and Christian law-tracts formulating ancient custom, merged with periodic fairs where chiefs proclaimed laws and poets praised chiefs, and where all freemen were attracted by a periodic market as well as by sports including horse-racing. These open-air gatherings, appropriate to a nonurban people, were often held in the midst of ancient tumuli or near sacred well shafts.[2]

It is not difficult to read back into the Wessex culture gatherings of like purpose, during which new chiefs were selected when the old were superannuated or killed in battle. Indo-European traditions everywhere have it that the king or chief is elected from a council of nobility of which he is a kinsman; in the oldest substrate of the ancient Brehon Laws of Ireland the range of kinsmen for this purpose included four generations, so much more cause for contention. Genealogical reckoning is important to the validation of leadership, the one indispensable subject of any oral tradition in aristocratic chiefdoms for which there must be a specialist occupation. The Druids of Gaul were evidently carriers of this role, ancient by the time of Caesar as he himself remarks. They were also responsible for computing the rota of annual festivals and assemblies from a traditional calendar. The old tribal round of life among Wessex warriors may have some echoes in the Celtic calendar of historical times.

The Ceremonial Year

The oldest extensive sample of writing in a Celtic language is, in fact, a calendar: a fragmentary bronze calendar found at Coligny (in France, near the Swiss border) and which dates to the late first century B.C., during the reign of Augustus. The appearance is Roman in lettering and layout, but the writing is Gaulish, perhaps the work of Druids on the verge of their final suppression, but more likely the work of Augustus, who set out to bring native festivals and lucky and unlucky days within the cult of the Roman pantheon. Significantly, the bronze fragments were found at the site of a temple to Apollo near a Roman road. The calendar itself is a very sophisticated one, calculated on the luni-solar year—lunar months are squared or nearly squared with the solar year by the insertion of an intercalary month of 30 days every 2¹/₂ years—and if Druidical would suggest a history of astronomy and calendar making. This would lend hope to those who wish to see Stonehenge as an observatory, assuming a very long history for astronomy going all the way back to the proto-Celts. But the science is Roman, and the clincher is the notation here and there on the Coligny calendar of NS DS, signifying *NefastuS DieS,* a day in Roman law during which it is illegal to transact business. What is more, Celtic festivals are not named as such and the one corresponding to Samain, the Celtic New Year, is missing altogether.[3]

If we are to look for a written record of the great festivals that mark the Celtic round of life, we will find it in the so-called Brehon Laws of Ireland; they have their roots not in Roman law but in preliterate Indo-European custom. These Irish law tracts were meant to codify Christian law in native terms at the time of the conversion when Dubthacn, the high king's chief poet, dictated pagan usages in verse to St. Patrick in A.D. 438.[4] This started a process of cultural self-reflection that provides us with additional material worthy of study in the *Glossary* of the ninth century Archbishop Cormac Mac Cullenan, King of Cashel, who took it upon himself to recover the meaning of obsolete words in Old Irish. The persistence among highland folk of the many usages appearing in these sources has been described by eighteenth century folklorists, whose observations on the Beltine fires have been gathered together by Sir James Frazer in *The Golden Bough.*[5]

Beltine is a pastoralist festival, marking the beginning of the summer season when cattle are driven from winter quarters into open grazing. On our calendar it is the first of May, that is, May Day, but the Celts marked it on the preceding night. Relics of the Celtic way of counting nights and not days survive in our use of the terms "fortnight" and "senight" and in our marking of Christmas Eve, New Year's Eve, and Allhallows Eve. Beltine probably means "Bel's Fire," after one of the oldest of the Celtic Gods, Belenus, known throughout the continent and always associated with a pastoral element there. It is in Cormac's *Glossary* that the chief event of Beltine is recorded. The cattle on their way to summer grazing grounds, and men as well, are driven between two fires kindled close together by Druids, who pronounce the purpose as a preservative against disease for the coming year. Other fires were kindled during Samain for sacrificial purposes, with children and beasts as victims, if Cormac's dark allusions can be believed. If so, it would not be fantastic to recall the holocausts of men and cattle in burning wicker figures described by Caesar and Strabo, and the cleft skull of a child at Woodhenge.

Two other Irish seasonal festivals are Imbolc (first of February) and Lugnasad (first of August). Imbolc corresponds with the Feast of Saint Brigit on the Christian calendar, and beyond the fact that her name is cognate with the Sanskrit *Bhrati*, "the Exalted One," little is known about her festival. If Imbolc means sheep's milk, as it seems, then it would be the name for the lambing season when the ewes begin to lactate. Lugnasad means feast of Lug, a god associated with ripening crops, and not with a pastoralist economy in the midst of transhumance, which is when his feast date falls. The festival is obviously an imported one of later agrarian settlers to Ireland. Lug is well known as the name behind Lyons and other continental towns.

The most outstanding of the truly archaic festivals is Samain, the reassembling or gathering together of the tribe at the end of the grazing season. This is an age-old practice, older than the Irish traditions, older than heroic Europe, older than Stonehenge. The evidence for it among the very first Neolithic settlers in Britain is in Windmill Hill, where the circular causewayed ditches enclose a temporary encampment for the reunion of isolated homesteaders. Here they round up their cattle at the year's end for slaughter and feasting, a time and place for making tribal alliances.

As we have noted many times, campsites of the Windmill Hill type are continuous with henge monuments; the latter may be described as causewayed camps reduced to one encircling bank and ditch with only one or two causeways leading into them. Stonehenge I is the premier example. And because the pastoral element long remained the dominant half of Neolithic mixed farming in Britain, it would seem evident that some continuity of function as well as form must have obtained. Yet the usual interpretation of Stonehenge I, apart from the astronomical one, is that it served a Neolithic cult of the great goddess, insofar as the Aubrey holes may be taken as "ritual pits" with which the priestess in charge communicated with the underworld spirits of procreation.

But more than one meaning may be attached to the pouring of libations into the Aubrey holes. The evidence for this is associated with cremated remains and thus suggests a purpose other than that of a botanical fertility cult. Recall that Stonehenge I is contemporary with the Cursus, that the Cursus may be a racetrack, and that the footraces run there may have been conducted as part of funeral games whose origin is evidently not the Mediterranean but barbarian Europe. The implicit theory of cremation, which in Homer takes place at funeral games, may also have its origin in the practices of pre-Homeric society. The bones of Patroklos (in the *Iliad*) and those of Achilles (in the *Odyssey*) are taken from the ashes, quenched in wine, and laid in "two fold fat." Wine, fat, and grease represent the liquefiable element of life that departs the bones during the drying process of age and death; cremation finalizes the drying process. Death, by definition, is "dryness." The need of the dead is liquid, and offerings to the dead are "pourings." Perhaps this is why there seems to be an almost worldwide belief that water barriers will prevent the spirits of the dead from rising to haunt the living.[6] Over the fourth Shaft Grave at Mycenae is an altar with a tube leading to the grave underneath, a device for pouring liquid down to the dead. In Homer, the bones of the dead are given their "portion of fire" and dried even as seeds are dried before spurting into new life. The rites of death thus imply the begetting of new life.[7]

Something similar comes from the Irish *Battle of Magh Tuired*, in which the god Dan Cecht puts dying warriors in a well, sings over it, and they come out whole again, though without speech. This, again, is a function of the ritual shaft. It is possible, too, that cauldrons served in place of shafts. Vessels are, of course, the source of food and may symbolize eternal life (perhaps that is one meaning of cinerary urns). One of the most brilliant pieces of Celtic art, the Gundestrup bowl found in a Danish peat bog, shows a god placing a warrior in a cauldron head first.[8] This is thought by some to mean warrior sacrifice. More likely it is related to the myth of Dan Cecht and symbolizes a return to life.

Funeral games in honor of some tribal dignitary, cremation rites, libation ceremonies—any of these religious exercises would provide a good pretext for the annual gathering at Stonehenge I, a reassembly of the tribe as at Windmill Hill, with its autumnal cattle roundup and unlimited feasting. By the time heroic society blossomed with the Wessex warriors, other occasions for assembly would arise with the capture and redistribution of cattle taken in spoiling raids. Achilles recalls his cattle reiving days and how the spoils were driven home; how the criers went out and gathered an assembly of all who had claims against the enemy; and how the leading men took charge of the assembly and did the dividing.

> The old King chose out carefully a herd of cattle and a large flock of sheep, three hundred, with the drovers. For a great debt was owing to him in Elis, a chariot and four horses, prize-winners, which had been sent there to the Olympic games: they were to run for a tripod. These Augeias the King held fast, but he let the driver go and mourn for his horses. So the old man took revenge for their deeds and their words, and chose a mort of stuff himself, but left the rest to be divided up, that everyone might have his rights.[9]

In pre-Christian Ireland, the regular annual assembly was the *oenach*. This was the chief event of Samain, the autumnal reuniting of the *tuath*, or tribe.

Scene from the Gundestrup Bowl, Denmark.

Tribal Alliances

The *Book of the Dun Cow*, part of the Ulster cycle, says that the *oenach* was

> that period of time which the Ultonians devoted to the holding of the fair of Samain in the plain of Murthemne every year: and nothing whatever was done by them during that time but games and races, pleasure and amusement, eating and feasting: and it was from this circumstance that the *Trenae Sumna* ("three days of Samain") are still observed throughout Erin.[10]

These fairs were attended by people from various clans within a tribe and sometimes between different tribes, their eternal wars with each other held in suspension temporarily by a sacred armistice or "sword truce," as in the Olympic and Isthmian games of Greece. Each day was given to the games of a particular tribe and each provincial king had a separate house for himself and his retinue at the time.

As there were three degrees of kingship and overkingship in ancient Ireland, there were three kinds of *oenach*. Overkingship in the Irish as in every mature heroic society that has left us a literature, is the product of personal alliances between kings and chieftains. The alliance may be cemented by marriage. In *Beowulf*, the Swedish king Onela is married to a sister of the Danish king Hrothgar. Another basis for alliance is a relationship named after fatherhood and sonship. In the Anglo-Saxon Chronicles (anno. 924), a Scottish king accepts Edward the Elder as "father and lord," who may ask his son in arms to render aid when required. In the Irish hero tales, the dominant king in the alliance takes young sons of the subordinate king into adoption, a form of hostage holding, and gives them military training.[11] In all cases, these forms of alliance replace wars and feuds.

In our opinion, Stonehenge was long a spatial marker for a seasonal gathering of the tribe that built the first phase under communal leadership, but with the rise of an aristocratic chiefdom it acquired new dimensions. Eventually the place gained intertribal significance for making alliances under centralized leadership; none of the other henge monuments in the region have been sufficiently altered to serve this purpose, over and above local gatherings. All are located in or near cemeteries, but the one around Stonehenge is not only the biggest; it is also the only one to contain burials of nonlocal chiefs.

Cemeteries are precisely the location in which the tribal assemblies of the Celts were held. One of Cuchullain's friends, Garman, asks that a "fair of mourning" *(oenach n-guba)* be held in his name at his grave and that the fair and the place bear his name forever.[12] Like instances of this in the Irish sagas indicate that assemblies are held in cemeteries because the fairs associated with them took their rise in funeral games in honor of the heroes buried there. Tribal assemblies and festivities are held in the midst of the tribal ancestors. This would explain the sepulchral aspects of Stonehenge III, for example, the transept of chambered tombs carried over as open-air trilithons. If ceremonies of ancestor worship took place in front of megalithic tombs belonging to small communal chiefdoms, then Stone-henge must have defined the space in which the enlarged activities of an aristocratic chiefdom took place; there funeral games in honor of departed warriors would coincide with a general assembly, a market, and intertribal sports. The tombs of lesser chiefs from outside the area (as their grave goods show) would then be counted as memorials to living parties making alliances with the overchief.

Overlordship, as known from Irish literature, is a position held in relation to other royal persons, and insofar as it tends to break down tribal and local identities, it does so only in the highest ranks of society. Chiefs make the alliances, but the hierarchy they form under one big chief is enlarged at odds with their followers. Alliances are difficult to contract because warriors, in assembly with their chief, will prefer that he continue to lead them in raids for booty and vengeance. Otherwise, warbands have no basis for allegiance.

The War Band as Circle of Followers

As Tacitus points out in his *Germania* of A.D. 98, Celtic band leaders often are drawn into war by the restless spirit animating their retinues. He writes that among the ancient Germans,

> renown is easier won among perils, and you cannot maintain a large body of companions except by violence and war. The companions are prodigal in their demands on the generosity of their chiefs. It is always "give me that war-horse" or "give me that bloody and victorious spear." As for meals with their plentiful, if homely fare, they simply count as pay. Such open-handedness must have war and plunder to feed it.[13]

Indeed, it is perhaps a misnomer to describe the bodies ruled by heroic chieftains as tribes. They are more accurately described as war bands.

Tacitus says, "the *princeps* or chiefs fight for victory, the *comites* or companions for their chiefs." The council of elders that sit with the chief when he holds court do not represent a tribal constituency; they are simply the close relatives of the leaders, the higher nobility from among whom the chief or king himself has been elected by his wider following. The business of the war band is war, to raid others like it for spoils and glory, and for the pleasures of acting out the resentment that comes from being a target of spoiling raids. Thus do redistributing chiefs seek out material goods to pass out in order to keep their position. Initially, war bands spread throughout temperate Europe as roaming pastoral units, on the lookout for genuinely tribal communities of peaceful Neolithic farmers to dominate. In time this opportunity for settling in would be used up, and bands would turn more and more to confront each other in war-making, or to the resolution of conflict by alliance-making in tribal assemblies. At all events, the government of heroic society, centered around the petty courts of rustic chieftains, is just the opposite of civilized government, with its rulers, priests, and gods speaking for their urban constituents. In time the court society of the heroic age turned in upon itself and evolved its own form of civic society, as alliances grew and population density increased—until the kingdoms and principalities of Medieval Europe were transformed into the nations of modern Europe. In this way the heroic tradition became a part of western society as it reinvented civic order for itself, unlike the ancient Mediterranean civilizations that *began* with civic society.

A striking element of continuity is the crown worn by magistrates and archons of ancient Greece and later by European monarchs. The crown is a stylized bandage wrapped around the head, symbolizing the way a band of men are bound together as followers of the same chief. In fact, the word for band in the Indo-European languages takes in both meanings. For example, German *Bund* means band as a circle of followers and band as a flat strip of material which is wrapped, tied, or knotted around something. In Homer the word is *telos*, related to Sanskrit *kula-m*, an assembly of men that, when breaking up, is "loosed." That is, the men are bound to each other until "loosed" or untied like a cloth band around the head. The crown of the European monarch is the embodiment of a band in the double meaning of the word, as is the mayoral chain.

Indeed, the war band when assembled forms a circle, as in the *Iliad*, when the followers of Menelaos gather about him. One of the scenes of Achilles's shield is a council of elders seated on polished stones "in a sacred circle." The agora is a circular embodiment of the same kind of assembly place. One is reminded of the "circle of judgment" formed by the council of the gods in the Northern mythology. Ole Worm correctly identified stone circles in Sweden and Denmark as chief-places where the electors stood in electing kings. In Denmark, this method persisted into the fourteenth century, until abrogated by Emperor Charles the Fourth. And all is mirrored in the heavenly sphere or the ring of the gods.

It would seem that of all the writers who through nine centuries of speculation have attempted to explain Stonehenge, Walter Charleton is the one who came closest to hitting on the truth. Drawing upon the pioneering archaeological field work and personal advice of Olaus Wormius, he concluded that Stonehenge was an ancient court royal, designed for the election and inauguration as king the Viking chief who most distinguished himself from among those who led their warriors to victory over King Alfred. Allowing for Charleton's ignorance of prehistoric dating, John Dryden's tribute to him rings true:

> Stone-heng, once thought a *temple*, You
>   have found
> A *throne*, where Kings, our Earthly Gods,
>   were Crown'd.
> Where by their wondering Subjects They
>   were seen,
> Chose by their Stature, and their
>   Princely meen.

Perhaps the best recommendation for Charleton's theory is John Webb's repudiation of it. Webb in upholding Stonehenge as a magnificent Roman

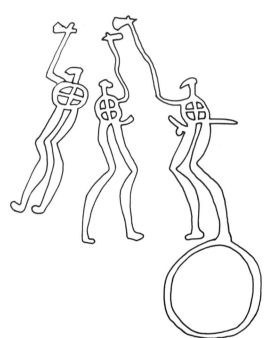

Dancing figures with axes and sun shields. Note phallic projections indicating "heroic nudity." The impression conveyed in this group is of a fertility ceremony and one that links with mythology. The axe was the symbol of the thundering god who was also a fertility deity. The ring at the foot of the right-hand figure may indicate a circle in which the dancers moved, perhaps symbolic of the sun's circular movement (after Gelling and Davidson, 1969).

temple was wroth to find Charleton comparing it with rude stone circles in the land of Ole Worm, "with such riff-raff Rubble in Denmark, as never any more contemptible and vile was read of." Charleton's interest in "riff-raff rubble" is ours exactly, and accords with the judgment of all modern prehistorians who see in Stonehenge a product of barbarian Europe in the heroic age, of which the Vikings happen to be a late extension.

Reviewing Charleton's political interpretation of Stonehenge in light of its correct place in time, it emerges as a tribal assembly place of the proto-Celts during the second millennium B.C., just as heroic society is forming in Europe as a result of Bronze-Age metal trade. A cow chief at Stonehenge then would have presided over at least one annual assembly, held in the midst of a vast burial ground in which generations of warrior/herdsmen and chieftains were interred with their battle axes and finery. Perhaps the main assembly of the living warriors was held at Samain; undoubtedly the men would have gathered for a number of purposes, not alone to continue another season of work on the structure itself. Tacitus describes the Germans standing around their chief, signaling approval by clashing their spears together; at Stonehenge, one may rightly listen for the thundering of battle axes against leather shields, for as Tacitus says, "No form of approval can carry more honor than praise expressed by arms." And if Tacitus describes the assembly as an occasion when a young man is inducted into the manhood of warrior society, it is easy to visualize each budding hero at Stonehenge receiving his first public recognition with the present of a stone ax or copper dagger from his chieftain or father or some other kinsman. If the fairs of ancient Ireland serve as historical memories, the assembly would include feasting and marketing and sporting events. Feasting would be a part of the autumnal cattle roundup. Marketing would play an emphatic role, given the position of Stonehenge at the crossroads of important prehistoric trade routes; it is a commonplace in the anthropological study of primitive economics to find trade located within a wider social, often festive, context than is the case in our own specialized marketing practices. Such is the nature of the kula ring and potlatching festivals. The sporting events could very well have been forerunners of the Greek Olympics, considering the fact that the Cursus at Stonehenge antedates the hippodromes of Greece and Rome.

Funeral Games at Stonehenge

The Cursus was built at the time of Stonehenge I by the people of the Windmill Hill culture. There is no reason why the footraces run there could not have continued to play a part in the tribal gatherings of the Wessex warriors, who after all had carried forward the Beaker practice of building round barrows, and the Beakers in turn had done this themselves by way of carrying forward the general pattern of round structures such as the Neolithic henge monuments. At all events, a clue to the way in which footracing could have figured in the annual assembly is given by an account of Celtic funeral games in ninth century Prussia. The account comes from the pen of King Alfred, who records the observations of one Wulfstan made during a voyage of geographic exploration in the Baltic, somewhere to the east of Gdansk.

Alfred says that when a wealthy man dies, his corpse is kept until the time of the annual fair, when most of his possessions are laid out in piles at some distances from a point marked by the corpse.

> Then all those are to be summoned together who have the fleetest horses in the land, for a wager of skill, within the distance of from five or six miles from these heaps; and they all ride a race toward the substance of the deceased.[14]

Certain other weapons and clothing of the deceased were reserved for cremation with him and the remains buried under a tumulus thrown up by the racers. Old Prussian, like the Lithuanian is a conserving Indo-European language and this custom might be very old indeed.

The presence of a race course near Stonehenge, itself located within a great cemetery, is enough to imply funeral games; if so, then the other events that go with tribal assemblies in heroic society.

Note that heroic society, for all its cruelty and barbarism, is more of a meritocracy than our own society which evolved out of it. A warrior may earn his place as a warrior by his valor as well as inherit a warrior's status from the established nobility; even kings or chiefs are elected, if only from the top ranks of the nobility, by the sovereign body of all men in arms. And where funeral games are played, the accumulated wealth of the hero is put up for grabs, perhaps as a means of avoiding a dispute over rights of inheritance. Nonetheless it is put up for the taking by the most skillful in some art connected with war. In our reflective urban civilization we despise war yet ask for a society in which all men may have an equal chance to strive for achievement within the limits of their abilities. These are contradictory wants from the viewpoint of heroic society, in which upward mobility is achieved only by war or by warlike sport at the cost of self-awareness and any reflections upon the ideal nature of a peaceful society this might entail. Peace itself was a "sword truce," in the words of the Irish epics, a condition forged by the strength of the armed man who keepeth his own house.

Symbolism of the Trilithons

If Stonehenge served the Wessex warriors as a tribal assembly, what political symbolism may be discovered in the layout of the monument itself? The sepulchral tradition in the overall design is fairly evident. Whatever tribal or military bodies gathered at Stonehenge for their joint celebration of funeral games and other events, the primary symbolism is drawn from a mortuary cult associated with the chambered tomb. By the time of Stonehenge III, collective burial had been replaced by individual burial. Large earth-covered tombs still continued to be built, but for individual heroes and their families. In the old-style chambered tomb, each chamber evidently was reserved for some special branch of the clan or family. The archways leading into these different chambers have been magnified and placed outside at Stonehenge as trilithons. Five trilithons representing five what? Perhaps five dynasties of aristocratic chieftains who met together in council before their respective portals. At one level of meaning, then, the trilithons symbolize the political geography of an alliance between at least five dynastic parties.

Stonehenge is surrounded by an immense cemetery which includes the round barrows of its warrior nobility going back to Beaker times. While consideration of the work entailed in the construction of Neolithic long barrows might suggest the emergence of stratified chiefdoms even

Plate 21.   **Trilithon imposts no. 51 and 52.** (Hans Schaal)

earlier, we have no evidence for the social units buried in them. The groups at Wor Barrow and Nutbane, however, comprise very special structures with elaborate mortuary houses and architecturally complex facades; here is something different. Indeed, these well-defined groups of long barrows may well have been dynastic.[15]

In addition to Stonehenge, four other major cemeteries are located in the Wessex area, five in all. From north to south they are at Lambourn on Berkshire Down, at Avebury on Marlborough Downs, at Stonehenge (the biggest one of all), at Cranborne Chase at Oakley Downs in Dorset, and at Dorchester, also in Dorset. Five trilithons, five cemeteries. One trilithon, at the heel of the horseshoe layout, is bigger and taller than the other four; one cemetery is bigger than the other four. Great archways that once led to burial chambers within the tomb of different kinship units, now lead outward to chiefly families united by marriage and by a common ceme-

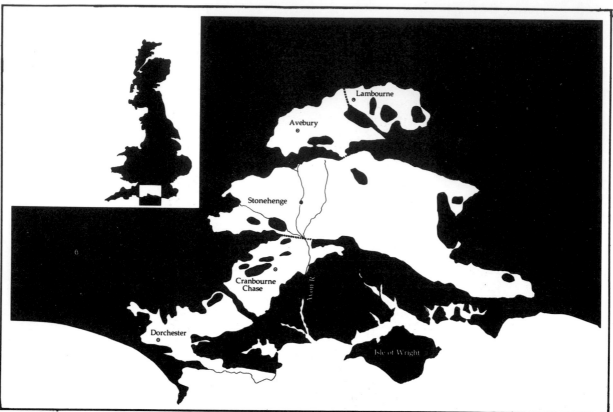

Map 9.   The five big cemeteries associated with stone circles in southern Britain. White areas are pastoral clearings on highground in the midst of lowland forest cover.

tery on the dynastic burial grounds of the dominant partner. These relationships suggest that the five trilithons in some way represent five tribal areas brought together into alliance under the influence of one preeminent tribe or war band. One "overking," to put it in the language of ancient Ireland, held hegemony over four "underkings," a relationship of moral authority symbolized in the very structure of Stonehenge; here the five political units of the Wessex warriors met at least once a year to rehearse their intertribal relationships in competitive funeral games as well as in the political business that called them together in the first place. In Irish mythology five does have sacred connotations; in the *Battle of Magh Tuired* five gods with five functions appear. This number may be related to the fivefold divisions of ancient Ireland, its four quarters and a navel at the center. All this, of course, has cosmic implications since four of the divisions correspond to the cardinal directions turning on the *axis mundi*.[16] Perhaps the doorways in the sarsen ring represent the portals of lesser chiefdoms, allied to the Big Five each after another during the course of construction. As the monument grew larger, so would authority of the "overking," whose influence would attract more and more war bands on the periphery and invite their smaller cow chiefs to participate in a single tribal forum with the big chiefs.

Plate 22. Sarsen ring imposts no. 4 and 5. (Hans Schaal)

173

Plate 23.   Another view of the same part of the sarsen ring, showing imposts no. 6 and 7 to the right. (Hans Schaal)

While we can only speculate about the parliamentary function of Stonehenge, it is less difficult to guess at the symbolic meaning of the spatial layout of the trilithons themselves. They are arrayed, to the modern eye, in the shape of a horseshoe. This is a significant perception. The horseshoe, in popular superstition, is a good luck charm to be nailed over one's door, and as such it is the heritage of Indo-European pastoral society. The horseshoe acquired its good luck symbology from its resemblance to the upcurved horns of the bull; in fact, the custom of nailing up a horseshoe over the door is a substitute for mounting the horns of a steer, still a current custom where they are available. The Celts wore an ornamental set of horns around the neck in the form of a golden torc, or as we would perceive it, a golden horseshoe. The horseshoe array of trilithons, then, is a symbolic set of horns.

The remains of both horns and hooves have been found at some Neolithic long barrows, including those around Stonehenge. The possibility
that heads or even stuffed carcasses were set up atop them should not be
excluded; according to Herodotus, the grave mounds of Scythian kings
were surmounted with stuffed horses. The great masses of ox bones found
at the forecourts of these same barrows may suggest that the animals
slaughtered there served more than a carnival of the living; in Celtic
mythology, the afterworld is a Land of Promise where the dead warrior
will feast upon unlimited herds of beef, not to say drink from bottomless
flagons of wine.[17] Perhaps Stonehenge itself was adorned with cattle
emblems, whole carcasses or perhaps only horns. These would have been
fixed to wooden dowels set three inches deep into the lintel tops of the
sarsen ring, although the discoverer of the holes in question prefers to see
them as holders for astronomically aligned sighting wands.[18] We prefer to
see them as holders for bovine esoterica, perhaps even gilded horns or
copper replicas (see Drawing 5).

Symbolic cattle horns are traceable all the way back to Old European
society. The most famous example is the horn motif in the decoration of
Cretan palace buildings, repeated end to end along the edge of every roof-
top like so many golden crenelations. But what is the intellectual content
of that symbolism? The answer can be found in Democritus, in his explanation of how horns grow on animals. Behind this ancient work of
natural history lie beliefs and assumptions about the natural world even
more ancient. Horns, Democritus explains, grow out of the head because
the life-substance of the body is drawn to the head and brains; what grows
out of the head is an issuance of whatever is within the head, an outcrop-
ping of the life-substance. Horns grow forth, watered by the same body
moistures that are lost at death, and which are supplied by the living to
"the dry ones" by means of libations. Horns, then, are outcroppings of the
stuff of life that is concentrated in the brain. In the Indo-European languages, the words for horn and brain are cognate (*cornu* and *cerebrum*, for
example). The horn of plenty, detached from the head and which supplies
the Celtic otherworld with beef and wine, is another embodiment of the
same procreative and regenerative power that causes the growth of horn
in the first place.[19]

The symbolic pair of cattle horns built into the horseshoe array of
trilithons at Stonehenge is most appropriate for a meeting place where
cow chiefs of different war bands will come together and deliberate alliances or celebrate them once formed. Cows are an important possession,
the object of raiding and a measure of wealth. What could be more important to the heroes of a pastoral society than control over cattle? And
what symbol of this wealth more fitting than the horns of the cattle themselves, the very outgrowth of power and the life-substance, the symbol of
fertility in the heavens as on earth?

It is perhaps not going too far to suggest that the eastward orientation
of the open end of the trilithon array was designed to catch the fire of the
sun as between the horns of a bull, redoing on earth what the horns of the
constellation Taurus do with the Pleiades shining between them. This

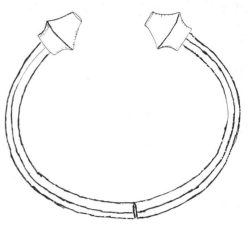

Golden neck ring or torque, Madrid.

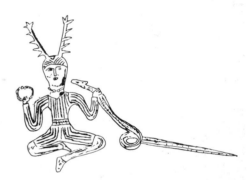

Figure from the Gundestrup Bowl holding a torc
and snake. He is normally interpreted as the
Celtic Cernunnos, the horned god.

Image of Celtic warrior wearing bull horn
helmet, Denmark.

Drawing 5.   Inaugurating a minor chieftain. (David Alexovich)

176

venerable and powerful cosmic symbolism, made immanent in the imposing architecture of an open-air tomb, would convey all the supernatural clout required to bring contentious warriors into line with their chief's political ambition to form alliances and thus enlarge his reach.

In sum, we think of Stonehenge as a monument built under the forceful leadership of some great cow chief, with one eye on the cosmos and another on the burial mounds of his predecessors, followers and allies. Chieftains such as he, archaeology reveals, belong to an Indo-European tradition known throughout Europe during the formative period of Celtic culture. In Wessex they raised their biggest monument to a tribal meeting place, a prehistoric forerunner of Parliament, that great legislature of Great Britain.

Because Parliament served as a model to other democratic nations, John Bright, one of its members, was moved in 1865 to say that "England is the mother of parliaments." But surely, his Parliament was itself the end-product of a long history of similar Indo-European institutions, beginning perhaps with Stonehenge and its assembly of chieftains, and moving through the Roman Senate—all places where men fought with words in strong debate. Improving John Bright's famous aphorism, we say that it was the proto-Celtic orators at Stonehenge who fathered the mother of parliaments.

The warrior heroes of the Indo-European tradition celebrated in its epic literature, for example, Homer's *Iliad*, were more than fierce and courageous aristocrats fighting for spoils. The Wessex warriors who built Stonehenge lacked the bronze swords of Homer's heroes, but they were Homeric for all that—militarized barbarians on the far edge of Bronze Age civilization, who fought with stone battle axes, and whose battle lust is remembered in the so-called *Iliad* of Europe, the *Táin*. But the heroics of Indo-European society throughout its conservative history were not confined to deeds of combat and pillage. Heroism included speeches leading to these actions, or to ending them by way of alliances.

Recall, if you will, how Homer describes Old Phoinix instructing Achilles in the particulars of heroism:

> You are in my charge; your aged father sent me with you on that day when he sent you from Phthia to King Agamemnon, just as a child, knowing as yet nothing of the combats of war, nothing of debate, where men can make their mark. So he sent me out to teach you all that, how to be a fine speaker and a man of action too.[20]

The Wessex warriors, whose sacred battle axes were buried with them in their graves surrounding Stonehenge, were undoubtedly no less trained to be articulate.

As Cato the Elder observed of the Celts in his day:

> *Pleraque Gallia dua res industriosissime perquitur, rem militarem et argute loqui.* They have two great passions, to be brave in warfare and to speak well.[21]

In other words, it took both a strong arm and a big mouth to be a warrior in the heroic tradition, a tradition that surely goes back to Stonehenge days, when chieftains gathered to speechify about war and alliances for peace in their great stone-built assembly place, located in the midst of their national cemetery. They would find effete the parliamentarians of our own day, who lack a strong arm and a cosmic mythos to animate it; in the West, a big mouth is all that survives of the heroic tradition.

Conclusion

What is Stonehenge? Who were the people who built it? These are questions that must be linked together in order to make any sense of the "mystery of Stonehenge." For above all else Stonehenge is a cultural monument; it cannot be taken out of its time and place. That place was the Britain of some four thousand years ago. It was not the present, the people were not modern Englishmen. And they were not scientists.

Stonehenge is the product of a nonliterate chiefdom society, presided over by warriors who dominated the local agricultural peoples but who depended on cattle for their wealth and political power. They lived by raiding their fellow chiefs in much the same ways that are described in heroic literature of somewhat later periods. When metals were introduced among them it strengthened their hold on the subpopulations. To seek the derivation of these warrior herdsmen we must look both to the east—to the north of the Black Sea and, paradoxically, to Britain itself. The rise of chiefs is accomplished in both places.

The earliest farmers of Britain, entering the islands in the late fifth millennium, flourished during the course of centuries of occupation. Their populations grew apace as they tilled small plots of land and herded their cattle. Organized tribally, they built great hillforts, corrals really, where they gathered their cattle each year to celebrate seasonal festivals of the harvest and perhaps, on the other side of the year, to the coming vernal season. Out of this activity there arose the political institution of chiefdoms and also the tradition of celestial observation. Both have to do with the building of Stonehenge.

Probably because of the growth of Neolithic populations and the size of their cattle herds (who, incidentally, denuded the Salisbury plain of most of its tree cover) pastoral tribes began to define their own separate territories and to defend them against their neighbors. Proof of the regional organization lies in both the hillforts and in the burial mounds belonging to the families and clans that surrounded them. Through the normal course of events tribal society began to crystallize around the more important families and clan heads. This was as much for defense as for internal reasons, that is, as a result of natural competition among families in the tribal grouping, some came to the fore. The process of dominance begins with the potlatch involving the meager goods and food that such a simply organized economy can muster. When the most successful competitors emerge as Big Men of the potlatch we see the beginnings of true tribal chiefs. Under the impetus of warfare and increased internal competition the chief accumulates more and more wealth (cattle, later metals) which he distributes among his followers. The chief lives in a tribal center among sedentary populations, migrates with his tribe in pastoral societies. Soon the whole social organization is ordered around an aristocratic caste which stands at one end of an imbalanced economic scale. When tribal meetings are held it is at the behest of the chief and his aristocratic followers.

Enter the warrior tribesmen of the east. The model of chieftain growth more or less fits Britain of the early third millennium save for one point. The warrior aristocracy was supplied by a mixture of native chief and migrating peoples who derive from the Continent. Immediately, they came from central Europe via the Low Countries but ultimately they originated in the steppelands north of the Black Sea. These new people were clearly chiefs since they buried their dead in single graves accompanied by the wealth befitting their station. By the end of the millennium they are ancestral Celts.

All the while chieftains developed their power, or brought it with them, the farmers and herders who constituted the main body of the population went about living their everyday lives and worshipping the same gods. While burial ritual changed from the old communal form to the new one of single inhumation, the basic ideas of an afterlife related to the rising of the sun in the east carried over. The cult of the moon, one aspect of the goddess of fertility, did also. Though the new gods of the chiefs were warriors who bore sacred axes, the same axes had some of the older fertility power of the Great Goddess. The axe symbol is to be found carved on the trilithons of Stonehenge.

With this background in mind we can see how and why Stonehenge was built. It was the meeting place of a particularly powerful tribe, probably under the influence of several strong chiefs or chiefly dynasties, who could muster the manpower to build a permanent tribal center. This was the symbol of one tribe's authority over others. Stonehenge is not a unique structure; it has many wooden parallels even in its vicinity. It is, in fact, likely one of five major circles in the region. Like later tribal hegemonies it was subject to the winds of fortune, inevitably adverse. Stonehenge could not be completed. It is a henge monument of stone not only because it was meant to be the most imposing structure on the plain but because its form is based on wooden prototypes; it was made of stone because this particular stone resembles wood and could be split like wood. It is also the same construction as the round barrows under which the chiefs of Wessex were buried. Thus the symbol of authority on earth is the same as the symbol of authority in the afterlife.

Stonehenge contains within it, then, considerable religious significance, but the exact nature of that is in doubt. Many would have it that Stonehenge is a monument dedicated to astronomical observation, to predicting the risings of many heavenly bodies and the eclipses of the sun and the moon. Much of the evidence for these conclusions is dubious. Stonehenge is astronomically oriented only insofar as it reflects the cosmology of the peoples who built it. And that, in turn, is an analog of their political and social organization. Stonehenge does seem to be aligned with celestial indicators of the four main seasons; that is to be expected of farmers, herders, and sea navigators. It is a circle because the heavens are a circle centered around a central pillar. Society is a circle. Once it was grouped around a central tribal hillfort, now it embraces the warchief and his circle of warriors. As in heaven, so on earth.

These are the "mysteries of Stonehenge." They are the secrets of a dead society that can never speak to us directly but can only offer up mute testimony to the archaeologist or at best pass the faintest of whispers through the epic literature of its descendants. There is no magic here, no alien beings, no far-ranging visitors from the civilized world. Stonehenge is the most visible remaining artifact of a primitive people; it represents their technology, their society, their politics, and their mental processes. That we can actually begin to glimpse these things is the real magic. And that is the magic of the historical imagination.

Notes

Introduction

[1] For the enormous bibliography accumulated up until the turn of the century, see W. J. Harrison, *Great Stone Monuments of Wiltshire: A Bibliography of Stonehenge and Avebury* (Devizes: C. H. Woodward, 1901).

[2] See W. Long, "Stonehenge and its Barrows," *The Wiltshire Archaeological and Natural History Magazine* 16 (June 1876).

Chapter 1
History of Ideas about Stonehenge

[1] This section is based principally upon R. W. Hanning, *The Vision of History in Early Britain: From Gildas to Geoffrey of Monmouth* (New York: Columbia University Press, 1966) and S. Piggott, "The Sources of Geoffrey of Monmouth. II. The Stonehenge Story," *Antiquity* 15 (December 1941): 305–19.

[2] Geoffrey of Monmouth, *The History of the Kings of Britain*, trans. by L. Thorpe from the Latin original (Baltimore: Penguin Books, 1966), p. 196.

[3] G. A. Kellaway, "Glaciation and the Stones of Stonehenge," *Nature* 233 (3 September 1971): 30–35.

[4] This section is based on J. A. Gotch, "Inigo Jones: A Modern View," *Essays by Divers Hands*, ed. M. L. Woods, *Transactions of the Royal Society of Literature of the United Kingdom*, n.s., vol. 8 (London: Oxford University Press, 1928), pp. 55–80; J. Lees-Milne, *The Age of Inigo Jones* (London: B. T. Batsford, 1953); and Inigo Jones, *The Most Notable Antiquity of Great Britain* (London: D. Browne, 1655).

[5] Thomas Carew and Inigo Jones, *Coelum Britannicum: A Maske at White-Hall In the Banqueting House, on Shrove-Tuesday-Night, the 18th of February* (London: Thomas Walkley, 1642).

[6] Jones, *Notable Antiquity*.

[7] John Webb, *A Vindication of Stone-Heng Restored* (London: R. Davenport for Tho. Bassett, 1665).

[8] This section is based on N. Moore, "Walter Charleton," in *Dictionary of National Biography*, vol. 4 (Oxford University Press, 1921–22), pp. 116-19; and the works of Walter Charleton, including *Chorea Gigantum* (London: Henry Henigman, 1663).

[9] Charleton, *Chorea Gigantum*.

[10] Samuel Pepys, quoted in *After Worcester Flight*, ed. A. Fea, (London: John Lane, 1904), p. 36.

[11] The nobility of John Dryden's poem is estimated in the article on Charlton in the *Dictionary of National Biography* cited above (n. 8). Less well known is the fact that his brother-in-law, Robert Howard, also prefixed an epistle to the same book, dedicating it "To my worthy friend, Dr. Charleton, on his clear discovery of Stone-Heng to have been a Danish Court-Royal, for the election of Kings, and not a Roman Temple, as supposed by Inigo Jones." Howard's poem closes with these lines, resembling Dryden's:

> Nor is Thy Stone-Henge a less Wonder grown,
> Though once a Temple thought, is now
> prov'd a *Throne*:
> Since we, who are so blest with *Monarchy*,
> Must gladly learn, from Thy Discovery,
> That great Respects not only have been
> found
> Where *Gods* were *Worshipped* but where *Kings*
> were *Crowned*.

[12] This section is based on three works by S. Piggott: *William Stukeley, An 18th Century Antiquary* (Oxford: Clarendon Press, 1950); *Celts, Saxons, and the Early Antiquarians* (Edinburgh: Edinburgh University Press, 1967); and *The Druids* (London: Thames and Hudson, 1968). And also the major work by William Stukeley himself, *Stonehenge, A Temple*

Restor'd to the British Druids (London: W. Innys and R. Manby, 1740).

[13]John Aubrey, *"Monumenta Britannica,"* MS of 1665 in the Bodleian Library, Oxford.

[14]Stukeley, *Stonehenge.*

[15]Quoted by Piggott, *The Druids,* p. 138.

[16]Malachi Mouldy [pseud.], *Stonehenge; or, the Romans in Britain. A Romance of the Days of Nero,* 3 vols. (London: Richard Bentley, 1842).

[17]G. S. Hawkins, *Stonehenge Decoded* (New York: Doubleday, 1965). This book may be regarded as an updated version of the work of Sir Norman Lockyer, *Stonehenge and Other British Monuments Astronomically Considered* (London: Macmillan, 1906).

[18]R. R. Newton and R. E. Jenkins, "Possible Use of Stonehenge," in *Nature* 239 (27 October 1972): 511-12.

[19]For a more recent example of Stonehenge idolatry, see the advertisement placed by Republic Steel on the back cover of *Fortune* magazine, May 1965. A color photograph of Stonehenge, with the sun rising behind one of the trilithons, is used to herald the scientific dependability of the company's metallurgical research. The photograph is captioned with the words, "Dependable then, dependable now—Stonehenge, a permanent solar and lunar calendar erected more than three thousand years ago." All the same, this ad speaks more truth than it intended. As we shall see, Stonehenge has closer connections with metallurgy than with astronomy.

[20]For a critique of Hawkins, see for example R. J. C. Atkinson, "Moonshine on Stonehenge," *Antiquity* 40 (1966): 212-16; and J. Hawkes, "God in the Machine," *Antiquity* 41 (1967): 174-80.

[21]F. Hoyle, *From Stonehenge to Modern Cosmology* (San Francisco: W. H. Freeman, 1972).

[22]Ibid., chap. 2.

Chapter 2
Europe before Stonehenge

[1]G. J. Larson, "Introduction: The Study of Mythology and Comparative Literature," in *Myth in Indo-European Antiquity,* ed. G. J. Larson (Berkeley: University of California Press, 1974), pp. 1-17.

[2]B. Klima, "The First Ground-plan of an Upper Paleolithic Loess Settlement in Middle Europe and Its Meaning," in *Courses toward Urban Life,* ed. R. J. Braidwood and G. R. Willey (Chicago: Aldine, 1962), pp. 193-210.

[3]R. J. Braidwood and B. Howe, "Southwestern Asia beyond the Lands of the Mediterranean Littoral," in Braidwood and Willey, *Urban Life,* pp. 132-46.

[4]K. M. Kenyon, *Digging Up Jericho* (London: Ernest Benn, 1957).

[5]O. Klindt-Jensen, *Denmark* (London: Thames and Hudson, 1957); C. A. Moberg, "Northern Europe," in Braidwood and Willey, *Urban Life,* pp. 309-29; V. G. Childe, *The Dawn of European Civilization,* 6th ed. (London: Routledge and Kegan Paul, 1957), pp. 177, 179; J. G. D. Clark, *Prehistoric Europe: The Economic Basis* (London: Methuen, 1952), pp. 33 ff.

[6]M. Gimbutas, "Old Europe c. 7000-3500 B.C.: The Earliest European Civilization before the Infiltration of the Indo-European Peoples," *Journal of Indo-European Studies* 1 (1973): 2.

[7]See V. G. Childe, *What Happened in History* (Harmondsworth: Penguin Books, 1942) among his many other books.

[8]Gimbutas, "Old Europe," pp. 1-20.

[9]M. Harris, *Cows, Pigs, Wars and Witches: The Riddles of Culture* (New York: Random House, 1974), pp. 11-34. The Indian elite, however, eat beef, perhaps even encouraging the taboo against it by way of reserving a scarce supply for themselves.

[10]E. Ishida, "Japan Rediscovered," *Japan Quarterly* 11: 276-82.

[11]C. Renfrew, *Before Civilization: The Radiocarbon Revolution and Prehistoric Europe* (New York: Knopf, 1973).

[12]Gimbutas, "Old Europe."

[13]M. Gimbutas, *The Gods and Goddesses of Old Europe, 7000 to 3500 B.C.: Myths, Legends and Cult Images* (Berkeley: University of California Press, 1974), p. 34.

[14]R. Redfield, *The Primitive World and Its Transformations* (Ithaca: Cornell University Press, 1953).

[15]Gimbutas, *Gods and Goddesses,* p. 34.

[16]Ibid., pp. 196-200.

[17]E. C. Baity, "Archaeoastronomy and Ethnoastronomy So Far," *Current Anthropology* 14 (1973): 416-17.

[18]Gimbutas, *Gods and Goddesses,* pp. 174-79.

[19]It is just possible that Old Europeans set down their religious ideas in symbolic notations on clay tablets, which may have been the precursor of writing. If so, these tablets antedate Mesopotamian writing by two millennia. For a discussion of this highly controversial matter, see M. S. F. Hood, "The Tartaria Tablets," *Antiquity* 41 (1967): 91-98; Renfrew, *Before Civilization,* pp. 176-82.

[20]Childe, *Dawn of European Civilization,* pp. 105 ff.; Gimbutas, *Gods and Goddesses,* pp. 27-29; R. Tringham, *Hunters, Fishers and Farmers of Eastern Europe, 6000-3000 B.C.* (London: Hutchinson University Library, 1971).

[21]A. G. Sherratt, "Socio-economic and Demographic Models for the Neolithic and Bronze Ages of Europe," in *Models in Archaeology,* ed. D. L. Clarke (London: Methuen, 1972), pp. 493-500; W. L. Rathje, "Models for Mobile Maya: A Variety of Constraints," in *The Explanation of Culture Change: Models in Prehistory,* ed. C. Renfrew (Pittsburgh: University of Pittsburgh Press, 1973), pp. 731-57.

22S. Piggott, *Ancient Europe: From the Beginnings of Agriculture to Classical Antiquity* (Chicago: Aldine, 1965), p. 52.

23B. Trigger, "The Archaeology of Government," *World Archaeology* 6, (1974): 95–105.

24B. Malinowski, *Argonauts of the Western Pacific* (London: George Routledge and Sons, 1922); see also J. P. Singh Uberoi, *Politics of the Kula Ring* (Manchester: Manchester University Press, 1962).

25A. Fleming, "The Genesis of Pastoralism in European Prehistory," *World Archaeology* (1972): 179–91; W. H. Goodenough, "The Evolution of Pastoralism and Indo-European Origins," in *Indo-European and Indo-Europeans*, ed. E. Cardona, H. M. Hoenigswald, and A. Senn (Philadelphia: University of Pennsylvania Press, 1970), pp. 253–66.

26Gimbutas, "Old Europe," pp. 166–67.

27Renfrew, *Before Civilization*, pp. 171–73; R. J. Forbes, *Studies in Ancient Technology* (Leiden: Brill, 1955 et seq.); C. Singer, E. J. Holmyard, and A. R. Hall, *A History of Technology*, vols. 1 and 2 (London: Oxford University Press, 1954 and 1956).

28J. A. Charles, "Where Is the Tin?" *Antiquity* 49 (1975): 19–24; J. E. Dayton, "The Problem of Tin in the Ancient World," *World Archaeology* 3 (1971): 49–70.

29C. Burney and D. M. Lang, *The Peoples of the Hills: Ancient Ararat and the Caucasus* (New York: Praeger, 1972), pp. 43 ff.

30See editorial comments in R. A. Crossland and A. Birchall, eds., *Bronze Age Migrations in the Aegean* (London: Duckworth, 1973), pp. 323–46.

31G. Clark, "The Invasion Hypothesis in British Archaeology," *Antiquity* 40 (1966): 165–71.

32G. E. Smith, "The Influence of Ancient Egyptian Civilization in the Near East and America," *Bulletin of the John Rylands Library* 3 (1916–17). Smith's best known work on heliocentrism is *In the Beginning: The Origin of Civilization* (New York: Norton, 1928).

33A. L. Kroeber, "Stimulus Diffusion," *American Anthropologist* 42 (1940): 1–20.

Chapter 3
Political History of Stonehenge

1A. Keiller, *Windmill Hill and Avebury* (London: Oxford University Press, 1965), p. 19.

2J. G. Evans, *The Environment of Early Man in the British Isles* (Berkeley: University of California Press, 1975), p. 104.

3Renfrew, *Before Civilization*, pp 228–36; A. Fleming, "Territorial Patterns in Bronze Age Wessex," *Proceedings of the Prehistoric Society* 37 (1971): 138–66.

4R. J. C. Atkinson, "Neolithic Engineering," *Antiquity* 35 (1961): pp. 292–99; C. Renfrew, D. Harkness, and R. Switsur, "Quanterness, Radiocarbon and the Orkney Cairns," *Antiq-*

uity 50 (1976): 194–205; P. Ashbee, *The Earthen Long Barrow in Britain* (Toronto: University of Toronto Press, 1970), p. 80.

5L. V. Grinsell and J. Dyer, *Discovering Regional Archaeology: Wessex* (Tring, Herts.: Shire Publications, 1971), p. 73; the standard work on long barrows in Britain is Ashbee, *Earthen Long Barrow*; an earlier work and companion to it is P. Ashbee, *The Bronze Age Round Barrow in Britain* (London: Phoenix House, 1960).

6G. Daniel, *The Megalith Builders of Western Europe* (London: Hutchinson, 1958). A useful guide to these monuments is E. S. Wood, *A Field Guide to Archaeology* (London: Collins, 1964), though readers should beware of a dated interpretation of Stonehenge.

7Renfrew, *Before Civilization*, pp. 228–36; Ashbee, *Earthen Long Barrow*.

8Renfrew, Harkness and Switsur, "Quanterness," pp. 194–205.

9E. R. Service, *Primitive Social Organization* (New York: Random House, 1971), p. 104.

10Ibid. p. 135.

11Ibid. p. 138.

12Childe, *Dawn of European Civilization*, pp. 222–28; R. J. Harrison, "Origins of the Bell Beaker Cultures," *Antiquity* 47 (1974): 99–109. See also the massive work done by D. L. Clarke, *Beaker Pottery of Great Britain and Ireland* (Cambridge: Cambridge University Press, 1970).

13Harrison, "Origins"; L. P. Louwe Kooijmans, *The Rhine/Meuse Delta: Four Studies on Its Prehistoric Occupation and Holocene Geology* (Leiden: Brill, 1974).

14S. Piggott, *A History of Wiltshire: Victoria History of the Counties of England*, vol. 1, pt. 2 (Oxford University Press, 1973), pp. 348–50.

15Ibid.

16Louwe Kooijmans, *Rhine/Meuse Delta*.

17R. J. C. Atkinson, *Stonehenge* (Harmondsworth: Penguin Books, 1960), pp. 72–77.

18M. Gimbutas, *The Prehistory of Eastern Europe* (Cambridge, Mass.: Peabody Museum, 1956), pp. 56–94. Professor Gimbutas has reiterated her identification of Kurgan peoples in many subsequent works, some of which are cited here.

19Gimbutas, "Old Europe," p. 177.

20E. D. Phillips, *The Royal Hordes: Nomad Peoples of the Steppes* (London: Thames and Hudson, 1965), pp. 30–36; Burney and Lang, *Peoples of the Hills*, pp. 82–84.

21Sir L. Woolley, *Excavations at Ur* (New York: Barnes and Noble, 1955).

22Note the illustration in Piggott, *Ancient Europe*, p. 127, for a well known example, that of Leubingen in East Germany.

²³Childe, *Dawn of European Civilization,* p. 167.

²⁴See G. Clark and S. Piggott, *Prehistoric Societies* (New York: Knopf, 1965), p. 308 for a lovely word picture of the scene.

²⁵E. Neustupný and J. Neustupný, *Czechoslovakia* (New York: Praeger, 1961), pp. 87–108.

²⁶Sherratt, "Socio-economic and Demographic Models."

²⁷K. Polanyi, "The Economy as Institutionalized Process," in *Trade and Markets in the Early Empires,* ed. K. Polanyi, C. M. Arensburg, and H. W. Pearson (Glencoe, Ill.:Free Press, 1957), pp. 243-69.

²⁸Neustupný, *Czechoslovakia,* pp. 103–5.

²⁹Ibid., p. 100.

³⁰Charles, "Where Is the Tin?"; Dayton, "Problem of Tin"; J. D. Muhly and T. A. Wertime, "Evidence for the Sources and Use of Tin during the Bronze Age of the Near East," *World Archaeology* 5 (1973): 111–22.

³¹Piggott, *History of Wiltshire.* Piggott's evidence was drawn almost exclusively from barrows dug in the later nineteenth century by Canon Greenwall. His techniques, which it would be charitable to describe as crude, have been criticized heavily by F. Peterson, "Traditions of Multiple Burial in Later Neolithic and Early Bronze Age England," *Archaeological Journal* 129 (1972): 22–40 and by others as having concentrated on the central part of each barrow, thus missing other burials within it. We now know that Bronze Age burial traditions in England were very complex. Very often, for example, both beakers and food vessels, inhumations and cremations, appear in the same barrow.

³²Piggott, *History of Wiltshire,* p. 363.

³³C. Renfrew, "Wessex as a Social Question," *Antiquity* 37 (1973): 221–24.

³⁴Ibid.; R. J. C. Atkinson, F. Vatcher, and L. Vatcher, "Radiocarbon Dates for the Stonehenge Avenue," *Antiquity* 50 (1976): 239–40; R. M. Clark, "A Calibration Curve for Radiocarbon Dates," *Antiquity* 49 (1975): 251–66. The dates come from an antler pick found in the erection ramp of one of the sarsens and which has been dated 1720 ±150 B.C. (recalibrated to about 2100 B.C.); debris from the double bluestone circle of Stonehenge II after its abandonment dated 1620 ±110 B.C. (recalibrated to about 2080 B.C.); and from an antler pick from a portion of the Avenue adjacent to Stonehenge in its third phase dated 1728 ±68 B.C. (recalibrated to about 2130 B.C.).

³⁵Renfrew, "Wessex as a Social Question."

³⁶W. B. Stanford and J. V. Luce, *The Quest for Ulysses* (New York: Praeger, 1974), pp. 126–27.

³⁷J. V. Luce, *Homer and the Homeric Age* (London: Thames and Hudson, 1975).

³⁸A. Fleming, "Models for the Development of Wessex Culture," in *The Explanation of Culture Change: Models in Prehistory,* ed. C. Renfrew (Pittsburgh: University of Pittsburgh Press, 1973), pp. 571–88.

³⁹J. F. S. Stone, *Wessex* (New York: Praeger, 1960), pp. 102–4, 147–48.

⁴⁰Cited by W. J. Harrison, *Great Stone Monuments,* p. 43.

⁴¹J. J. Tierney, "The Celtic Ethnography of Posidonius," *Proceedings of the Royal Irish Academy* 60, sec. C, no. 5 (1960): 271-272.

⁴²A. Burl, *The Stone Circles of the British Isles* (New Haven and London: Yale University Press, 1976), p. 316.

Chapter 4
The Stones of Stonehenge

¹W. M. F. Petrie, *Stonehenge* (London: Edward Stamford, 1880).

²R. S. Newall, *Stonehenge,* 3d ed. (London: Her Majesty's Stationery Office, 1959).

³T. B. L. Webster, *From Mycenae to Homer* (New York: W. W. Norton, 1964), p. 174.

⁴G. Smith, "Excavations of the Stonehenge Avenue at West Amesbury, Wiltshire," *Wiltshire Archaeological Magazine* 68 (1973): 53.

⁵Ibid., p. 54.

⁶M. MacNeill, *The Festival of Lughnasa: A Study of the Survival of the Celtic Festival of the Beginning of Harvest* (London: Oxford University Press, 1962), pp. 62 ff., 311 ff.

⁷E. H. Stone, *The Stones of Stonehenge* (London: Robert Scott, 1924), pp. 44–57.

⁸Kellaway, "Glaciation," pp. 30–35.

⁹Stone, *The Stones of Stonehenge,* pp. 77–78. For a dramatization of this method of splitting sarsen stone, see the novel by H. Harrison and L. E. Stover, *Stonehenge* (New York: Scribner's, 1972), chap. 21.

¹⁰J. Coles, *Archaeology by Experiment* (New York: Scribner's, 1973), pp. 73–74.

¹¹Ibid, p. 94.

¹²Stone, *The Stones of Stonehenge,* pp. 99–108.

¹³Coles, *Archaeology by Experiment,* p. 94; Atkinson, "Neolithic Engineering," pp. 134–39.

¹⁴Coles, *Archaeology by Experiment,* p. 94.

¹⁵Sir A. J. Evans, "Stonehenge," *Archaeological Review* 2 (1899): 313–14.

¹⁶R. S. Newall, "Stonehenge," *Antiquity* 3 (1929): 75–88.

¹⁷L. E. Stover and T. K. Stover, *China: An Anthropological Perspective* (Pacific Palisades: Goodyear, 1976), pp. 23–24.

¹⁸L. V. Grinsell, *The Archaeology of Wessex* (London:

Methuen, 1958), map II, pp. 346–47; see also Patrick Crampton, *Stonehenge of the Kings* (New York: John Day, 1968), p. 62.

[19]HMSO, *Royal Commission on Historical Monuments: County of Dorset,* vol. 2, pt. 3 (London: Her Majesty's Stationery Office, 1970), pp. 421–27.

[20]Peterson, "Traditions of Multiple Burial," pp. 22–40.

[21]S. Piggott, *British Prehistory* (Oxford University Press, 1949), pp. 129–30.

[22]Baity, "Archaeoastronomy," p. 404.

[23]Gimbutas, *Gods and Goddesses,* pp. 124–31.

[24]O. G. S. Crawford, *The Eye Goddess* (London: Phoenix House, 1958).

[25]A. Fleming, "The Myth of the Mother Goddess," *World Archaeology* 1 (1969): 247-61.

[26]Gimbutas, *Gods and Goddesses,* pp. 227–30.

[27]C. S. Coon, *The Story of Man,* 3d. ed. (New York: Knopf, 1969), p. 179.

[28]J. E. Pfeiffer, *The Emergence of Man* (New York: Harper and Row, 1969), p. 335.

[29]Evans, *Environment of Early Man,* p. 106.

[30]Baity, "Archaeoastronomy," pp. 404–5.

[31]For a discussion of Near Eastern elements in Homer see, for example, C. H. Gordon, *Before the Bible* (New York: Harper and Row, 1962); M. Astour, *Hellenosemitica* (Leiden: Brill, 1967); Webster, *From Mycenae to Homer,* chap. 3.

[32]H. R. E. Davidson, *Gods and Myths of Northern Europe* (Baltimore: Penguin Books, 1964), pp. 26–27.

[33]Gimbutas, "Old Europe," p. 203.

[34]Gimbutas, *Gods and Goddesses,* pp. 67–68.

[35]Davidson, *Gods and Myths,* p. 29.

[36]M. Gimbutas, "Perkunas—The Thunder God of the Balts and Slavs," *Journal of Indo-European Studies* 1 (1973): 466–78; J. P. Maher, "*HaEḰMON: 'Stone Axe' and 'Sky' in Indo-European/Battle Axe Culture," *Journal of Indo-European Studies* 1 (1973): 51–54; M. Gimbutas, "Battle Axe or Cult Axe?" *Man* 53 (1953): 51–54.

[37]Davidson, *Gods and Myths,* p. 83.

[38]Evans, "Stonehenge," p. 327.

[39]P. Grimal, ed., *Larousse World Mythology* (London: Hamlyn, 1965), pp. 437–39. Note illustration, p. 439.

[40]Davidson, *Gods and Myths,* pp. 26–27; Grimal, *Larousse,* p. 438.

[41]J. Forde-Johnston, *Prehistoric Britain and Ireland* (London: J. M. Dent & Sons, 1976), pp. 136–37.

[42]E. Neustupný, "Factors Determining the Variability of

the Corded Ware Culture," in *Explanation of Culture Change,* ed. C. Renfrew, p. 728.

[43]S. Ferguson, "On the Ceremonial Turn Called 'Desiul,'" *Proceedings of the Royal Irish Academy,* 2d ser. 1 (1879): 359.

[44]B. Rhys and A. Rhys, *The Celtic Heritage* (New York: Grove Press, 1961) pp. 140–85.

[45]Forde-Johnston, *Prehistoric Britain,* p. 143.

[46]R. Hertz, *Death and the Right Hand,* translated from the German of 1909 by R. Needham and C. Needham (Aberdeen: Cohen and West, 1960), pp. 101-2.

[47]L. L. Cederquist and F. Fuchs, "Antenatal Sex Determination," *Clinical Obstetrics and Gynecology* 13 (1970): 160.

[48]Ferguson, "Ceremonial Turn," p. 360.

[49]Piggott, *Ancient Europe,* p. 127.

[50]Piggott, *History of Wiltshire,* p. 354; Stone, *Wessex,* p. 108.

[51]Stone, *Wessex,* p. 108.

[52]Burl, *Stone Circles.*

[53]A. Burl, "Dating the British Stone Circles," *American Scientist* 61 (1973): 167–74; A. Thom, *Megalithic Sites in Britain* (Oxford: Clarendon Press, 1967).

[54]R. J. C. Atkinson, "Megalithic Astronomy—A Prehistorian's Comments," *Journal of the History of Astronomy* 6 (1975): 49.

[55]Burl, "British Stone Circles," p. 170.

[56]Baity, "Archaeoastronomy," p. 407.

[57]Burl, "British Stone Circles," p. 169.

[58]Ibid., p. 168.

[59]Burl, *Stone Circles,* p. 73.

[60]Hawkins, *Stonehenge Decoded.*

[61]Atkinson, "Moonshine on Stonehenge;" Baity, "Archaeoastronomy," pp. 388–400.

[62]Atkinson, *Stonehenge,* p. 50. Hawkins recently has changed his mind about his original theory and now proposes only solar and lunar azimuthal sight lines for Stonehenge. He contends that the trilithons and the outer stones of phase III were genuine sighting devices but that the sarsen circle was a later addition built for unknown purposes. Unfortunately, his sightlines are based on a building date of 1800 B.C. which is, perhaps, two hundred years too late. See G. S. Hawkins, "Astronomical Alignments in Britain, Egypt and Peru," in *The Place of Astronomy in the Ancient World,* ed. F. R. Hodson, (Oxford University Press, 1974), pp. 157–68.

[63]C. A. Newham, *The Astronomical Significance of Stonehenge* (Leeds: Blackburn, 1972); Baity, "Archaeoastronomy," p. 418.

64A. Thom, A. S. Thom, and A. S. Thom, "Stonehenge," *Journal for the History of Astronomy* 5 (1974): 71–90.

65Renfrew, "Before Civilization," pp. 240–41.

66J. E. S. Thompson, "Maya Astronomy," in *The Place of Astronomy*, ed. Hodson, p. 87.

67Thom, Thom, and Thom, "Stonehenge"; A. Thom, "Astronomical Significance of Prehistoric Monuments in Western Europe," in *The Place of Astronomy*, ed. Hodson, pp. 149–56.

68Atkinson, "Megalithic Astronomy," pp. 50–51.

69L. E. Maistrov, "Remarks," in *The Place of Astronomy*, ed. Hodson, pp. 267–68.

70See R. S. Richardson, "Headstones for Astronomers," *Astounding Science Fiction* (July 1944), pp. 104–12.

71P. Gelling and H. E. Davidson, *The Chariot of the Sun* (New York: Praeger, 1969), pp. 5, 43–67.

72D. Lewis, "Voyaging Stars: Aspects of Polynesian and Micronesian Astronomy," in *The Place of Astronomy*, ed. Hodson, pp. 133–48.

73H. H. Lamb, "Climate, Vegetation and Forest Limits in Early Civilized Times," in *The Place of Astronomy*, ed. Hodson pp. 195–230. It should be remarked that periods of warm/dry climate were not uninterrupted. To the contrary, centuries of wet spells intervened, such as the one sometime between 2000 and 1800 B.C. Nor were climatic factors uniformly localized, so that in places like Ireland there were many more cold/wet periods than on Salisbury Plain.

74Atkinson, "Megalithic Astronomy," p. 51.

75The word "Druid" in English is derived not from Celtic usage but from plural forms in the Greek *druidae* or *druides* in Latin. See Piggott, *The Druids*, p. 105. The derivation is *id* or *wid* ("wise") with an intensifying prefix *dri* or *tri* ("three"), hence "thrice wise." See A. R. Burn, "Holy Men on Islands in Pre-Christian Britain," *Glasgow Archaeological Journal* 1 (1969): 2-6.

76Burl, "British Stone Circles," p. 173.

77Baity, "Archaeoastronomy."

78R. J. C. Atkinson, "Silbury Hill," *Antiquity* 42 (1968): 299.

79Gelling and Davidson, *Chariot of the Sun*, pp. 68–78.

80C. N. Parkinson, *Parkinson's Law* (Boston: Houghton Mifflin, 1957).

81Service, *Primitive Social Organization*; Sherratt, "Socio-economic and Demographic Models."

82Renfrew, *Before Civilization*, chap. 8; J. D. Evans, *Malta* (London: Thames and Hudson, 1959).

83H. Frankfort, *The Birth of Civilization in the Near East* (New York: Anchor Books, 1956); J. A. Wilson, "Egypt," in *Before Philosophy*, ed. H. Frankfort and H. A. Frankfort (Harmondsworth: Penguin, 1949), pp. 39–133.

84K. Mendelssohn, *The Riddle of the Pyramids* (London: Thames and Hudson, 1974), pp. 141–70.

85Atkinson, "Neolithic Engineering," pp. 292–99.

86G. J. Wainwright, "Durrington Walls: A Ceremonial Enclosure," *Antiquity* 42 (1968): 20–26; Renfrew, *Before Civilization*, pp. 231–32.

87Atkinson, "Neolithic Engineering"; Coles, *Archaeology by Experiment*, pp. 73–74. See also R. J. C. Atkinson, "Neolithic Science and Technology," in *The Place of Astronomy*, ed. Hodson, p. 128.

Chapter 5
Indo-Europeans & the Heroic Tradition

1All quotations from these Posidonian authorities are translated by J. J. Tierney, "Celtic Ethnography," pp. 247–75.

2Ibid., p. 272.

3Ibid., p. 267.

4See J. Whatmough, *The Dialects of Ancient Gaul* (Cambridge, Mass.: Harvard University Press, 1970).

5T. G. E. Powell, *The Celts* (New York: Praeger, 1958), p. 17.

6M. Dillon and N. K. Chadwick, *The Celtic Realms* (New York: New American Library, 1967), p. 142.

7Powell, *The Celts.*

8Clark and Piggott, *Prehistoric Societies*, p. 308.

9Coon, *The Story of Man*, chap. 8.

10Dillon and Chadwick, *The Celtic Realms*, p. 214.

11S. Piggott, *Prehistoric India* (Harmondsworth: Penguin, 1950), pp. 250–62.

12 F. J. Tritsch, "The 'Sackers of Cities' and the Movement of Populations," in *Bronze Age Migrations*, ed. Crossland and Birchall, p. 235.

13Piggott, *Prehistoric India*, p. 259; see also Dillon and Chadwick, *The Celtic Realms*, p. 97.

14Piggott, *Ancient Europe*, p. 80.

15Dillon and Chadwick, *The Celtic Realms*, pp. 10, 209.

16R. Graves, *The Anger of Achilles* (New York: Pyramid Books, 1966), pp. 21–22.

17Sir M. Wheeler, *Civilizations of the Indus Valley and Beyond* (London: Thames and Hudson, 1966), pp. 72–83. The Harappān civilization is now thought to have declined due to a deteriorating environment and flooding sometime before the arrival of the Aryans. The cities they occupied were mostly abandoned, thus the boasting hymns of self-glory and city smashing are typical warrior hyperbole.

[18]There is a vast literature on this subject. For a recent summary see J. Mallory, "A Short History of the Indo-European Problem," *Journal of Indo-European Studies* 1 (1973): 21–65.

[19]P. Friedrich, "Proto-Indo-European Kinship," *Ethnology* 5 (1966): 1–37.

[20]Piggott, *Prehistoric India*, p. 263. One possible basis for the cow chief's hospitality may be seen at Windmill Hill. There the animal bones are all from adults, which means killing and feasting on cows at seasonal festivals.

[21]M. Gimbutas, "An Archeologist's View of PIE in 1975," *Journal of Indo-European Studies* 2 (1974): 289–308.

[22]Goodenough, "The Evolution of Pastoralism."

[23]For an example of this process, see V. I. Georgiev, "The Arrival of the Greeks in Greece: The Linguistic Evidence," in *Bronze Age Migrations*, ed. Crossland and Birchall, pp. 243-53.

[24]Piggott, *History of Wiltshire*, p. 396.

[25]Piggott, *Ancient Europe*, p. 232.

[26]Piggott, *The Druids*, pp. 54–89.

[27]Powell, *The Celts*, pp. 50–51.

[28]Tierney, "Celtic Ethnography," p. 272.

[29]Ibid., p. 269.

[30]Ibid., p. 250.

[31]Ibid., 269.

[32]A. G. Ross, *Pagan Celtic Britain* (London: Routledge and Kegan Paul, 1967), p. 106.

[33]K. H. Jackson, *The Oldest Irish Tradition: A Window on the Iron Age* (Cambridge: Cambridge University Press, 1964), p. 20.

[34]Tierney, "Celtic Ethnography," p. 250.

[35]Ibid., p. 247.

[36]Dillon and Chadwick, *The Celtic Realms*, pp. 247-48. See also T. R. Cross and C. H. Slover, eds., *Ancient Irish Tales* (New York: Henry Holt, 1936), pp. 205–6.

[37]Piggott, *Ancient Europe*, p. 257.

[38]Homer, *Iliad*, trans. W. H. D. Rouse (New York: Mentor Books, 1950), p. 138.

[39]N. K. Sandars, trans., *The Epic of Gilgamesh*, (Harmondsworth: Penguin Books, 1964), p. 59.

[40]Piggott, *Ancient Europe*, p. 78.

[41]Sandars, *Gilgamesh*, p. 59.

[42]Homer, *Iliad*, p. 260.

[43]G. N. Garmonsway, trans., *Beowulf*, in *Beowulf and Its Analogues*, by G. N. Garmonsway, J. Simpson, and H. E. Davidson (New York: J. P. Dutton, 1971), p. 38. See also G. N. Garmonsway, "Anglo-Saxon Heroic Attitudes," in *Franciplegius: Medieval and Linguistic Studies in Honor of Francis Peabody Magoun, Jr.*, ed. J. B. Bessinger, Jr. and R. P. Creed (New York: New York University Press, 1965), pp. 139–46.

[44]J. Brønsted, *The Vikings* (Harmondsworth: Penguin Books, 1965), p. 250.

[45]C. O'Rahilly, *Táin Bó Cúalnge* (Dublin: Dublin Institute for Advanced Studies, 1967), p. 164. See also H. M. Chadwick and N. K. Chadwick, *The Growth of Literature, Vol. 1: The Ancient Literatures of Europe* (Cambridge: Cambridge University Press, 1932).

[46]It is perjury, however, that makes him somewhat suspect as a hero. He could thus not be trusted to behave like a typical hero, that is, a boasting mutton-head. Here again is found a later feature in Homer; Odysseus is the hero of a trading, mercantile audience for whom Hermes the cunning thief was especially popular. N. O. Brown, *Hermes the Thief* (Madison: University of Wisconsin Press, 1947). See also M. I. Finley, *The World of Odysseus*, rev. ed. (New York: Viking Press, 1965), pp. 68–69.

[47]P. Friedrich, "Defilement and Honor in the *Iliad*," *Journal of Indo-European Studies* 1 (1973): 127–44.

[48]D. Ward, "On the Poets and Poetry of the Indo-Europeans," *Journal of Indo-European Studies* 1 (1973): 127–44. Note the same theme in A. L. Bates, "Beowulf and Odysseus," in *Franciplegius*, ed. Bessinger and Creed, pp. 88–89.

[49]Tierney, "Celtic Ethnography," pp. 249–250.

[50]Ibid, p. 248.

[51]See R. L. S. Bruce-Mitford, *The Sutton Hoo Ship Burial: A Handbook* (London: Trustees of the British Museum, 1968).

Chapter 6
Stonehenge: Parliament of Heroes

[1]Jackson, *Oldest Irish Tradition*, p. 5.

[2]Piggott, *The Druids*, p. 49.

[3]T. D. Kendrick, *The Druids: A Study in Keltic Prehistory* (London: Methuen, 1928), pp. 118–19.

[4]P. W. Joyce, *A Social History of Ancient Ireland*, 2 vols. (1913; reprint ed., New York: Benjamin Blom, 1968), vol. 1, p. 173.

[5]Sir J. G. Frazer, *The Golden Bough* (New York: Macmillan, 1922), chap. 62; MacNeill, *Festival of Lughnasa*.

[6]R. L. Hall, "Ghosts, Water Barriers, Corn, and Sacred Enclosures in the Eastern Woodlands," *American Antiquity* 41 (1976): 360–64.

[7]R. B. Onians, *The Origins of European Thought about the Body, the Mind, the Soul, the World, Time and Fate* (Cambridge: Cambridge University Press, 1951).

[8]J. V. S. Megaw, *Art of the European Iron Age* (New York:

Harper and Row, 1970), pp. 131–33. A recent theory holds that the whole of the Gundestrup bowl represents a number of scenes in the *Táin Bó Cúalnge*. The argument is very persuasive with this one exception: the "dunking" scene does not really correspond with the battle in the river between Fergus and Cuchullain. If the Gundestrup version has a *Táin* cognate, it is where Cuchullain is purified by a priest by being dipped into three different cauldrons. See G. S. Olmstead, "The Gundestrup Version of the *Táin Bó Cúailinge*," *Antiquity* 50 (June 1976): 95–103.

[9]Homer, *Iliad*, p. 138.

[10]Joyce, *Social History*, vol. 2, p. 438.

[11]H. M. Chadwick, *The Heroic Age* (Cambridge: Cambridge University Press, 1912), p. 374.

[12]Joyce, *Social History*, vol. 2, p. 434.

[13]Tacitus, *On Britain and Germany*, trans. H. Mattingly (Harmondsworth: Penguin Books, 1948), pp. 112–13.

[14]The Rev. J. Ingram, *An Inaugural Lecture on the Utility of Anglo-Saxon Literature, to Which Is Added the Geography of Europe by King Alfred* (Oxford University Press, 1807), p. 83. See also E. S. Duckett, *Alfred the Great* (University of Chicago Press, 1958), pp. 162–68.

[15]Ashbee, *Earthen Long Barrow*, p. 108.

[16]Rhys and Rhys, *The Celtic Heritage*, pp. 148, 187.

[17]Ashbee, *Earthen Long Barrow*, p. 84; Herodotus, *The Histories*, trans. Aubrey de Selincourt (Harmondsworth: Penguin Classics, 1954), p. 281; Powell, *The Celts*, p. 157.

[18]R. F. Brinckerhoff, "Astronomically-Oriented Markings on Stonehenge," *Nature* 263 (7 October 1976): 465–69.

[19]Onions, *Origins of European Thought*.

[20]Homer, *Iliad*, p. 110.

[21]Quoted by Dillon and Chadwick, *The Celtic Realms*, p. 17.

Glossary

Age (technological)   The scheme for dividing prehistory into a *Stone Age, Bronze Age,* and *Iron Age* was devised by Christian Thomsen (1788-1865), the first curator of the National Museum of Denmark, to classify the various prehistoric tools and weapons of different materials in his charge. This is known as the "Three Age System," and it was progressively elaborated by others to include an *Old, Middle,* and *New Stone Age,* and even a *Copper Age* between that of New Stone and Bronze. The scheme is all but moribund, yet its vocabulary is all we have, limited as it is. For one thing, it is strictly technological, reduced to artifacts, voiding other matters of culture and social thought. For another, it implies a scaled development of stages without reference to time and place, when in fact, cultures may exist "in" different "ages" at the same time, even to interact so as to create new cultures that have no place in the scheme. Such an example is "Secondary Neolithic."

alignments   Single or multiple rows of standing stones.

amalgamation   The process whereby cultures at different levels of evolutionary development are melded into a new culture that fits none of the simple slogans of the Three Age System (q.v.), usually the result of steady interaction, such as through trade, as when a migrant culture settles in the midst of an established one. This was the process behind the evolution of Britain's Windmill Hill culture, otherwise known as Secondary Neolithic.

arsenic   A metal found with copper, especially in the ore deposits of central Germany; a hardening agent in the casting of bronze used by the Beaker folk until the development of tin bronze.

Aryans   The Indo-European speaking people of the *Rig Veda* who migrated into India from the northwest at the beginning of the second millenium B.C.

Atkinson, R. J. C.   Professor of archaeology in the University College of South Wales at Cardiff, and the foremost authority on Stonehenge. No work on this monument can be done without reference to his work. (See Bibliography.)

Aubrey, John (1626-97)   The father of British archaeology and the first to recognize within the bank of Stonehenge the circle of pits we know as the *Aubrey holes.*

Avebury   The largest of the British henge monuments, 5 miles west of Marlborough in Wiltshire. Its outer bank encloses almost 29 acres and is broken by four entrances. The southern one leads on to Kennet Avenue, consisting of two parallel rows of sarsen stones $1^1/_2$ miles long and ending at the so-called Sanctuary, which may have been once occupied by a circular timber building of Neolithic origin, perhaps a kiva. Around the inner lip of the ditch (which lies within the bank) is a great circle of sarsens, enclosing two smaller stone circles. Beaker burials have been found beneath the base of some stones.

avenue   Dating to the Secondary Neolithic or Beaker periods, these are ceremonial trackways leading up to stone circles. The one at Stonehenge, defined by a bank and ditch, is some $13^1/_2$ feet wide and runs almost 2 miles to the Avon River. Avebury's is the most spectacular, defined by a row of one-hundred parallel standing stones, each pair of an alternate size and shape.

axe   An implement used for chopping or cutting, it is perhaps the earliest tool used by man's ancestors. Hafted axes were used in the Mesolithic and Neolithic ages for woodworking (sometimes as adzes), though at least one type of polished axe (greenstone, q.v.) had ritual purpose. The metal axe and its imitator, the Battle axe, are hallmarks of early Indo-Europeans and, as such, were clearly implements of war. The axe is also associated with the Indo-European god of thunder and male fertility.

axe factories　Places where axes of a particularly desirable stone were manufactured in the Mesolithic and Neolithic periods. These axes were traded out either as rough blanks or finished products.

banderkeramik (linear pottery)　The Danubians' form of pottery, decorated with ribbons of parallel lines forming spirals and meanders.

barrow　A round or elongated tumulus raised over one or more burials, which may be contained in a cist, mortuary house, or chamber tomb. (See *round barrow, long barrow.*)

battle axe　A shaft-hole axe, the characteristic weapon of early Indo-Europeans in western Europe. Beautifully polished battle axes, (imitating in stone, down to the casting seams, copper axes of Kurgan peoples) were buried with high status males as symbols of their authority. Indeed, few of these show signs of wear; they must be taken as symbolic implements.

Battle Axe culture　Designation of early Indo-European peoples in northern and central Europe. Also known as Corded Ware peoples, from characteristic pottery found in their graves.

beaker　A general term for a pottery vessel used for drinking or as a pitcher, it applies specifically to early migrating Indo-European people found in western Europe.

Beaker culture　Named after a pot typically found in round barrows belonging to wide-ranging groups of metal using people, the first metal users in western Europe. Probably originating in central Europe, small bands of Beaker folk migrated west by land and sea where they settled into static Neolithic communities, sometimes dominating them by their ferocity and weaponry (metal dagger, bow and arrow) or by intermarrying with the locals. In Britain, such a merger of cultures took physical form in round barrows associated with long barrow cemeteries and in the construction of stone circles, not the least of which is Stonehenge II.

Bronze Age　One of the periods in the *Three Age System.* (See *Age.*) Because the system was meant to periodize the technology of prehistoric cultures, it becomes anomalous with the Bronze Age, which of course takes in the literate civilizations of the ancient Near East. (The anomaly

is all the more apparent with the Iron Age). In Europe, centers of bronze making coincide with the rise of heroic society in the Aegean (Mycenae), central Europe (Ūnětice), and Britain (Wessex).

cattle　The wild species, *Bos primigenius*, often portrayed in Upper Paleolithic cave art, were brought under domestication during the early Neolithic, with a number of breeds, notably *B. longifrons* in Europe and southwest Asia, and *B. indica* (the zebu) in India. Thereafter, cattle became the measure of wealth among pastoral societies subdivided out of Neolithic mixed farming and retained symbolic value long after the rise of metal-wealthy chiefs. The very word for "wealth" in many Indo-Europeans' traditions is derived from a word for cow, e.g., *pecunia* in Latin.

causewayed camps　The characteristic enclosure of the Windmill Hill culture, whose concentric ditches with internal banks delimited a meeting place used by the population of a wide area for seasonal fairs or carnivals.

celt (with a soft "c")　A special term for shoe-last hoe blades and axe heads.

Celts　The barbarian peoples of central and western Europe, organized in aristocratic chiefdoms, belonging to the La Tène and Halstatt cultures, but with direct origins in the Beaker folk of the European Bronze Age and connections with peoples of the Eurasian steppe.

Chalcolithic　See *Copper Age.*

chamber tomb　The general name for tombs of Neolithic date in which any number of dead were deposited in a stone-built charnel house over which a mound was constructed. These were focal points for local communities or families whose members were interred with considerable ritual. The ongoing rituals to the dead and constant re-use of the burial vault distinguish chamber tombs from long barrows (q.v.).

Charleton, Walter (1619-1707)　Physician to Charles II. Thanks to advice from the Danish antiquary, Ole Worm, he formulated the first political interpretation of Stonehenge.

chariot　An aristocratic vehicle of war with two spoked wheels and drawn by horses and usually carrying two men, a warrior and a driver. It first appears in West Asia in about the 21st century B.C. and is associated with Indo-European invaders from the north who became the Hyksos, Kassites, and Hittites. The Aryans took it to India, and the forebears of the Mycenaeans introduced it to Europe, where it spread widely and rapidly, and where later it gave dominance to the La Tène Celts before their defeat by the legions of Caesar.

chiefdom   On a scale of social organization between tribe and state, the chiefdom may best be described as a hierarchical society based on status, with a chief as political leader and main redistributer of goods and social prestige. An ambiguous typology at best, and perhaps not truly a step in the process of cultural evolution, several types of chiefdoms may be discerned, ranging from communal through petty to aristocratic.

Childe, V. Gordon (1892-1957)   The Australian Professor of Archaeology at London University (formerly at Edinburgh University) who made a large synthesis of prehistoric material from the whole of Europe and whose interest in human society, recognized behind mere artifacts, remains the inspiration for all workers in the field of cultural interpretation—this despite the radiocarbon revolution, which has reversed the arrows of cultural diffusion he had directed from the ancient Near East toward Europe.

Cimmerians   Warrior herdsmen of the Russian steppes, successors to the Kurgan homeland, who were driven out by the Scythians in the 8th century B.C., whereupon they entered Anatolia and fought many wars with civilized Near Eastern empires, notably Assyria.

cist   A box-shaped burial container of Mesolithic origin, made of stone slabs set on edge, covered by a single capstone, and sunk beneath the ground. Carried over into Neolithic tombs in Europe, it is built on the ground surface and covered by a barrow.

civil society   A state-organized society; a civilized end product of evolutionary change out of tribal society, either directly out of Neolithic townships (as in West Asia) or indirectly out of Neolithic villages through chiefdoms imposed by warrior herdsman (as in Europe).

civilization   A level of human social organization that produces an elite-focused, high cultural tradition. It represents new levels of social organization, the city and state, and technology such as writing, wheelmaking, and metallurgy.

collective tombs   See *chamber tombs*.

copper   Like gold, one of the first metals used by man, because it can be found in a pure state with no need for smelting; only later was it extracted from a variety of ores. The molten form, produced by smelting, led to casting, but not without flaws. These were remedied only by alloying copper with arsenic or tin to produce bronze.

Copper Age   Supposedly a period at the end of the Stone Age before the start of the Bronze Age when copper was the main raw material for tools and weapons. (See *Age*.)

The term *Chalcolithic,* implying joint use of stone and copper, is no better, since stone continued in use beside bronze and even iron. The fact is, copper was alloyed to produce bronze almost as soon as it was smelted, except in Old Europe—if the term has any validity at all, this is the only place it would apply.

corded ware   A pot style. Decorated by impressing cords around the neck of the vessel, it is typically found in single-graves associated with early Indo-Europeans. Also, capitalized, a variant name for Battle Axe culture.

Cuçuteni culture   The Romanian branch of the Tripolye culture, thus part of the Old European culture complex.

culture   The sum total of procedures by which humans adapt to their environment and which is learned by one generation after another. A specific culture is an instance of such procedures at any given place and period of time. Archaeologically, a culture is the total assemblage of remains belonging to a people or group of related peoples.

cultural evolution   Cumulative change resulting from one or more historical processes, including local invention of new traits (be they tools, beliefs, or social institutions), the borrowing of traits by way of diffusion, the amalgamation of traits or peoples by way of trade or other forms of contact, or the stratification of society by way of conquest.

cursus   A type of monument, named by William Stukeley, found only in Britain and constructed during the later Neolithic, although use may have continued long after that. It consists of a long avenue embanked on both sides and around the ends, with quarry ditches on the outside. Two are located in the Stonehenge region, where the Greater Cursus measures 3000 by 110 feet; the largest one of all, in Dorset, runs over six miles.

cyclopean masonry   Walls built of large, irregular but close-fitting stones, as those walls around the hill-top palace compound at Mycenae, so called by later Greeks who fancied that such walls could only have been made by giant Cyclops.

Danubian culture   The first farming culture in central Europe, based on slash and burn cultivation of the easily tilled loessial soils occurring there. Its diagnostic pottery is Banderkermik and its most famous site is at Köln-Lindenthal.

diffusion   Process whereby culture traits pass from one group to another.

Dolní Věstonice   A camping site of Upper Paleolithic mammoth hunters in southern Moravia indicating long phases of occupation in semi-permanent houses in association with a burial ground. Thus is the settled life of Neolithic villagers adumbrated by a hunting culture favored by a supply of game almost as reliable on the spot as domesticated food.

double axe   A shaft-hole axe with two opposed cutting edges, especially those in bronze of the Minoans. It acquired religious significance besides its functional use, drawing its common symbolism from that of the great goddess in Old European Culture.

Druids   Shaman/priests in the service of Celtic warrior chiefs; by extension, similar religious specialists among the proto-Celts and other early Indo-European peoples.

Durrington Walls   A large, twin-entrance henge monument, about 1500 feet in diameter, within 2 miles of Stonehenge, and close by the Avon river. Its reconstruction is Secondary Neolithic, but, like many other henges in the region, it attracted the interest of Beaker immigrants, shards of whose pottery have been found there. Within are several sets of post holes, suggesting roofed and walled buildings. Possibly it was the center of a tribal territory.

Ertebølle   The climax of Mesolithic culture in the west Baltic region, whose late phase is marked by the introduction of pottery as a result of contact with newly arrived TRB farmers to the south, but which Neolithic phase may otherwise have been independently developed. (Its huge kitchen middens indicate a settled life of long standing.)

Evans, Sir Arthur (1851-1941)   Keeper of the Ashmolean Museum, Oxford, in 1884, he later turned to field work in Crete, where he began excavations at Knossos in 1899 at his own expense. During the next thirty-five years he laid bare most of what we now know of Minoan palace culture.

food vessel   A funerary vessel found with cremations (now subsumed under the name of grooved ware) which lends its name (capitalized) to an early Bronze Age culture originating in northern Britian. Resulting from a fusion of Beaker folk and Secondary Neolithic peoples, members of this amalgamated culture migrated to various other parts of the Isles.

funnel beaker   A necked beaker, not related to the Beaker culture. The original German word, *Trichterbecher* (abbreviated to TRB) is diagnostic of the Neolithic cultures of northern Europe. This tradition is probably related to that of the Danubian people, though the pottery style is very different.

Gimbutas, Marija   Professor of European Archaeology at the University of California, Los Angeles, who, in working out the two major layers of European prehistory, Old European and Indo-European, not only conceived the former, but was a major figure in establishing the latter as a cultural complex, as well—in defiance of most professional opinion that Indo-European is a linguistic concept merely, never to be a cultural concept.

Glastonbury   A lake village in Somerset, which has yielded more data on the British Iron Age of La Tène times than any other site.

great goddess   A single fertility deity of multiple aspect, or a group of deities glossed as one, associated with all Near Eastern and European Neolithic cultures. Symbols related to her cult include female figurines, eye-motifs, chevrons, lozenges, and spirial meanders. Elements of the goddess were remembered in later mythologies, e.g., the Greek Demeter. Considerable nonsense has been written about such a goddess, and the reader should be advised that the deity may have been only one among many in the Neolithic; nor does worship of her imply a matriarchal social organization.

greenstone   A lay expression comprising a variety of rocks the geologist would distinguish as serpentine, jadeite, nephrite, and others. Nonetheless, prehistoric Europeans used these materials interchangeably for making the best quality of polished stone axes, just as jade was popular among the Chinese and Mayans.

Hallstatt   The earlier period of the European Iron Age, named after its type site in Austria, 30 miles east of Salzburg.

Hawkins, Gerald S.   Chairman of the Department of Astronomy at Boston University in association with the Smithsonian Astrophysical Observatory in Cambridge, Massachusetts, his theory of Stonehenge as a "Neolithic computer," although largely discredited, did stimulate research into the matter of prehistoric "science."

henge   A class of monument found only in the British Isles, defined in 1932 by Thomas Kendrick. Henges consist of a circular area, from 150 to 1,700 feet in diameter, delimited by an embankment whose quarry is normally outside it. Some have a single entrance, others have two entrances opposite each other (as at Durrington Walls). Most are late Neolithic. Those in southern England, to judge from their proximity to causewayed camps such as Windmill Hill, seem to be simplified or formalized versions of these hilltop sites. Many henges have extra features such as burials, pits, stone circles (e.g., Avebury and Stonehenge) or post holes for free standing timber uprights (as at Woodhenge). The secondary structure now standing at Stonehenge is Bronze Age, erected by the Wessex culture, which replaced that erected in the early Bronze Age by the Beaker culture.

Heroic Age   The time whensoever aristocratic chiefdoms flourished in barbarian Europe, and known in such literary sources as *Beowulf,* the *Táin,* and the *Iliad.*

heroic society   Indo-European society during the Heroic Age, with its tripartite layering.

Holocene epoch   The second epoch of the Quaternary period, commencing with the end of the Pleistocene epoch, and during which most of the present species of mammalian fauna arose.

Homo erectus   The first humans, who lived up into the middle Pleistocene, and whose cultures occupy the Lower Paleolithic.

Homo sapiens   The successor species of *H. erectus,* appearing about 400,000 years ago with transitional forms such as Swanscombe Man in Britain (who is sometimes, as in this book, classed with *erectus*). Modern *sapiens,* however, does not appear in the fossil record until the later part of the upper Pleistocene, and its culture is associated with the Upper Paleolithic.

horse   A widespread game animal in the Pleistocene, in post-glacial times it was restricted to the Eurasian steppes and forests. Its domestication by nomadic Kurgan herdsmen occurred much later than did the domestication of cattle, sheep, goats, and pigs by Neolithic settlers elsewhere. This was the breed of horse trained to pull Indo-European war chariots, which were not replaced by mounted warriors or knights until a new variety of sufficient strength had been bred in late and post-Roman times. Its use for commercial draft and plow agriculture came much later still. All the same, admiration for horses by Europeans has outlasted that for cattle. A man of honor was lately still a "horseman," that is, a *cavalier,* a *chevalier,* a *ritter,* a *caballero.* But the Western passion for mobility persists in the use of the automobile, and perhaps the honor-object has been switched from horse to car.

Ice Age   See *Pleistocene.*

Indo-European   A group of languages, first recognized by William Jones in 1786, originating in the Kurgan homeland and carried out from there by folk movements during the second millenium B.C. Now also a specific group of cultures with a common heritage.

Iron Age   Strictly speaking, Hallstatt and Le Tène, although in this book we allow for its full development under the Roman empire. At this point, the technological "Age" system, designed for the periodization of prehistory, overlaps with written history. In fact, the Iron Age may be said to have lasted up until the Industrial Revolution. The system is thus an awkward one at best.

Jarmo   An early Neolithic village in the Zagros mountains (bordering the Mesopotamian valley), excavated by Prof. Robert Braidwood, sited in a region where food production (the Neolithic) may first have emerged out of food collecting (the Mesolithic).

kiva   An underground chamber, found in Pueblo villages of the American southwest, used as a men's clubhouse and for performance of religious ceremonies. In a society lacking overt political leadership, the *kiva* brought a village's elders together on a regular basis to form a consensus on informal social controls. We translate the *kiva* into a cross-cultural concept for any meeting place in a Neolithic village or township of villages where the secular matters of society are brought under informal study in concert with religious observances under shamanistic guidance. Thus do we speculate on *kiva* controls among the Neolithic townships of Old Europe and even postulate *kiva* housing on the grounds of the Sanctuary at Avebury and within the confines of Durrington Walls.

Knossos   A major palace site of the Minoans, on the north central coast of Crete. Its excavation was the life work of Sir Arthur Evans, from 1899 to 1935.

Köln-Lindenthal   A well-known excavated village of the Danubian culture, located on the outskirts of Cologne, Germany. The post holes and house plans reveal a large settlement of substantial timber houses that were abandoned once the fertility of the soil was exhausted. After the land lay fallow for sufficient time, in the course of conducting slash and burn agriculture, the site was re-occupied and the village rebuilt. This cycle was repeated seven times over widely separated phases of occupation at Köln-Lindenthal.

kurgan   Russian word for barrow which covers single-grave burials, used by Marija Gimbutas to denote early Indo-European burials. By extension, Kurgan culture is the life-way of the various Kurgan peoples who built these barrows.

Kuro-Araxes Culture   An early bronze using culture, located in the Caucasus region, from whom early Indo-Europeans (Kurgan folk) obtained their metallurgy.

La Tène   A later period of the European Iron Age, whose type site is a votive deposit in the shallow water at the east end of Lake Nuechâtel in Switzerland. Its art style, the beautiful curvilinear, was influenced by Scythian art from the steppelands to the east.

linear pottery   See *Banderkeramic.*

loess   A fine, wind-deposited soil composed of silt-sized particles. Belts of this soil cross Europe and were first exploited agriculturally by the Danubian farmers.

long barrow   Long earthen or chalk mounds, anywhere from 150 to 300 feet in length and 30 to 100 feet wide, which covered wooden or turf mortuary houses, dating to the Neolithic period (Windmill Hill). These collective tombs are found in southern and eastern England and seem to be modelled on the longhouse of northern Europe. Although the mortuary house was likely used as a charnel house over a period of time, once covered with earth it was permanently sealed. This practice differs from that of the chamber tombs.

Lower Paleolithic   The hunting cultures of *Homo erectus* and early *H. sapiens,* associated in Europe with Acheulian technology.

Maglemosian   The Mesolithic culture of the north European plain, adapted to a forest and lakeside environment and marked by woodworking tools such as knapped stone axes and adzes. Its earliest manifestation is known from the Star Carr site in northern England.

Maikop   One of the richest of the Kurgan burials, located in the northern Caucasus, dating to about the early or middle of the third millenium B.C. The royal burial within the timbered mortuary house shows that chieftainship must have been evolving in the Indo-European homeland long before the out migration to Europe a millenium earlier.

Malta   A Mediterranean island 60 miles south of Sicily, noted for its series of megalithic temples, and dating from at least 3000 B.C., whose objects of worship were the avatars of a female deity of Old European provenance.

megalithic   Structures built of large stones, such as menhirs and alignments, stone circles, and chamber tombs.

magalithic tombs   Loosely, any chamber tomb, passage grave, or long barrow, built with large stones or not, and often grouped in cemeteries. They are Neolithic in origin, with Mesolithic carry overs (especially notable in cases where a cist burial is retained), and they contain collective deposits.

menhir   A single vertical standing stone, sometimes observed as marking Beaker burials in southwest England.

Mesolithic   (*Middle Stone Age,* see *Age.*) The cultures of the skilled hunting peoples, with wide regional variations, who lived between the end of the Würm glaciation and the beginnings of Neolithic plant and animal domestication.

Middle Paleolithic   The hunting cultures of Neanderthal Man, associated in Europe with Mousterian technology.

Minoan   The people of Bronze Age Crete, whose palace culture at Knossos is the near civilized high point of Old European culture.

Mother Goddess   See *great goddess.*

mortuary house   A wooden or stone copy of a dwelling, buried under a barrow of Kurgan mound or a Neolithic long barrow.

multilineal evolution   An approach to culture change, less doctrinaire than unilineal evolution (q.v.), and which accounts for changes in human society along its many lines in specific developmental sequences.

Mycenae   One of the chief citadels of the Mycenaean Bronze Age, surrounded by massive walls of cyclopean masonry and entered by the famous Lion Gate. The home of the leader of the expedition against Troy, Agamemnon, hence the possible seat of a high king of the Achaeans.

Mycenaeans   Strictly speaking, the inhabitants of Mycenae, but generally, the Bronze Age peoples of the entire Argolid. In Homer, they are the Achaeans, whose forebears arrived in the third millenium B.C., speaking an Indo-European language. Later cultural borrowings from the Minoans led to the rise in the 16th century B.C. of the so-called Mycenaean civilization.

Neanderthal Man   An extinct subspecies of *Home sapiens,* some of whose populations are the direct ancestors of modern men, living during the Riss-Würm interglacial and into the Würm glacial period. In Europe, Neanderthal cave burials with funerary offerings provide the oldest surviving evidence for religious belief in an afterlife.

Neolithic   (*New Stone Age,* see *Age.*) A way of life involving the use of polished stone tools, plant domestication, animal husbandry, or any combination of these traits. This may include the domination of herders over farmers in a layered society, as typified in the history of the Indo-Europeans.

New Grange   The most notable passage grave in Ireland, formerly part of a cemetery on the banks·of the river Boyne 25 miles north of Dublin. Like that in the Stonehenge region, this megalithic site was later infiltrated and occupied by Beaker folk.

Recent   See *Holocene.*

Old Europe   Coined by Marija Gimbutas to describe the great Neolithic culture complex of the Balkans, Greece, and southern Russia. Its dates are c. 7000 to c. 3500 B.C., when it was infiltrated by the warrior peoples of the Kurgan culture. The same term is used by a German philologist, Hans Krahe, to identify a series of old river names in Europe which may be of Proto-Indo-European origin.

oppidum (pl. *oppida*)   A Roman town serving as an administrative center for the surrounding area. Caesar applied the term to hillforts of the Celts in Gaul. These, at the time of the conquest, were large, permanent settlements, the first true towns in transalpine Europe.

Paleolithic   (*Old Stone Age,* see *Age.*) The hunting cultures of the Pleistocene geological epoch. (See *Lower, Middle,* and *Upper Paleolithic.*)

passage grave   A type of chamber or magalithic tomb characterized by a round barrow in which a burial chamber is placed and approached by a long passage. It is mainly found in the western parts of the British Isles. The classic example is New Grange.

peristalith   A ring of stones around a megalithic tomb.

Petrie, Sir Flinders (1853-1942)   Renowned English Egyptologist who began his career in archaeology with a survey of Stonehenge yet to be matched for precision. The numbers he assigned to the stones are still in use, and his determination that the monument was built during the course of three major phases of construction (I, II, and III) remains the basis for all modern theory.

Piggott, Stuart   Until recently, long-time Professor of Prehistoric Archaeology at Edinburgh University, successor in that post to V. Gordon Childe. He is one of the most influential British archaeologists of this century and a voluminous writer on many fields, ranging from prehistoric India to studies in British antiquarianism, and perhaps best known for his work on the British Neolithic and Bronze Age, which includes his identification of the Wessex culture.

Pleistocene   The first epoch of the Quaternary period, or Ice Age, beginning two or three million years ago. The glacial ice which gives this epoch its popular name was not a constant feature, however, but a recurring one of four major movements. In Europe, the sequence is named Gunz, Mindel, Riss, and Würm. Times between these are interglacials; for example, the Riss-Würm interglacial.

postglacial period   Another name for the Holocene geological epoch, associated with sub-stages of climate in northern Europe based on pollen analysis. The sequence is Pre-Boreal (from about 11,000 to 7700 B.C.), Boreal (7700-5550), Atlantic (5550-3000), Sub-Boreal (3000-500), and Sub-Atlantic (500 B.C. to the present). Each period, however, takes in several climatic fluctuations, e.g., the "Little Ice Age" of the period c. 1550 to c. 1850 A.D.

Primary Neolithic   The culture of the first farmers in Britain; early Neolithic. (See *Wessex farmers.*)

proto-Celts   Like the word Indo-European, once taken to mean only those peoples of prehistory who would clearly emerge as Celtic-speaking peoples (e.g., those of the Hallstatt culture), if taken as a cultural term, it should apply to the Beaker folk.

proto-Indo-Europeans (PIE)   A language theoretically ancestral to all Indo-European languages, hence spoken in the Kurgan homeland. It is a construct made by linguists, often working back through Sanskrit, and much disputed among members of that profession. As a cultural term, it applies to the earliest peoples whose traits may be linked to those of known Indo-European peoples, i.e., Kurgan folk or perhaps Battle Axe/Corded Ware folk.

Quaternary   The present period in the geological history of the earth, subdivided by the Pleistocene and Holocene (or Recent) epochs.

radiocarbon dating   A method for the absolute dating of organic remains up to 50,000 years old by measuring the amount of radioactive decay in Carbon 14. The method was conceived by the American chemist Willard L. Libby in 1946. For the correction of flaws in the method, see *radiocarbon revolution.*

radiocarbon revolution   A phrase coined by Colin Renfrew in response to a recent reevaluation of Carbon 14 dates. A recalibration of these dates shows that the prehistory of Europe is much older than had been thought and, in fact, that such monuments as the Maltese temples and megalithic tombs are older than any similar constructions in the centers of early civilization in the Near East. Therefore, the arrows of cultural diffusion may be reversed from West to East.

redistribution   An economic system in which goods from diverse production zones are brought to a political or religious center and then handed out on a roughly equitable basis. It is a market system (in modern terms) only by default of the social relations between givers and senders, which may have a ritualistic basis, as in the gift exchange of the Melanesian *kula* ring and the potlatching or give-away banquets of American Indians native to the Northwest coast. These ethnographic examples are by no means to be taken as exact parallels of ancient practice (which we can never know), yet they offer the only possible hints as to the workings of a pre-marketing economy in the past. At all events, the system provides the power base for chiefs of all kinds and, it seems, must give a rationale for the rise of urban centers.

Rig Veda   The most sacred book of Hinduism, finally recorded in about 1800 B.C., after centuries of oral transmission from the date of composition by the Aryan immigrants of India. Its language is Sanskrit, dead apart from the priests who conserve it in the recitation of their scripture. They are the praise poets or Druids of the Aryan tradition, still singing the glories of warrior heroes come to the Punjab, now gods. The *Rig Veda* is, in fact, a compilation of 1,028 poems in praise of various gods, chief of whom is Indra, the same Chariot-riding, bolt-hurling thunder god who is Jupiter with the Romans, Zeus with the Greeks, and Thor with the Scandinavians. *Rig* in Sanskrit means "laudatory stanzas," and *veda* means "knowledge," cognate with English *wit*, which, at bottom, comes from the Indo-European root for "to see." It is therefore cognate also with *video*. The word for what we see on TV springs from the same root that names the sacred lore of the Hindus.

Riss   The third and next to last of the glacial movements into the valleys and plains of Europe during the Pleistocene.

ritual shafts   Found among Celts, early and late, these were repositories for votive objects. The symbolism derives from cosmology: sunk into the earth, shafts were the negative aspect of the world tree which connected the heavens and underworld. The dry dead, who dwelt in the nether regions, required liquid which was poured down the shafts, as in Mycenaean graves, or flowed down the cosmic tree, as perhaps was implied by the stelae surmounting Kurgan graves. Such symbolism was reinforced by finds of trees in ritual shafts. (See *shaft grave*.)

round barrow   The most common monument in the British archaeological landscape. The term usually applies to Bronze Age single-grave burials. Neolithic passage graves, by contrast, are set in large round barrows, and pagan Anglo-Saxons buried their chiefs under them. Round barrows take several distinct forms, but the meaning of the differences is not clear.

sarsens   Boulders of sandstone found on the chalk downs of Wiltshire, used without shaping by the builders of Avebury and several megalithic tombs. Those boulders employed in the building of Stonehenge were often split into tabular sections and sometimes abraded to conform to an older tradition of carpentry, which called for mortise and tenon joints, as in fitting lintels of the trilithons on their imposts.

Scythians   Warrior herdsmen who displaced the Cimmerians from the Eurasian steppes in the eighth century B.C. In the royal graves of their kingly chiefs are luxury goods they traded for with Greek colonies along the Black Sea coast. A reverse influence is to be seen on the developing Celtic art of Europe, namely the fluid animal style of the steppes. Herodotus, who visited the Scyths in about 450 B.C., reported on their customs in his book of *Histories*. From it we have obtained some knowledge of nomadic chiefdoms of the steppes.

Secondary Neolithic   An amalgamation of Mesolithic and Primary Neolithic cultures, as in southern Britain, which resulted in the Windmill Hill culture (q.v.).

shaft grave   In the royal cemeteries at Mycenae, richly furnished tombs at the bottom of deep narrow pits. In two series, the richest of these date to the 16th century B.C. The form runs in a continuous line from the early Kurgan graves. (See *ritual shafts*.)

shaman/priest   A religious specialist in a chiefdom society who is not yet a bureaucratic hierophant as is a priest in civil society, but whose caste organization and service to a political leadership makes him more than an individual shaman in a tribal society.

Silbury Hill   A huge mound, the largest man-made hill in Europe, standing about 130 feet in height, 550 feet across the base and covering about 5½ acres. Excavated in the late 1960s, it reveals a complex construction (though not a burial barrow) and seems to have been a flat topped pyramid used for as yet unknown purposes. It is generally contemporary with the Great Pyramids of Egypt.

single-grave cultures   A general term for the new, intrusive cultures which appear in the midst of static Neolithic farming cultures in most of Europe. The burial rite in question is inhumation of a single corpse laid in a pit or within a mortuary house under a round barrow. This rite, together with the stone battle axe and cord-marked pottery among the grave goods, links the single-grave cultures with a complex derived from the south Russian Kurgan cultures.

slash and burn (swidden)   A primitive type of agriculture in which fields are cleaned from forests by cutting trees, burning them; and permitting the ash to wash into the soil. Since the land is not irrigated and, in Europe, is confined to light soils, the fertility lasts only a few years, whereupon those who work the land move on to a new patch of forest. This was the method employed by the first farmers in Europe, the Danubians.

Star Carr   The oldest Maglemosian site in northern Europe and the best preserved Mesolithic site in Britain, located 6 miles north of Richmond, Yorkshire.

state   A level of social organization typified by social classes and a sharply defined political organization in the hands of an elite who hold a monopoly on power through military and supernatural means, and who rule by means of impersonal law administered by a bureaucracy.

stimulus diffusion   Process whereby the idea of a culture trait is communicated to another.

stone circle   A type of monument confined to the British Isles. It consists of a circular array of stones which may stand alone or within the banks of a henge monument.

Stukeley, William (1687-1765)   After John Aubrey, the first English antiquarian to associate Stonehenge with the Druids. He made the association with such romantic force as to rank it with the lunatic fringe of archaeology, simply because it has been acted upon by the mock-Druids of the present day. It is possible, however, that proto-Druids have been thrown out with the romance.

suttee   The Hindu rite of a widow taking her own life in order to go with her dead spouse into the afterlife. This is the last living vestige of an Indo-European burial custom, derived from the single-grave cultures. That the tomb of a male skeleton may have been reopened for the burial of a female later is a compromise in these cultures, perhaps, with the collective burials of the megalithic tomb builders they encountered on the way of their westward migration.

Sutton Hoo   The cenotaph of a seventh century East Anglian king, made in a ship burial in the Sutton Hoo estate alongside the river Deven in Suffolk opposite the town of Woodbridge. It is now in the British Museum and is one of the greatest archaeological discoveries made in the British Isles.

swidden   See *slash-and-burn.*

tell   A word from the Arabic meaning hill or mound, used in the archaeology of the Near East to name a dead heap of mud brick villages, built and rebuilt, over the accumulation of their refuse. By extension, any pile of successive settlements, yielding to stratigraphic excavation, as the towns of Old Europe.

Teutons   The Germanic-speaking branch of the Indo-Europeans in northern Europe. The linguistic and social distinction made between them and the Celts proper in Gaul is of little or no significance when dealing with the general pattern of Indo-European culture in barbarian Europe at that time.

torc (also torque)   A neck-ring, so called from the Latin *torquere,* to twist, because many examples of this Celtic ornament, known from the early Bronze Age until the Roman occupation, are made of spirally twisted gold or bronze. But the twist is not its only meaningful attribute; its curvature may suggest a pair of cattle horns.

TRB   See *funnel beaker.*

tribe   An amorphous concept for a stage of cultural evolution organized on the basis of family, band, and clan, the normal limits of Neolithic society. Sometimes acephalous, it more often is arranged as a communal chiefdom, as among the Wessex farmers. They may also attain to the unusual townships of Old Europe and their semi-formal governance. Later chiefdoms build upon and incorporate elements of tribal culture.

trilithon   A structure consisting of two imposts and a lintel across the space between them, named by William Stukeley, five of which stand at the center of Stonehenge. Similar structures in Neolithic Britain occur as transept entrances in some megalithic tombs. The shaman/priests of the Wessex warriors who brought these outside to stand as a political monument to an intertribal meeting place, sanctified with funereal overtones, may also have read into these trilithons an Indo-European triplism. This may have been a set of universal principles (one for each stone) known in both surviving wings of the Indo-European culture areas, Ireland and India. They are the principles of creation, destruction, and possession, named in the Hindu tradition as the deities Brahma, Shiva, and Vishnu. (See *triplism.*)

triplism   The power of three in the divine triads of some Indo-European deities, such as Brahma, Shiva, and Vishnu in the Hindu tradition. Threes, in fact, permeate all aspects of Indo-European culture. (See *trilithon.*)

Tripolye   The eastern province of the Old European culture complex, located in the Ukraine. Related in some ways to the emerging Kurgan culture to which it was a neighbor.

type site   The place name of an archaeological culture where it was first discovered or where it was best excavated, and applied to its widest known distribution.

Únětice   Early Bronze Age culture located in Czechoslovakia. From the mid-late third millenium, it developed over the course of a millenium into a Bronze Age chiefdom society which had wide trade contacts. It is, thus, related to both Mycenae on the one hand and Wessex on the other.

unilineal evolution   Doctrine holding that, ideally, there are certain fixed stages through which all human societies must pass, as through the three age system of technological development. (See *Age.* Also see *multilineal evolution.*)

Upper Paleolithic   The cultures of the hunting peoples who lived during the latter half of the Würm glaciation.

Ur   One of the chief cities of ancient Sumer in Mesopotamia, hence a foundation stone in the ediface of western civilization. The royal tombs of Ur, excavated by Sir Leonard Woolley in the 1920s and 1930s, yielded magnificent, rich goods yet are unique in the annals of Mesopotamian archaeology. Perhaps the dynasty buried there (dating to c. 2800 B.C.) was somehow related to Indo-Europeans, among whom similar funerary practices (including human sacrifice) was normal.

urnfield   Specifically, cemeteries in which cremated human remains are placed in urns. The term usually refers to a late Bronze Age culture in central Europe. Urnfielders expanded outward to many parts of Europe and the Mediterranean during the late second millenium B.C. and thereafter. In Italy, they may have been Proto-Italic speakers; clearly some were Celts. They took up iron making and, in Europe, developed into the Hallstatt folk.

Val Camonica   A valley in northern Italy in which many rock carvings have been found. Most date to the Bronze Age, and some are among the earliest representations of Indo-European deities, especially the war god.

Vikings   A general term for Scandinavian sea-going marauders who began raiding in Europe and down even to the Black Sea and Mediterranean in the late eighth century A.D. They represent the last of a long series of migratory movements by barbarian Indo-European peoples, which began with Kurgan folk.

Vučedol   An early Bronze Age site in northern Yugoslavia representing a culture in which bronze working was developed in Europe and from which Beaker folk may have borrowed the techniques.

Wessex culture   Early Bronze Age culture, identified by Stuart Piggott, which occupied southwestern Britain and whose members constructed the last phases of Stonehenge. Excavation of Wessex barrows (no habitations have yet been found) reveals it to have been a chief-led society in contact with similar cultures on the Continent, e.g., Únětice.

Wessex farmers   Primary Neolithic farmers in southern England. They belong to the Western Neolithic tradition represented in France by Chassey culture, whose ancestors had migrated along the Mediterranean coasts beginning in the eighth millenium B.C. Later these farmers would come in contact with the Continental descendants of Danubian farmers, from whom they would obtain the earthen long barrow.

West Kennet   A famous chamber tomb located near Windmill Hill and related to that culture. The tomb and probably an associated mortuary temple were used throughout the whole later Neolithic and Beaker period, perhaps for a millenium, before being finally sealed.

Windmill Hill   Type site for the middle Neolithic (Secondary) culture of southern England. The site is a multivalate causewayed camp covering some 21 acres. Artifacts and evidence indicate that Windmill Hill was a tribal ceremonial center, a place for redistribution.

Windmill Hill culture   Once thought to have been primary Neolithic, this culture is now seen as middle Neolithic (Secondary), dating at least to the mid fourth millenium.

Woodhenge   Classed technically as a henge monument and located adjacent to Durrington Walls, 6.2 miles from Stonehenge. Within a bank and ditch roughly 12 to 15 feet in diameter were found six concentric rings of post holes at the center of which was the grave of a child whose skull had been cloven. The rings have been variously interpreted as a ritual structure (perhaps a *kiva*), a henge monument not unlike Stonehenge, or as free standing posts analogous to wooden circles found among North American Indians.

Worm, Ole (1588-1654)   The Danish court physician and antiquarian who published the first drawings of megalithic monuments. He further advised Walter Charleton on parallel structures in Britain, which led to his work on Stonehenge.

Wormius, Olaus   See *Worm, Ole.*

Würm   The fourth and last glacial advance of the Pleistocene, followed by the Holocene, or Recent epoch.

Bibliography

Ashbee, P. *The Bronze Age Round Barrow in Britain.* London: Phoenix House, 1960.

———. *The Earthen Long Barrow in Britain.* Toronto: University of Toronto Press, 1970.

Astour, M. *Hellenosemitica.* Leiden: Brill, 1967.

Atkinson, R. J. C. *Stonehenge.* Harmondsworth: Penguin Books, 1960.

———. "Neolithic Engineering," *Antiquity* 35, (1961): 292–99.

———. "Moonshine on Stonehenge." *Antiquity* 40, (1966): 212–16.

———. "Silbury Hill." *Antiquity* 42, (1968): 299.

———. "Neolithic Science and Technology," In *The Place of Astronomy in the Ancient World,* edited by F. R. Hodson, pp. 123–32. London: Oxford University Press, 1974.

———. "Megalithic Astronomy—A Prehistorian's Comments." *Journal of the History of Astronomy* 6, (1975): 42–52.

Atkinson, R. J. C.; Vatcher, F.; and Vatcher, L. "Radiocarbon Dates for the Stonehenge Avenue." *Antiquity* 50, (1976): 239–40.

Aubrey, John. "Monumenta Britannica; or Miscellany of British Antiquities. Vol. 1, Section 1, Templa Druidum; Stoneheng." MS in the Bodleian Library, Oxford. 1665.

Baity, E. C. "Archaeoastronomy and Ethnoastronomy So Far." *Current Anthropology* 14, (1973): 389–449.

Barclay, Edgar. *Stonehenge and Its Earthworks.* London: D. Nutt, 1895.

Bessinger, J. B., Jr., and Creed, R. P., eds. *Franciplegius: Medieval and Linquistic Studies in Honor of Francis Peabody Magoun, Jr.* New York: New York University Press, 1965.

Braidwood, R. J., and Howe, B. "Southwestern Asia beyond the Lands of the Mediterranean Littoral." In *Courses Toward Urban Life,* edited by R. J. Braidwood and G. R. Willey, pp. 132–46. Chicago: Aldine, 1962.

Braidwood, R. J., and Willey, G. R., eds. *Courses toward Urban Life.* Chicago: Aldine, 1962.

Brinckerhoff, R. F. "Astronomically-Oriented Markings on Stonehenge." *Nature* 263 (7 October 1976): 465–69.

Brønsted, J. *The Vikings.* Harmondsworth: Penguin Books, 1965.

Brown, N. O. *Hermes the Thief.* Madison: University of Wisconsin Press, 1947.

Bruce-Mitford, R. L. S. *The Sutton Hoo Ship Burial: A Handbook.* London: Trustees of the British Museum, 1968.

Burl, A. "Dating the British Stone Circles." *American Scientist* 61 (1973): 167–74.

———. *The Stone Circles of the British Isles.* New Haven and London: Yale University Press, 1976.

Burn, A. R. "Holy Men on Islands in Pre-Christian Britain." *Glasgow Archaeological Journal* 1 (1969): 2–6.

Burney, C., and Lang, D. M. *The Peoples of the Hills: Ancient Ararat and the Caucuses.* New York: Praeger, 1972.

Cardona, E.; Hoenigswald, H. M.; and Senn, A., eds. *Indo-European and Indo-Europeans.* Philadelphia: University of Pennsylvania Press, 1970.

Carew, Thomas, and Jones, Inigo. *Coelum Britannicum: A Maske at White-Hall in the Banqueting House, on Shrove-Tuesday-Night, the 18th of February.* London: Thomas Walkley, 1642.

Cederquist, L. L., and Fuchs, F. "Antenatal Sex Determination." *Clinical Obstetrics and Gynecology* 13 (1970): 159-66.

Chadwick, H. M. *The Heroic Age.* Cambridge: Cambridge University Press, 1912.

Chadwick, H. M., and Chadwick, N. K. *The Growth of Literature, Vol. 1: The Ancient Literatures of Europe.* Cambridge: Cambridge University Press, 1932.

Charles, J. A. "Where Is the Tin?" *Antiquity* 49 (1975): 19–24.

Charleton, Walter. *Chorea Gigantum, or, The most Famous Antiquity of Great-Britain, Vulgarly called Stone-Heng, Standing on Salisbury Plain, Restored to the Danes.* London: Henry Henigman, 1663.

Childe, V. G. *What Happened in History.* Harmondsworth: Penguin Books, 1942.

———. *The Dawn of European Civilization,* 6th ed. London: Routledge and Kegan Paul, 1957.

Clark, G. "The Invasion Hypothesis in British Archaeology." *Antiquity* 40 (1966): 165–71.

Clark, G., and Piggott, S. *Prehistoric Societies.* New York: Knopf, 1965.

Clark, J. G. D. *Prehistoric Europe: The Economic Basis.* London: Methuen, 1952.

Clark, R. M. "A Calibration Curve for Radiocarbon Dates." *Antiquity* 49 (1975): 251–66.

Clarke, D. L. *Beaker Pottery of Great Britain and Ireland.* Cambridge: Cambridge University Press, 1970.

Clarke, D. L., ed. *Models in Archaeology.* London: Methuen, 1972.

Coles, J. *Archaeology by Experiment.* New York: Scribner's, 1973.

Coon, C. S. *The Story of Man,* 3rd ed. New York: Knopf, 1969.

Crampton, P. *Stonehenge of the Kings.* New York: John Day, 1968.

Crawford, O. G. S. *The Eye Goddess.* London: Phoenix House, 1958.

Cross, T. R., and Slover, C. H., eds. *Ancient Irish Tales.* New York: Henry Holt, 1936.

Crossland, R. A., and Birchall, A., eds. *Bronze Age Migrations in the Aegean.* London: Duckworth, 1973.

Daniel, G. *The Megalith Builders of Western Europe.* London: Hutchinson, 1958.

Davidson, H. R. E. *Gods and Myths of Northern Europe.* Baltimore: Penguin Books, 1964.

Dayton, J. E. "The Problem of Tin in the Ancient World." *World Archaeology* 3 (1971): 49–70.

Dillon, M., and Chadwick, N. K. *The Celtic Realms.* New York: New American Library, 1967.

Duckett, E. S. *Alfred the Great.* Chicago: University of Chicago Press, 1958.

Evans, Sir A. J. "Stonehenge." *Archaeological Review* 2 (1889): 312-30.

Evans, J. D. *Malta.* London: Thames and Hudson, 1959.

Evans, J. G. *The Environment of Early Man in the British Isles.* Berkeley: University of California Press, 1975.

Fea, A., ed. *After Worcester Flight.* London: John Lane, 1904.

Ferguson, S. "On the Ceremonial Turn Called 'Desiul'." *Proceedings of the Royal Irish Academy,* 2nd ser., 1 (1879): 355–64.

Finley, M. I. *The World of Odysseus,* rev. ed. New York: Viking Press, 1965.

Fleming, A. "The Myth of the Mother-Goddess." *World Archaeology* 1 (1969): 247–61.

———. "Territorial Patterns in Bronze Age Wessex." *Proceedings of the Prehistoric Society* 37 (1971): 138–66.

———. "The Genesis of Pastoralism in European Prehistory." *World Archaeology* 4 (1972): 179–91.

———. "Models for the Development of Wessex Culture." In *The Explanation of Culture Change,* edited by C. Renfrew, pp. 571–88. Pittsburgh: University of Pittsburgh Press, 1973.

Forbes, R. J. *Studies in Ancient Technology.* Leiden: Brill, 1955 et seg.

Forde-Johnston, J. *Prehistoric Britain and Ireland.* London: J. M. Dent & Sons, 1976.

Frankfort, H. *The Birth of Civilization in the Near East.* New York: Anchor Books, 1956.

Frankfort, H., and Frankfort, H. A., eds. *Before Philosophy.* Harmondsworth: Penguin Books, 1949.

Frazer, Sir J. G. *The Golden Bough.* New York: Macmillan, 1922.

Friedrich, P. "Proto-Indo-European Kinship." *Ethnology* 5 (1966): 1-37.

———. "Defilement and Honor in the *Iliad.*" *Journal of Indo-European Studies* 1 (1973): 127–44.

Garmonsway, G. N. "Anglo-Saxon Heroic Attitudes." In *Franciplegius,* edited by J. B. Bessinger, Jr., and R. P. Creed, pp. 139–46, New York: New York University Press, 1965.

Garmonsway, G. N., trans. *Beowulf.* In *Beowulf and Its Analogues,* by G. N. Garmonsway, J. Simpson, and H. E. Davidson. New York: J. P. Dutton, 1971.

Gelling, P., and Davidson, H. E. *The Chariot of the Sun.* New York: Praeger, 1969.

Geoffrey of Monmouth. *The History of the Kings of Brit-*

ain. Translated by L. Thorpe from the Latin original. Baltimore: Penguin Books, 1966.

Georgiev, V. I. "The Arrival of the Greeks in Greece: The Linquistic Evidence." In *Bronze Age Migrations in the Aegean,* edited by R. A. Crossland and A. Birchall, pp. 243–53. London: Duckworth, 1973.

Gimbutas, M. "Battle Axe or Cult Axe?" *Man* 53 (1953): 51–54.

———. *The Prehistory of Eastern Europe.* Cambridge, Mass.: Peabody Museum, 1956.

———. "Old Europe c. 7000-3500 B.C.: The Earliest European Civilization before the Infiltration of the Indo-European Peoples." *Journal of Indo-European Studies* 1 (1973): 1–20.

———. "Perkunas—The Thunder God of the Balts and Slavs." *Journal of Indo-European Studies* 1 (1973): 466–78.

———. *The Gods and Goddesses of Old Europe, 7000 to 3500 B.C.: Myths, Legends and Cult Images.* Berkeley: University of California Press, 1974.

———. "An Archaeologist's View of PIE in 1975." *Journal of Indo-European Studies* 2 (1974): 289–308.

Goodenough, W. H. "The Evolution of Pastoralism and Indo-European Origins." In *Indo-European and Indo-Europeans,* edited by E. Cardona, H. M. Hoenigswald, and A. Senn, pp. 253–66. Philadelphia: University of Pennsylvania Press, 1970.

Gordon, C. H. *Before the Bible.* New York: Harper and Row, 1962.

Gotch, J. A. "Inigo Jones: A Modern View." In *Essays by Divers Hands,* edited by Margaret L. Woods, a volume in the *Transactions of the Royal Society of Literature of the United Kingdom,* n.s. 8: 55–80. London: Oxford University Press, 1928.

Graves, R. *The Anger of Achilles.* New York: Pyramid Books, 1966.

Grimal, P., ed. *Larousse World Mythology.* London: Hamlyn, 1965.

Grinsell, L. V. *The Archaeology of Wessex.* London: Methuen, 1958.

Grinsell, L. V., and Dyer, J. *Discovering Regional Archaeology: Wessex.* Tring, Herts.: Shire Publications, 1971.

Hall, R. L. "Ghosts, Water Barriers, Corn, and Sacred Enclosures in the Eastern Woodlands." *American Antiquity* 41 (1976): 360–64.

Hanning, R. W. *The Vision of History in Early Britain: From Gildas to Geoffrey of Monmouth.* New York: Columbia University Press, 1966.

Harris, M. *Cows, Pigs, Wars and Witches: The Riddles of Culture.* New York: Random House, 1974.

Harrison, H., and Stover, L. E. *Stonehenge* [a novel]. New York: Scribner's, 1972.

Harrison, R. J. "Origins of the Bell Beaker Cultures." *Antiquity* 47 (1974): 99–109.

Harrison, W. J. *Great Stone Monuments of Wiltshire: A Bibliography of Stonehenge and Avebury.* Devizes: C. H. Woodward, 1901.

Hawkes, J. "God in the Machine." *Antiquity* 41 (1967): 174–80.

Hawkins, G. S. *Stonehenge Decoded.* New York: Doubleday, 1965.

———. "Astronomical Alignments in Britain, Egypt and Peru." In *The Place of Astronomy in the Ancient World,* edited by F. R. Hodson, pp. 157–68. London: Oxford University Press, 1974.

Hérodotus. *The Histories.* Translated by Aubrey de Selincourt. Harmondsworth: Penguin Classics, 1954.

Hertz, R. *Death and the Right Hand.* Translated from the German of 1909 by R. Needham and C. Needham. Aberdeen: Cohen and West, 1960.

HMSO. *Royal Commission on Historical Monuments: County of Dorset,* vol. 2, part 3. London: Her Majesty's Stationery Office, 1970.

Hodson, F. R., ed. *The Place of Astronomy in the Ancient World.* London: Oxford University Press, 1974.

Homer. *Iliad.* Translated by W. H. D. Rouse. New York: Mentor Books, 1950.

Hood, M. S. F. "The Tartaria Tablets." *Antiquity* 41 (1967): 91–98.

Hoyle, F. *From Stonehenge to Modern Cosmology.* San Francisco: W. H. Freeman, 1972.

Ingram, Rev. J. *An Inaugural Lecture on the Utility of Anglo-Saxon Literature, to Which Is Added the Geography of Europe by King Alfred.* London: Oxford University Press, 1807.

Ishida Eiichirō. "Japan Rediscovered." *Japan Quarterly* 11: 276–82.

Jackson, K. H. *The Oldest Irish Tradition: A Window on the Iron Age.* Cambridge: Cambridge University Press, 1964.

Jones, Inigo. *The Most Notable Antiquity of Great Britain, Vulgarly Called Stone-Heng, on Salisbury Plain, Restored, by Inigo Jones, Esquire, Architect General to the Late King.* London: D. Browne, 1655.

Joyce, P. W. *A Social History of Ancient Ireland.* 2 vols. 1913. Reprint. New York: Benjamin Blom, 1968.

Keiller, A. *Windmill Hill and Avebury.* London: Oxford University Press, 1965.

Kellaway, G. A. "Glaciation and the Stones of Stonehenge." *Nature* 233 (3 September 1971): 30–35.

Kendrick, T. D. *The Druids: A Study in Keltic Prehistory.* London: Methuen, 1928.

Kenyon, K. M. *Digging Up Jericho.* London: Ernest Benn, 1957.

Klima, B. "The First Ground-plan of an Upper Paleolithic Loess Settlement in Middle Europe and Its Meaning." In *Courses toward Urban Life,* edited by R. J. Braidwood and G. R. Willey, pp. 193-210. Chicago: Aldine, 1966.

Klindt-Jensen, O. *Denmark.* London: Thames and Hudson, 1957.

Kroeber, A. L. "Stimulus Diffusion." *American Anthropologist* 42 (1940): 1–20.

Lamb, H. H. "Climate, Vegetation and Forest Limits in Early Civilized Times." In *The Place of Astronomy in the Ancient World,* edited by F. R. Hodson, pp. 195–230. Oxford University Press, 1974.

Larson, G. J. "Introduction: The Study of Mythology and Comparative Literature." In *Myth in Indo-European Antiquity,* edited by G. J. Larson, pp. 1–17. Berkeley: University of California Press, 1974.

Lees-Milne, J. *The Age of Inigo Jones.* London: B. T. Batsford, 1953.

Lewis, D. "Voyaging Stars: Aspects of Polynesian and Micronesian Astronomy." In *The Place of Astronomy in the Ancient World,* edited by F. R. Hodson, pp. 133–48. London: Oxford University Press, 1974.

Lockyer, Sir N. *Stonehenge and Other British Monuments Astronomically Considered.* London: Macmillan, 1906.

Long, W. "Stonehenge and Its Barrows." *The Wiltshire Archaeological and Natural History Magazine* 16 (June 1876).

Louwe Kooijmans, L. P. *The Rhine/Meuse Delta: Four Studies on Its Prehistoric Occupation and Holocene Geology.* Leiden: Brill, 1974.

Luce, J. V. *Homer and the Homeric Age.* London: Thames and Hudson, 1975.

MacNeill, M. *The Festival of Lughnasa: A Study of the Survival of the Celtic Festival of the Beginning of Harvest.* London: Oxford University Press, 1962.

Maher, J. P. "HaEKMON: 'Stone Axe' and 'Sky' in Indo-European/Battle Axe Culture." *Journal of Indo-European Studies* 1 (1973): 51-54.

Maistrov, L. E. "Remarks." In *The Place of Astronomy in the Ancient World,* edited by F. R. Hodson, pp. 267–68. London: Oxford University Press, 1974.

Malinowski, B. *Argonauts of the Western Pacific.* London: George Routledge and Sons, 1922.

Mallory, J. "A Short History of the Indo-European Problem." *Journal of Indo-European Studies* 1 (1973): 21–65.

Megaw, J. V. S. *Art of the European Iron Age.* New York: Harper and Row, 1970.

Mendelssohn, K. *The Riddle of the Pyramids.* London: Thames and Hudson, 1974.

Moberg, C. A. "Northern Europe." In *Courses toward Urban Life,* edited by R. J. Braidwood and G. R. Willey, pp. 309–29. Chicago: Aldine, 1962.

Moore, N. "Walter Charleton." *Dictionary of National Biography,* vol. 4, pp. 116–19. London: Oxford University Press, 1921–22.

Mouldy, M. [pseud.] *Stonehenge; or, the Romans in Britain. A Romance of the Days of Nero.* 3 vols. London: Richard Bentley, 1842.

Muhly, J. D., and Wertime, T. A. "Evidence for the Sources and Use of Tin during the Bronze Age of the Near East." *World Archaeology* 5 (1973): 111–22.

Neustupný, E. "Factors Determining the Variability of the Corded Ware Culture." In *The Explanation of Culture Change,* edited by C. Renfrew, pp. 725–30. Pittsburgh: University of Pittsburgh Press, 1973.

Neustupný, E., and Neustupný, J. *Czechoslovakia.* New York: Praeger, 1961.

Newall, R. S. "Stonehenge." *Antiquity* 3 (1929): 75–88.

———. *Stonehenge.* 3d ed. London: Her Majesty's Stationery Office, 1959.

Newham, C. A. *The Astronomical Significance of Stonehenge.* Leeds: Blackburn, 1972.

Newton, R. R., and Jenkins, R. E. "Possible Use of Stonehenge." Nature 239 (27 October 1972): 511–12.

Olmstead, G. S. "The Gundestrup Version of the *Tain Bo Cuailinge.*" *Antiquity* 50 (1976): 95–103.

Onians, R. B. *The Origins of European Thought about the Body, the Mind, the Soul, the World, Time and Fate.* Cambridge: Cambridge University Press, 1951.

O'Rahilly, C. *Táin Bó Cúalnge.* Dublin: Dublin Institute for Advanced Studies, 1967.

Parkinson, C. N. *Parkinson's Law.* Boston: Houghton Mifflin, 1957.

Peterson, F. "Traditions of Multiple Burial in Later Neolithic and Early Bronze Age England." *Archaeological Journal* 129 (1972) 22–40.

Petrie, W. M. F. *Stonehenge.* London: Edward Stamford, 1880.

Pfeiffer, J. E. *The Emergence of Man.* New York: Harper and Row, 1969.

Phillips, E. D. *The Royal Hordes: Nomad Peoples of the Steppes.* London: Thames and Hudson, 1965.

Piggott, S. "The Sources of Geoffrey of Monmouth. II. The Stonehenge Story." *Antiquity* 15 (1941): 305-19.

———. *British Prehistory*. London: Oxford University Press, 1949.

———. *William Stukeley: An 18th Century Antiquary*. Oxford: Clarendon Press, 1950.

———. *Prehistoric India*. Harmondsworth: Penguin, 1950.

———. *Ancient Europe: From the Beginnings of Agriculture to Classical Antiquity*. Chicago: Aldine, 1965.

———. *Celts, Saxons, and the Early Antiquarians*. Edinburgh: Edinburgh University Press, 1967.

———. *The Druids*. London: Thames and Hudson, 1968.

———. *A History of Wiltshire: Victoria History of the Counties of England*. Vol. 1, part 2. London: Oxford University Press, 1973.

Polanyi, K. "The Economy as Institutionalized Process." In *Trade and Markets in the Early Empires*, edited by K. Polanyi, C. M. Arensburg, and H. W. Pearson, pp. 243–69. Glencoe, Il.: Free Press, 1957.

Powell, T. G. E. *The Celts*. New York: Praeger, 1958.

Rathje, W. L. "Models for Mobile Maya: A Variety of Constraints." In *The Explanation of Culture Change*, edited by C. Renfrew, pp. 731–57. Pittsburgh: University of Pittsburgh Press, 1973.

Redfield, R. *The Primitive World and Its Transformations*. Ithaca: Cornell University Press, 1953.

Renfrew, C. *Before Civilization: The Radiocarbon Revolution and Prehistoric Europe*. New York: Knopf, 1973.

———. "Wessex as a Social Question." *Antiquity* 47 (1973): 221–24.

Renfrew, C., ed. *The Explanation of Culture Change: Models in Prehistory*. Pittsburgh: University of Pittsburgh Press, 1973.

Renfrew, C.; Harkness, D.; and Switsur, R. "Quanterness, Radiocarbon and the Orkney Cairns." *Antiquity* 50 (1976): 194–205.

Rhys, B. and Rhys, A. *The Celtic Heritage: Ancient Tradition in Ireland and Wales*. New York: Grove Press, 1961.

Richardson, R. S. "Headstones for Astronomers." *Astounding Science Fiction*, July 1944, pp. 104–12.

Ross, A. G. *Pagan Celtic Britain*. London: Routledge and Kegan Paul, 1967.

Sandars, N. K. trans. *Gilgamesh*, Harmondsworth Penguin Books, 1964.

Service, E. R. *Primitive Social Organization*. New York: Random House, 1971.

Sherratt, A. G. "Socio-economic and Demographic Models for the Neolithic and Bronze Ages of Europe." In *Models in Archaeology*, edited by D. L. Clarke, pp. 493–500. London: Methuen, 1972.

Singer, C.; Holmyard, E. J.; and Hall, A. R. *A History of Technology*. Vols. 1 and 2. London: Oxford University Press, 1954 and 1956.

Singh Uberoi, J. P. *Politics of the Kula Ring*. Manchester: Manchester University Press, 1962.

Smith, G. "Excavations of the Stonehenge Avenue at West Amesbury, Wiltshire." *Wiltshire Archaeological Magazine* 68 (1973): 42–63.

Smith, G. E. "The Influence of Ancient Egyptian Civilization in the Near East and America." *Bulletin of the John Rylands Library* 3 (1916–17).

———. *In the Beginning: The Origin of Civilization*. New York: Norton, 1928.

Stanford, W. B., and Luce, J. V. *The Quest for Ulysses*. New York: Praeger, 1974.

Stone, E. H. *The Stones of Stonehenge*. London: Robert Scott, 1924.

Stone, J. F. S. *Wessex*. New York: Praeger, 1960.

Stover, L. E. and Stover, T. K. *China: An Anthropological Perspective*. Pacific Palisades: Goodyear, 1976.

Stukeley, W. *Stonehenge, A Temple Restor'd to the British Druids*. London: W. Innys and R. Manby, 1740.

Tacitus. *On Britain and Germany*. Translated by H. Mattingly. Harmondsworth: Penguin Books, 1948.

Thom, A. *Megalithic Sites in Britain*. Oxford: Clarendon Press, 1967.

Thom, A. "Astronomical Significance of Prehistoric Monuments in Western Europe." In *The Place of Astronomy in the Ancient World*, edited by F. R. Hodson, pp. 149–56. London: Oxford University Press, 1974.

Thom, A.; Thom, A. S.; and Thom, A. S. "Stonehenge." *Journal for the History of Astronomy* 5 (1974): 71–90.

Thompson, J. E. S. "Maya Astronomy." In *The Place of Astronomy in the Ancient World*, edited by F. R. Hodson, pp. 67–82. London: Oxford University Press, 1974.

Tierney, J. J. "The Celtic Ethnography of Posidonius." *Proceedings of the Royal Irish Academy* 60, sec. C, no. 5 (1960): 189–275.

Trigger, B. "The Archaeology of Government." *World Archaeology* 6 (1974): 95–105.

Tringham, R. *Hunters, Fishers and Farmers of Eastern Europe, 6000–3000 B.C.* London: Hutchinson University Library, 1971.

Tritsch, F. J. "The 'Sackers of Cities' and the Movement of Populations." In *Bronze Age Migrations in the Aegean*, edited by R. A. Crossland and A. Birchall, pp. 233–38. London: Duckworth, 1973.

Wainwright, G. J. "Durrington Walls: A Ceremonial Enclosure." *Antiquity* 42 (1968): 20–26.

Ward, D. "On the Poets and Poetry of the Indo-Europeans." *Journal of Indo-European Studies* 1 (1973): 127–44.

Webb, J. *A Vindication of Stone-Heng Restored.* London: R. Davenport for Tho. Basset, 1665.

Webster, T. B. L. *From Mycenae to Homer.* New York: W. W. Norton, 1964.

Whatmough, J. *The Dialects of Ancient Gaul.* Cambridge, Mass.: Harvard University Press, 1970.

Wheeler, Sir M. *Civilizations of the Indus Valley and Beyond.* London: Thames and Hudson, 1966.

Wilson, J. A. "Egypt." In *Before Philosophy,* edited by H. Frankfort and H. A. Frankfort, pp. 39–133. Harmondsworth: Penguin Books, 1949.

Wood, E. S. *A Field Guide to Archaeology.* London: Collins, 1964.

Woolley, Sir L. *Excavations at Ur.* New York: Barnes and Noble, 1955.

Index

UNIVERSITY OF
WOLVERHAMPTON

Wolverhampton Learning Centre
University of Wolverhampton
St Peter's Square
Wolverhampton WV1 1RH
Wolverhampton (01902) 322305

Telephone Renewals: 01902 321333
This item may be recalled at any time. Keeping it after it has
been recalled or beyond the date stamped may result in a fine.
See tariff of fines displayed at the counter.

0 3 DEC 1999	27/11/01	
04 FEB C9862		
07 MARCH D7585		
1 6 MAR 2001		
- 4 JUN 2001